HERALDRY IN
THE ROYAL NAVY

[Crown Copyright Reserved

EXAMPLES OF SHIPS' BADGES

Top, left to right. R.N.V.R. old design (Major ffoulkes), R.N.V.R. new design (College of Heralds), Fleet Air Arm Squadron badge (College of Heralds).
Centre, left to right. Standard design (College of Heralds), Battleship design (Carver, H. Maschek), Cruiser design (Carver, H. Maschek).
Bottom, left to right. Auxiliary design (Carver, H. Maschek), Destroyer design (Major ffoulkes), R.I.N. design (Carver, H. Maschek).

Frontispiece

HERALDRY IN THE ROYAL NAVY

CRESTS AND BADGES
OF H.M. SHIPS

by
ALFRED E. WEIGHTMAN

The Naval & Military Press Ltd

Published by

The Naval & Military Press Ltd
Unit 5 Riverside, Brambleside
Bellbrook Industrial Estate
Uckfield, East Sussex
TN22 1QQ England

Tel: +44 (0)1825 749494

www.naval-military-press.com
www.nmarchive.com

In reprinting in facsimile from the original, any imperfections are inevitably reproduced and the quality may fall short of modern type and cartographic standards.

FOREWORD

The Author, himself a designer of ships' badges of uncommon skill, has at long last written the book for which so many of us have been waiting. Here, in these pages, will be found much to interest not only the student of heraldry but also the more general reader whose interest lies in the ways and customs of ships and the sea.

The story of the ship's badge is an ancient one, for it was born in the desire of man partly to beautify his ship and partly to make of her a living personality which could readily absorb his love and devotion. We find its genesis, perhaps, in the Vikings' raven, in the lovely stern carvings which graced Tudor and Stuart ships, in the noble figureheads carried by eighteenth- and nineteenth-century sailing ships, and even in the gingerbread work which, not so very long ago, used to adorn even the humblest of the trading brigs and schooners.

In the Royal Navy the ship's badge, as well as being an adornment, serves an additional purpose in keeping bright the dignity and tradition which a ship's name may carry. Often enough a ship may be given a badge designed to keep alive the memory of one of her more famous exploits, or perhaps commemorate one of her more gallant captains. Sometimes the name itself will suggest the badge, as in the case of H.M.S. *Artful*, for whom the Ships' Badges Committee produced the appropriate design of a monkey proper. Nevertheless, whatever the mood of the design may be, the badge is always treasured, and regarded as a tangible form of the ship's personality.

Mr. Weightman has ranged wide over the field of naval heraldry, and his book is the result of diligent research and effort. In it he has, I think, captured much of the inward spirit of the badge in addition to its outward form, and he shows us how, behind the design resplendent in its heraldic colours, lies that age-old devotion with which men have always served the ships in which they have sailed. The story of ships' badges has long needed to be written. Here, in Mr. Weightman, it has at last found a worthy chronicler.

P. K. KEMP
(Admiralty Archivist)

CONTENTS

	Page
FOREWORD	v
INTRODUCTION	xvii
THEIR ORIGIN AND USE	1
CASTING THE BADGES	13
BATTLE HONOURS	15
SHAPES OF BADGES	23
RULERS OF GREAT BRITAIN SINCE 1588	24
H.M.S. ABERCROMBIE	25
H.M.S. ACHILLES	27
H.M.S. ACTAEON	28
H.M.S. ADVENTURE	30
H.M.S. AENEAS	31
H.M.S. AFRICA	32
H.M.S. AGAMEMNON	33
H.M.S. AGINCOURT	35
H.M.S. AISNE	37
H.M.S. AJAX	38
H.M.S. ALAMEIN	40
H.M.S. ALAUNIA	41
H.M.S. ALBEMARLE	42
H.M.S. ALBION	43
H.M.S. ALBRIGHTON	45
H.M.S. AMBROSE	46
H.M.S. AMETHYST	48
H.M.S. ANSON	50
H.M.S. ANZAC	52
H.M.S. APOLLO	53
H.M.S. ARCHER	56
H.M.S. ARETHUSA	58
H.M.S. ARGONAUT	61
H.M.S. ARGUS	63
H.M.S. ARIADNE	65
H.M.S. ARIEL	67
H.M.S. ARK ROYAL	69
H.M.S. ARMADA	71
H.M.S. ARROGANT	72
H.M.S. ARTEMIS	73
H.M.S. ATHERSTONE	74

	Page
H.M.S. AURORA	75
H.M.S. AUSONIA	77
H.M.S. BARFLEUR	78
H.M.S. BARROSA	81
H.M.S. BATTLE-AXE	83
H.M.S. BELFAST	84
H.M.S. BELLEROPHON	85
H.M.S. BELLONA	87
H.M.S. BERMUDA	88
H.M.S. BERWICK	89
H.M.S. BIRMINGHAM	90
H.M.S. BLACK PRINCE	91
H.M.S. BLACK SWAN	93
H.M.S. BLAKE	94
H.M.S. BONAVENTURE	96
H.M.S. BOXER	98
H.M.S. BRECON	99
H.M.S. BRITANNIA	100
H.M.S. BROADSWORD	103
H.M.S. BRUCE	104
H.M.S. BULWARK	105
H.M.S. CADIZ	107
H.M.S. CAMPANIA	108
H.M.S. CAMPERDOWN	109
H.M.S. CENTAUR	110
H.M.S. CENTURION	113
H.M.S. CERES	115
H.M.S. CEYLON	117
H.M.S. CHALLENGER	118
H.M.S. CHATHAM	120
H.M. DOCKYARD CHATHAM	121
H.M.S. CLEOPATRA	122
H.M.S. COCHRANE	124
H.M.S. COLLINGWOOD	126
H.M.S. COLOSSUS	128
H.M.S. COMMONWEALTH	130
H.M.S. CONQUEROR	131
H.M.S. CORNWALL	132
H.M.S. CORUNNA	134
H.M.S. COSSACK	135

	Page
H.M.S. COURAGEOUS	136
H.M.S. CROSSBOW	137
H.M.S. CRUSADER	138
H.M.S. CUMBERLAND	140
H.M.S. CURACOA	142
H.M.S. CYCLOPS	143
H.M.S. CYGNET	145
H.M.S. DAINTY	148
H.M.S. DARING	150
H.M.S. DARTMOUTH	152
H.M.S. DECOY	154
H.M.S. DEFENCE	156
H.M.S. DEFENDER	158
H.M.S. DEFIANCE	160
H.M.S. DELIGHT	163
H.M.S. DESPATCH	165
H.M.S. DEVONSHIRE	166
H.M.S. DIADEM	169
H.M.S. DIAMOND	171
H.M.S. DIANA	174
H.M.S. DIDO	177
H.M.S. DOMINION	179
H.M.S. DORSETSHIRE	180
H.M.S. DRAKE	181
H.M.S. DREADNOUGHT	183
H.M.S. DRYAD	184
H.M.S. DUBLIN	186
H.M.S. DUCHESS	188
H.M.S. DUKE OF EDINBURGH	190
H.M.S. DUKE OF YORK	191
H.M.S. DUNKIRK	192
H.M.S. EAGLE	194
H.M.S. EARL OF PETERBOROUGH	198
H.M.S. EDINBURGH	199
H.M.S. ENCHANTRESS	200
H.M.S. ENDEAVOUR	202
H.M.S. ESSEX	203
H.M.S. EURYALUS	204
H.M.S. EXETER	206
H.M.S. FALMOUTH	207

		Page
H.M.S. FINISTERRE	..	209
H.M.S. FORMIDABLE	..	210
H.M.S. FORESTER	..	212
H.M.S. FORTUNE	..	214
H.M.S. FRANKLIN	..	216
H.M.S. FURIOUS	..	217
H.M.S. GABBARD	..	218
H.M.S. GAMBIA	..	219
H.M.S. GANGES	..	220
H.M.S. GLASGOW	..	222
H.M.S. GLORIOUS	..	224
H.M.S. GLORY	..	225
H.M.S. GLOUCESTER	..	227
H.M.S. GRAVELINES	..	228
H.M.S. GREENWICH	..	229
H.M.S. GRENVILLE	..	230
H.M.S. GUARDIAN	..	231
H.M.S. HAMPSHIRE	..	232
H.M.S. HAWKINS	..	233
H.M.S. HERCULES	..	234
H.M.S. HERMES	..	237
H.M.S. HIBERNIA	..	240
H.M.S. HINDUSTAN	..	241
H.M.S. HOGUE	..	242
H.M.S. HOOD	..	244
H.M.S. HOWE	..	245
H.M.S. ILLUSTRIOUS	..	247
H.M.S. IMPLACABLE	..	249
H.M.S. INDEFATIGABLE	..	251
H.M.S. INDOMITABLE	..	254
H.M.S. INFLEXIBLE	..	256
H.M.S. INVINCIBLE	..	257
H.M.S. IRON DUKE	..	258
H.M.S. IRRESISTIBLE	..	260
H.M.S. JAMAICA	..	261
H.M.S. JUTLAND	..	263
H.M.S. KELLY	..	264
H.M.S. KEMPENFELT	..	265
H.M.S. KENT	..	266
H.M.S. KENYA	..	267

	Page
H.M.S. KING EDWARD VII	268
H.M.S. KING GEORGE V	269
H.M.S. LAGOS	271
H.M.S. LAUREL	272
H.M.S. LION	273
H.M.S. LIVERPOOL	275
H.M.S. LONDON	277
H.M.S. LOWESTOFT	279
H.M.S. MAGPIE	281
H.M.S. MANXMAN	283
H.M.S. MARLBOROUGH	284
H.M.S. MARNE	285
H.M.S. MARY ROSE	286
H.M.S. MATAPAN	289
H.M.S. MATCHLESS	290
H.M.S. MAURITIUS	291
H.M.S. MEDWAY	292
H.M.S. MELBOURNE	293
H.M.S. MERMAID	294
H.M.S. MILNE	295
H.M.S. MONARCH	296
H.M.S. MOON	297
H.M.S. MUSKETEER	298
H.M.S. MYNGS	299
H.M.S. NAPIER	300
H.M.S. NATAL	301
H.M.S. NELSON	302
H.M.S. NEPAL	303
H.M.S. NEWCASTLE	304
H.M.S. NEWFOUNDLAND	307
H.M.S. NEW ZEALAND	308
H.M.S. NIGERIA	309
H.M.S. NIZAM	310
H.M.S. NOBLE	311
H.M.S. NORMAN	312
H.M.S. NUBIAN	313
H.M.S. OBEDIENT	315
H.M.S. OBDURATE	316
H.M.S. OCEAN	317
H.M.S. OPPORTUNE	318

	Page
H.M.S. ORION	319
H.M.S. OROTAVA	321
H.M.S. ORWELL	322
H.M.S. OSEA	323
H.M.S. OWEN	324
H.M.S. PACTOLUS	325
H.M.S. PALADIN	326
H.M.S. PATUCA	327
H.M.S. PEGASUS	328
H.M.S. PELICAN	329
H.M.S. PEMBROKE	332
H.M.S. PENELOPE	334
H.M.S. PERSEUS	336
H.M.S. PETARD	338
H.M.S. PHOEBE	339
H.M.S. PIONEER	341
H.M.S. PORTIA	343
H.M.S. PRIMROSE	344
H.M.S. PRINCE OF WALES	345
H.M.S. PRINCESS ROYAL	346
H.M.S. PROTECTOR	347
H.M.S. QUEEN	349
H.M.S. QUEEN ELIZABETH	350
H.M.S. QUEEN MARY	352
H.M.S. QUILLIAM	353
H.M.S. RAMESES	354
H.M.S. RAPID	355
H.M.S. RELENTLESS	357
H.M.S. RENOWN	359
H.M.S. REPULSE	360
H.M.S. RESOURCE	362
H.M.S. REVENGE	363
H.M.S. ROBERTS	365
H.M.S. ROCKET	367
H.M.S. RODNEY	370
H.M.S. ROEBUCK	371
H.M.S. ROYAL SOVEREIGN	374
H.M.S. ROYALIST	375
H.M.S. RUBY	377
H.M.S. SAINTES	379

		Page
H.M.S. ST. JAMES	.. ..	380
H.M.S. ST. KITTS	.. ..	381
H.M.S. ST. VINCENT	.. ..	382
H.M.S. SATELLITE	.. ..	383
H.M.S. SAVAGE	.. ..	384
H.M.S. SCORPION	.. ..	385
H.M.S. SCOTT	.. ..	386
H.M.S. SEAGULL	.. ..	387
H.M.S. SEA ROVER	.. ..	388
H.M.S. SHAH	.. ..	389
H.M.S. SHANNON	.. ..	390
H.M.S. SHARK	.. ..	391
H.M.S. SHEFFIELD	.. ..	393
H.M.S. SIRIUS	.. ..	394
H.M.S. SLUYS	.. ..	396
H.M.S. SOLEBAY	.. ..	397
H.M.S. SORCERESS	.. ..	399
H.M.S. SOUTHAMPTON	.. ..	400
H.M.S. SUPERB	.. ..	401
H.M.S. SURPRISE	.. ..	404
H.M.S. SUSSEX	.. ..	406
H.M.S. SWIFTSURE	.. ..	407
H.M.S. TEAZER	.. ..	410
H.M.S. TEMERAIRE	.. ..	411
H.M.S. TENACIOUS	.. ..	412
H.M.S. TERMAGANT	.. ..	413
H.M.S. TERPSICHORE	.. ..	414
H.M.S. THESEUS	.. ..	415
H.M.S. THISTLE	.. ..	417
H.M.S. THUNDERER	.. ..	418
H.M.S. TIGER	.. ..	420
H.M.S. TORMENTOR	.. ..	421
H.M.S. TOTEM	.. ..	422
H.M.S. TOURMALINE	.. ..	423
H.M.S. TRAFALGAR	.. ..	424
H.M.S. TRIBUNE	.. ..	425
H.M.S. TRIDENT	.. ..	426
H.M.S. TRIUMPH	.. ..	427
H.M.S. TROUBRIDGE	.. ..	431
H.M.S. TRUCULENT	.. ..	432

		Page
H.M.S. TUMULT	.. ..	433
H.M.S. TUSCAN	.. ..	434
H.M.S. TYNE	.. ..	435
H.M.S. TYRIAN	.. ..	436
H.M.S. ULSTER	.. ..	437
H.M.S. ULYSSES	.. ..	438
H.M.S. UNA	.. ..	439
H.M.S. UNBEATEN	.. ..	440
H.M.S. UNBROKEN	.. ..	441
H.M.S. UNDAUNTED	.. ..	442
H.M.S. UNDINE	.. ..	443
H.M.S. UNICORN	.. ..	444
H.M.S. UPSTART	.. ..	447
H.M.S. URANIA	.. ..	448
H.M.S. URCHIN	.. ..	449
H.M.S. URSA	.. ..	450
H.M.S. VANGUARD	.. ..	451
H.M.S. VENGEANCE	.. ..	455
H.M.S. VENUS	.. ..	457
H.M.S. VERULAM	.. ..	458
H.M.S. VICTORIOUS	.. ..	459
H.M.S. VICTORY	.. ..	461
H.M.S. VIDAL	.. ..	463
H.M.S. VIGILANT	.. ..	464
H.M.S. VIGO	.. ..	465
H.M.S. VINDICTIVE	.. ..	466
H.M.S. VIRAGO	.. ..	467
H.M.S. VOLAGE	.. ..	468
H.M.S. VULCAN (DEFIANCE)	.. ..	469
H.M.S. WAGER	.. ..	472
H.M.S. WAKEFUL	.. ..	473
H.M.S. WARRIOR	.. ..	474
H.M.S. WARSPITE	.. ..	476
H.M.S. WATERWITCH	.. ..	478
H.M.S. WELLINGTON	.. ..	479
H.M.S. WEYMOUTH	.. ..	480
H.M.S. WHELP	.. ..	482
H.M.S. WHIRLWIND	.. ..	483
H.M.S. WIZARD	.. ..	484
H.M.S. WOOLWICH	.. ..	485

	Page
H.M.S. WRANGLER	486
H.M.S. YARMOUTH	487
H.M.S. ZAMBESI	489
H.M.S. ZEALANDIA	490
H.M.S. ZEALOUS	491
H.M.S. ZEBRA	492
H.M.S. ZENITH	493
H.M.S. ZEPHYR	494
H.M.S. ZEST	495
H.M.S. ZODIAC	496

ILLUSTRATIONS

EXAMPLES OF SHIPS' BADGES	*Frontispiece*
	Page
THREE MEMORIAL WINDOWS	499
FIGUREHEADS	500–1
EARLY UNOFFICIAL BADGES	502–7
FIGUREHEAD AND BADGES ON A ROWING BARGE	508
ENTRANCE, ADMIRAL SUPERINTENDENT'S OFFICE, CHATHAM DOCKYARD	509
MAIN GATE BADGE, R.N. DOCKYARD, CHATHAM	510
BADGE OF QUEEN ELIZABETH AT UPNOR	511
ARETHUSA BATTLE HONOURS	512
BADGE NEAR R.N. COLLEGE, GREENWICH	512
EXAMPLES OF ARMS AND SCROLL-WORK	513
PULPIT EX H.M.S. NEW ZEALAND	514

All Illustrations are Copyright.

INTRODUCTION

THIS book has been compiled in response to many requests from those interested in ships' badges for more information on this all-absorbing subject. More and more people are collecting examples, and as so little has appeared, either written or illustrated, this work may help to supply the demand. The matter contained herein might well form the basis of acquiring a wider knowledge of nautical heraldry, and a complete collection of ships' badges and crests would be well worth while making. In this book only a small proportion of those possible have been dealt with, for there are well over 2,000 official and unofficial badges, but those selected will give a good general idea of their types and the wide variety of designs used.

The language of heraldry has not been strictly adhered to and the descriptions which appear with the official badges are those which have been given officially. All the examples used I have drawn in line from the photographs of the original sealed patterns or photographs of the carvings, as supplied by the Admiral Superintendent, Royal Naval Dockyard, Chatham, where all the sealed patterns and negatives are held.

The battle honours have been taken from the Official List which is at the Admiralty Library, and I am greatly indebted to the Admiralty Archivist for allowing me access to this list. It is possible that there may be certain amendments to the list of battle honours at a later date.

In the book I have given a few of the unofficial badges which appeared before 1918, of which there were a great many, but these will serve to show the general pattern which they took. I have not shown all the badges any particular ship could have had, for it is known that they were changed quite often. A wide selection of various types have been shown covering many ships of the present fleet and those which have now gone out of service.

In some cases only brief historical notes have been given about a particular ship, and in other cases a more extended history covering other ships which have borne an individual name. It was impossible to cover all the histories of the vessels chosen, interesting as many of them are, as it would have limited to a great extent the number of badges which could have been shown. The expanded histories serve to show the many and varied services our ships have been called upon to perform and how a ship built up her battle honours and history scroll and then proudly displayed them on each succeeding ship of the name.

There are many other badges which deserve mention but which have not been shown, such as the badges of the Royal Naval Division of the 1914-18 war; the R.N.V.R. Divisions, such as *President, Sussex, Severn*, etc.; the Fleet Air Arm Squadrons; the mine-watching service badge; the Royal Naval Dockyards, which have recently been granted badges; the badge of the W.R.N.S.; the recent badge of the Royal Naval Reserve Officers' Club; and the badges of the navies of the Commonwealth.

In compiling this work I acknowledge with grateful thanks the help I have had from many sources in order to make up the story and to fill in the gaps in my own knowledge of the subject. First and foremost is the Admiral Superintendent of the Royal Naval Dockyard, Chatham, and the staff of the Drawing Office, especially Mr. Don Edser, for their generous help in getting this book under way; the Admiralty Archivist and his staff at the Admiralty Library for allowing me to consult their lists of naval ships' histories, ships' badges and battle honours; to Mr. H. Maschek, the carver of the badge patterns, for showing me how they were carved; to Mr. Edward A. Mitchell of the College of Arms for showing me how the badges were designed and painted; to Commander Peter Scott, R.N.V.R., for allowing me to use his father's letter; to Mr. W. J. Steeple for the benefit of his extensive knowledge of H.M. Ships' histories, and who checked the final proofs, and for the many valuable suggestions he gave me; to the Controller of Her Majesty's Stationery Office for permission to reproduce the Official Badges; to the Director of the Imperial War Museum for allowing me to use photographs shown in this book and for his information on Major ffoulkes; and I should like to make special mention of Mr. A. L. Kipling, of Messrs. Gale & Polden, for the advice he has given me and the splendid way in which he has arranged the layout of the book. A final appreciation must go to my wife for the constant encouragement she gave me and without whose help I could not have completed the work at all.

With all works of a compilation nature and where vessels are reconstructed or converted and change their classification it is possible that errors may have crept in, though everything has been done to try and prevent this, and in this connection I should appreciate that errors found may be brought to my notice so that any future edition may be corrected.

A. E. WEIGHTMAN

T.S. Arethusa,
 Lower Upnor, Rochester, Kent.

SHIPS' BADGES
OF THE ROYAL NAVY

THEIR ORIGIN AND USE

THE exact date when badges were first carried by R.N. Ships is not known, but there is no doubt that the origin was similar to that of the Army and has come down to the present form from the past, mainly for recognition purposes, though often influenced by decorative and prestige reasons. A study of heraldry would give the full story, and a very fascinating story it is too. There are some enthusiasts who would like to state that the first bearers of *cote armure* were Adam and Eve, and if this were so then present-day badges certainly had an early start, though one cannot help thinking that this carries heraldry a little too far back. In ships' badges we shall certainly find much that bears on heraldry, for many of the devices carried have been adopted and adapted from coats of arms. From history we learn that it was the custom from the earliest times for communities to adopt some device for identification, for there are the badges of the Scottish clans with their oak sprigs, fir club moss, wild myrtle, etc., and indeed in certain badges of the *Loch* class vessels of H.M. Navy we find these very same types of sprigs appearing. The Romans had their eagle standard, and the Athenian owl is familiar to all who study this subject; the Scriptures, too, tell us of standards or symbols of the Jewish tribes, and a very early instance of a badge being used for distinguishing an army is that now carried by the Welsh Guards, the leek. This emblem in its vegetable state, Cadwallader ordered his men to wear for recognition purposes in the year 640. When heraldic devices actually dated from as a science is probably about the twelfth century. Ships have carried banners, shields, figureheads and a variety of other decorations from the very earliest times, and to state that any one of these forms of decoration was responsible for the beginning of badges in ships might be as near the truth as we are likely to get. There have, of course, been times when there has been no decoration at all on ships, but these occasions have been rare and have been associated with economy more than anything else. Perhaps we can say, then, that the small piece of decoration which is the ship's badge evolves from the past decoration and recognition banners and shields and the seaman's own love of decoration. It is interesting to note that the present badge of H.M.S. *Swiftsure* is derived from the figurehead of the first *Swiftsure* of 1573. The badge of H.M.S. *Warrior* also comes from the figurehead carried by a previous *Warrior*, as also does the badge of *Orion*; and the lion of the *Vanguard's* badge is representative of the time when a lion was the most commonly used figurehead for a ship of the Navy. When the figurehead departed from the nautical scene its place was taken by another type of decoration, generally consisting of scroll-work and coats of arms. The *Minotaur* had such decoration as this, having the Royal Arms with scroll-work and a ribbon, whilst the *Agincourt* carried a lavish display showing the Royal Arms supported by the lion and the unicorn, flags and weapons, and underneath, the feathers and motto of the Prince of Wales. Badges of a present and past *Agincourt* are shown in this book. A variety of these types were carried, but were gradually dispensed with through changing bow shape and other needs. From about 1885 to 1890 this form of decoration went into a decline, and after this fewer and fewer ships carried decorations on the bow.

It is only in comparatively recent times that the badge as we know it has been official—December, 1918, to be exact—but these official badges grew out of the unofficial ones carried before that date. The unofficial badges were often crude in design; many were of a humorous character, though indeed there were many of very pleasing design which helped in some cases to form the basis of an official badge. The crude ones were often an initial letter and were concerned with the name of the ship and its class only, and made no pretence towards being highly decorative, having been made for the purpose of boat identification only. Decoration, however, appeared on the gun tampions and these were often splendidly done. It would appear that the well-executed designs we see on notepaper of the mid-nineteenth century were only for this crested notepaper which had just then become fashionable; that it should extend to having a badge made was only logical. Sometimes these badges were designed by, or at the request of, the Commanding Officers of the ships which desired to put them up. An instance of this can be seen from this letter to Lady Scott from Captain Scott:

"H.M.S. BULWARK,
Sunday Night.

"I've got a small piece of work for you. We want a crest for the *Bulwark*, a design from which castings can be made to form badges for the boats. Hitherto they have carried a flag, the usual sign of an Admiral ship. Now we have become a private ship, we must have something apropos. The name isn't easy to fix. I am enclosing a sheet with notes, and you've just got to rack your pretty head and suggest a design when I come up to see you, then make it in clay. What's the use of marrying a sculptor if she doesn't do such things? The design must convey an idea, quaintly or otherwise; (2) it must be simple so that it can be distinguished at a considerable distance. Do you see the requirements? Bulwark is a word of Scandinavian origin and signifies a rampart or something of that nature. It has come to signify protection and safety in modern language. It doesn't seem there is much choice but to adopt something that carries the meaning of the name, something, that is a play upon the word, as is often the case in Herald's crests—a plain B is rather hackneyed."

This letter, then, shows what was wanted and what it was for: that it was originally for distinguishing boats of the various H.M. vessels, and any other uses grew out of this particular need. It was not at all difficult to make out the senior officers' boats with their flag of rank flying, and so a need arose to supply some means by which the boats of officers of lower rank could be identified. It was only natural that the crest or design which resulted from this practice would be used on notepaper, for here again the Admirals' ships had a crest showing the flag in a naval crown with the name of the ship. This practice is still in operation on H.M. Ships, and we find as before that the ship's badge or a portion of the badge is used on the notepaper, on Christmas cards, invitation cards, and on entertainment programmes.

Boats' badges are not cast now, though I did see recently boats' badges being cast for the Royal Yacht, H.M.S. *Britannia*, and for use on the *Gothic* of the Shaw, Savill and Albion Line ready for the occasion when the Royal Family would be on board.

The ship's badge will be found in a number of places on board a ship, its principal position being on the fore part of the ship's bridge, on the after superstructure and quarterdeck, on boards at the head of companion ways, on notice boards, on battle honour plaques, and as tampions for the guns, though these latter are sometimes different in design. Unofficial badges are still to be seen on ships which are not entitled to carry a badge, and they are generally executed on board by some enthusiast who paints his design on a piece of wood, or gets some sympathetic "chippy" to carve one for him, or even a cast badge made secretly. I saw one a short while ago during Navy Days at Chatham on the H.M.C.T.B. P8108, showing a white swan on a blue sea with a light blue sky. Such an effort shows how keen the interest is in badges and how strong is the desire to have a badge on the part of the ship's company, a very commendable practice indeed.

Quite a number of H.M. Establishments have collections of badges ranged round their drill sheds, etc.; particularly is this so where collections are made with a purpose, such as representing the ships manned by a particular port division. In the Dockyard Museum at Chatham there are many examples of boats' badges, and on the training ship *Arethusa* at Lower Upnor on the Medway the boys in training are inspired by a collection, both official and unofficial, which is placed round the messdecks. A fine collection has been got together in the Nelson Hall at H.M.S. *Ganges*. At the Imperial War Museum will be found a collection of badges and also gun tampions; there also will be found much information on the part played by Major ffoulkes in the establishing of badges on an official footing, whilst at the National Maritime Museum at Greenwich will be found some examples of gun tampions, and a collection of printed samples of old and new badges. The Royal United Services Institute Museum in Whitehall has quite an interesting show of badges and tampions. The Admiralty Library, of course, has a very comprehensive collection of information and photographs on this subject, as is only natural, for the Admiralty Archivist is a member of the Ships' Badges Committee and the Library staff have to deal with many inquiries about badges. Never a day passes without getting some problems on them to answer. No doubt there are many others at home and abroad who are interested and who make collections of badges. Apart from our own Navy, badges are carried by the Dominion and other navies, the French having some very pleasing and noteworthy examples.

One of the finest sights which can be seen with reference to ship badges is that which is in St. George's Church at the Royal

Naval Barracks, Chatham. Here badges are displayed at their best, being incorporated in a set of stained glass windows forming the Chatham Port Division War Memorial. These windows by Mr. Hugh Easton have embodied in the design 94 crests of ships representative of those and their men lost by enemy action in the 1939-45 war. They are aglow with light and colour, and the emblems live on as a glorious and fitting tribute to the men and ships who served their country faithfully in its greatest need. Here we see the crossed swords and cinquefoils of the *Clacton*, sunk whilst escorting L.S.T. 411, which was itself lost, off the island of Corsica in the Mediterranean; there is the *Campbeltown* of St. Nazaire fame; the lightning flashes of the *Hurricane*; the rayed eye of the *Wakeful*; there is the badge of the *Cossack*, which achieved lasting fame in its rescue of imprisoned Merchant Navy men from the grounded prison ship *Altmark* at Josingfiord; there, too, is the *Salopian*, ex *Shropshire*, armed merchant cruiser; the *Jervis Bay*, whose self-sacrifice against overwhelming odds will never be forgotten; *Curacoa*, so tragically lost in collision with the *Queen Mary* in convoy; *Cornwall*, sunk in company with the *Dorsetshire* near the Maldive Islands by the Japanese; the badges of *Curlew* and *Veteran* and all those others portrayed here in glass, in this, which must be one of the loveliest sets of stained glass windows, glowing and impressive, a beautiful memorial to the noble deeds of seamen. The ends of the pews in this church are also being decorated with ships' badges and here we find such examples as *Aisne, Glory, Neptune, Defender, Triumph, Savage, St. Kitts, Cossack, Obdurate, Naiad, Whirlwind, Partridge, London, Zephyr*, and the W.R.N.S. Not only do they make lovely decorations on their ships, but also in places where the connections are nautical and where they serve to remind us of our ships and our men.

There are commercial firms which execute carvings and castings of these badges for private collectors and other interested parties, and as a result, of course, they have built up a considerable amount of knowledge in respect to these. Noteworthy amongst them is the firm of G. K. Beaulah & Co., of Hull, who have specialized in this form of work, and also in the production of designs and castings for the Merchant Navy ships which carry them.

The Toc H Church of All Hallows, Barking by the Tower,

in London, badly bombed during the war and now rising again, has some very interesting pieces of heraldry to show, including ships' badges. Once upon a time a number of carvings were displayed in the church, but since the bombing they have been stored elsewhere. When the church is being fitted out again these carvings will once more find their way into the South Aisle, where everything connected with the Royal and Merchant Navies will be placed. Incidentally this church is the earliest known Mariners' Chapel in England and dates from 1272 as such. The verger, ex Royal Navy, showed me their collection, and also told me that the *Pretoria Castle*, in which he served, carried a very smart badge depicting a castle, undoubtedly an unofficial one for I cannot find any record of it. The collection of very expertly carved ships' badges in this church have amongst them the following: *Cossack*, *Comet*, *Consort* and *Contest*, which were carved in Hong Kong; there are *Warspite*, *Howe*, *Cockade*, *Royalist*, *Kenya*, *Duke of York*, *Manchester*, Royal Marines Commando Brigade, and the boat badges of the *Furious* and *Tyne* (a repair ship). The gun tampion of the *Rodney* is there, and in the examples in the church is the badge of the *Hood*. Here, too, are the coats of arms of Nelson and Sir Francis Drake and the badge of the W.R.N.S. There is also the badge of the French battleship *Richelieu*, and a very fine example it is. It shows a shield on which there are three chevrons superimposed on an anchor; above is the Apostolic hat, and tassels at the sides and underneath a scroll motto. When this church is finally restored it should present a very fine sight.

We can quite safely say that the form and standard of the present ships' badges in the Royal Navy is due to the enthusiasm and hard work put into the task of producing them by the late Major Charles ffoulkes, C.B., O.B.E., O.St.J., Hon. D.Litt.Oxon, F.S.A., former master of the Tower Armouries and later Director of the Imperial War Museum. His work and interest in ships' badges for the Royal Navy is well known. From the first of his badges to the time when the work was turned over to the College of Heralds, Major ffoulkes produced about 556 designs. He first came into this fascinating work following a request from the commanding officer of a new destroyer, H.M.S. *Tower*, for a badge design appropriate to his ship. The finished design, representative of a part of the Tower of London, the White Tower, set him on the way to making the ships' badges official.

This pleasing design was taken note of by shipbuilders, and he was asked to supply designs for other vessels, amongst which were *Tintagel, Whitshed, Winter* and *Tara*. Brass badges were cast from these designs for boat badges, gun tampions were made, and dies were also struck for stamping the crests on notepaper. The interest displayed led him to inquire into the whole question of badges, for hitherto they had of course been unofficial, and where fitted on a ship they were only obtained by devious means in the dockyards and shipyards at home and abroad. The types of designs which were in evidence in those days can be seen in the examples of unofficial badges shown in this book. Many of the designs were totally unsuitable and not quite in keeping with that sense of tradition and continuity which we expect in the Royal Navy.

They were often, as mentioned before, very humorous, as we can see by the drawing of the badge used by H.M.S. *Osea*, which shows a blue devil in an egg-shell taking a sight and afloat on the sea, inspired by Rudyard Kipling's poem about this very same devil. Many of the designs were really excellent, and the examples selected by some of the ships were worthy of the highest commendation, but often these, excellent as they were, could not be satisfactorily used for casting owing to their complicated design. Very often a ship accumulated quite a number of badges of different design during her commissions, for the badge depended on what the commanding officer or the ship's company thought of it. On their whims depended whether the badge should remain or a new one be prepared, or whether no badge should be used at all. One officer of my acquaintance told me that while he was in H.M.S. *Africa* they had eight different badges through changes of commanding officers and other reasons. Of course, not all ships even after 1918 were entitled to badges, and many who were not made up their own, purely unofficial of course, and these, like the earlier ones, were not quite in keeping with what one should expect. There was a trawler during the last war named the *Stella Rigel*, and she carried a diamond-shaped badge which showed across its centre the caption "To Hell With Hitler". Two ships in which I served carried unofficial badges; one of them, a trawler, carried a badge representative of the United States, from whence the ship had come, and a star to represent the ship's name of *Luminary*. The motto carried was

"Libertas". The other ship, an L.S.T., carried a circular badge painted to represent a tropical scene and on it was a pelican disgorging tanks on to the beach. The motto was "Tanks Pal". Probably an intensive search amongst the ships of today which are not entitled to carry a badge would reveal many of an unofficial nature.

In order to give the unofficial badges closer study, Major ffoulkes advertised for collections of crests from notepaper and was lucky enough to obtain a book containing many examples of R.N. Ships' badges and notepaper crests with which to go ahead with his investigations. Even now it is possible to come across these books produced by printing firms which specialized in providing the books and the notepaper for making these collections. Only a short while ago I saw one in Foyles' bookshop in the Charing Cross Road. I understand, too, that a collection of these crests has found its way into the National Maritime Museum at Greenwich. Major ffoulkes came to the conclusion from his study of the designs that they made their appearance on H.M. Ships between 1850 and 1860 and were perhaps coincidental with the 1851 Exhibition, where die stamps were on show and soon became fashionable. On 10th December, 1918, the Admiralty accepted Major ffoulkes' offer to supply badges for H.M. Ships and for them to be made official. A committee was formed which became known as Ships' Badges Committee, and he became the Admiralty Adviser on Heraldry. It was now decided to make experiments on the form the official badges should take, and arrangements were made for various shapes to be tried out on a police launch between Westminster and Lambeth Bridges. Several shapes were made from cardboard, these being gilded, and were shown on the launch for observers to report on as they passed by. The observations were made from a captured German submarine used for propaganda purposes, which was moored near the Houses of Parliament. Even the traffic on the river was held up so that this work could proceed (unofficially, I might add). On completion of the experiments it was decided to use circular shapes for battleships, pentagon shapes for cruisers and light cruisers, shield shapes for destroyers, and a diamond shape for aircraft carriers, submarines, depot ships and sloops. Owing to the wide variety of names, a large amount of research work had to be done at the Zoological Gardens, the Natural

History Museum, the British Museum and Kew Gardens. Misprints in records caused some difficulties, for there were some ships whose names were not as they had been intended through these errors. For instance, it has been stated that the *Whitley* should have been *Whitby*, and in this connection it should be significant that the name is not to be used again; and the *Sterling* which should have been *Stirling* after Admiral Stirling. However, the difficulties were surmounted and badges produced appropriate to the names.

When the designs were passed by the Ships' Badges Committee they went on to Messrs. Martyns, the Palace Decorators of Cheltenham, who produced the necessary carvings ready for casting. When Martyns had completed the carvings, they came back to the Committee for inspection and if passed went on to Chatham for casting. A year's intensive work resulted in 113 carvings being exhibited in Gieves' Galleries in Bond Street. Later on the contract for carving went to Mr. H. L. Maschek, who originally worked for Martyns and who has now been doing this work for the Admiralty for over thirty years. The number of designs he has carved in his London studio would make a truly amazing show.

After seventeen years' association in the production of ships' badges, in which time Major ffoulkes had produced his 556 designs and accomplished an incredible amount of research work and hard labour and also provided suitable mottoes for the ships, his connection came to an end. In 1935 the designing of badges passed into the hands of the College of Heralds, where they were looked after by Clarenceux King of Arms. After the death of Sir Arthur Cochrane, Clarenceux King of Arms, the work was taken over by Somerset Herald, Mr. M. R. Trappes-Lomax. From this establishment come some very lovely designs, and they are most ably interpreted by the carver and most carefully handled in the foundry in the Royal Naval Dockyard at Chatham, where the casting of the badges is done.

Commanding Officers of ships entitled to badges can make suggestions with respect to the design of the badges, and they must give their reasons for their suggestions, so that the proper interpretation may be made of them, but these must be in before the final decision is made by the Ships' Badges Committee. When the badges have been decided upon, the resultant designs are often achieved only by intensive research work on the part of the College of Heralds and from the suggestions put forward by the committee and the ship's personnel, and is by no means the simple task one would imagine it to be. It is most difficult to strike an idea and a design which would be readily understood by everybody in the case of many of H.M. Ships' names, though a large number are readily seen. Often the crew of a ship, beholding their badge for the first time, cannot understand the reason for it. There should be some remedy for this. Take, for instance, the survey vessel H.M.S. *Vidal*, named after Admiral Vidal. The badge of this ship is a roasting grid. Unless you know the story such a design conveys nothing until it is explained that Admiral Vidal did survey work on the St. Lawrence River in Canada, and it was St. Lawrence, so the story goes, who was roasted on a grid. Very obvious badges are those of the *Trident* (a gold trident), *Liberty* (the Statue of Liberty), *Sparrow* (sparrow on a branch), or *Snipe* (a flying snipe).

When the College of Heralds has produced the necessary design, it is inspected and passed by the Ships' Badges Committee and is then sent to the contractor for carving. Later on, when the original design is finished with by the carver, this original design, together with the motto, is sent to Chatham Dockyard, where they are filed in the Drawing Office. This drawing is the sealed pattern. It is now necessary to make a facsimile of the designs which, after being passed by the Admiralty, goes to the ship for placing in the ship's book with a copy of the motto. The original drawing is also photographed, a print being sent to the Admiralty and also one to the ship. The negatives are stored at Chatham so that copies can be made for interested parties. These are obtainable for a nominal sum for a print and a copyright fee. If the badge is to be used in some commercial form, this has to be stated to the Admiral Superintendent so that the fee can be assessed. Due acknowledgement must be made for its use to the Chief Controller, H.M. Stationery Office, as these prints are Crown Copyright.

When badges are purchased by the public for any purpose it is often noted that there are three types of photographs. One shows a rather rough drawing, another shows the actual carving, and the present-day one shows the very fine work as done by the College of Heralds. The earlier ones were not very well drawn as the artist, despite his intense enthusiasm, was not skilled in such work, and he looked to the carver to interpret his ideas more skilfully, As the carvings were done with great skill it became the practice to photograph the carvings rather than the drawings. Then there came a special occasion when a photograph was required in a hurry, and as a carving was not available and the sealed pattern was, this was taken instead. As it happened to be one of the excellent pieces of work turned out by the painter at the College of Heralds it naturally photographed very well, and so this system has been adhered to ever since. Until all the negatives have been replaced by photographs of the present type of sealed pattern, the old ones will continue to be used when prints are required.

Mr. H. L. Maschek, of Wembley in London, has been connected with carving badges for the Admiralty since 1919, and has carved a very large number which includes some very interesting examples. When a badge is required, Mr. M. R. Trappes-Lomax, Somerset Herald, submits a sketch to the Ships' Badges Committee, which is then passed on to Mr. Edward A. Mitchell (Heraldic Designer and painter at the College) for detail drawing and colouring. Mr. Maschek, when preparing his carving, then enlarges the drawing to the size the casting is to be and carves the patterns in best yellow pine; the interpretation of the drawings being left to his skill and imagination. Being a very fine and experienced craftsman, the results have only to be seen to appreciate how ably he does this. The wood he uses, yellow pine, is found to be very suitable for casting work. When the patterns are carved these are submitted to the Admiralty Archivist for inspection, and then he delivers them to Chatham for castings to be made and for painting before they are set up on their individual ships.

He tells me that the most interesting pattern he has carved was the gun tampion of the battleship *King George V*, which portrayed the head of the late King George V. The badge of the battleship, it will be noted, is slightly different, having the Royal Cypher as can be seen in the illustration which accompanies information on the ship. The cutest design he considers was the *Espiegle*, depicting a cunning, tubby little fellow of the Middle Ages, with a roguish grin on his face, a perfect characterization of the practical joker Tilleulenspiegel. The most difficult problem was the Tyne R.N.V.R. badge. Major ffoulkes wanted the head of the Tyne river god as the emblem, and although he knew that there were illustrations to be found, somehow or other he could not unearth one. He asked Mr. Maschek to try and obtain one, and so he found his way into the South Kensington Library. After explaining his mission, the attendant was very obliging and brought out volume after volume about Newcastle. Just when he was giving up hope of finding it there, the very last volume brought success, for the frontispiece was the head of the river god with plaited beard, fishes and net entwined in his hair surmounted with a basket of coals and pick and shovel. Major ffoulkes was, of course, highly delighted, and always appreciated the work Mr. Maschek put into any research and to the final result in study and interpretations in the finished patterns.

The patterns for the badges of the ill-fated submarines *Thetis*, *Truculent* and *Affray* were carved by Mr. Maschek, and he is often asked whether he had any premonition in their impending disaster. Such a question is natural, for often in doing work of this kind one might have a certain difficulty to surmount, and then when something happens it could be connected and some kind of an interpretation put on it. But, as he says, the carving of the patterns was just routine work and therefore no premonition of their regretful fate was felt. In his connection with the Admiralty he has also been concerned in the carving of battle honour plaques, without which no ship with valiant predecessors or honours is really complete. He has also made patterns for the Indian, Pakistan and Chinese Navies.

When the carved patterns are finished they are delivered to Chatham, and usually Mr. Maschek delivers them himself so that they cannot come to any harm in transit. When this carving is received in the dockyard it goes to the pattern shop to be varnished prior to being sent to the foundry for casting. When it is finished with at the foundry it is returned to the pattern shop and then placed in store. I often think it would be a good plan if these could be shown on Navy Days. In fact it would be a good idea if the whole process could be on show to the public, for it is very difficult to realize what a lot of work and thought goes into these badges.

CASTING THE BADGES

All ships' badges are officially cast at the Royal Naval Dockyard, Chatham, at their foundry. When the carved wooden pattern for a ship's badge is received at the foundry and a start is to be made in casting it, it is passed to the moulder, who places the yellow pine carved pattern in a bottom box face upwards. Sand is then sieved into the box. The sand used at Chatham is Ryarsh sand, and this is mixed with oil to bond it together strongly. The moulder stands over the box with his sieve rubbing handfuls of sand through the mesh. This is then tightly pressed down in order to pack it all round the carving and ensure covering properly. This is essential, of course, for if the sand does not cover properly, then the resultant casting is useless and has to be scrapped. Sometimes these carvings are quite intricate and so the moulder certainly needs to know his craft very well indeed. When this is all ready the box is turned and a top box is brought in and placed over the bottom one, and into this is poured ordinary foundry sand, which is rather darker than the first lot of sand used round the face of the pattern, and the whole carefully rammed down and smoothed off. A hollow spigot is driven into this and the sand taken out, leaving a hole, called an in-gate, which allows the flow of molten metal to reach the interior. Then it is lifted off. Very careful smoothing is now done with a jointing trowel, and then when ready a loosening spike is carefully introduced into the back of the wooden pattern in order to lift it out, leaving a hollow impression of the badge in the sand ready for the molten metal. The sand is then scooped out to make the rest of the channel to the interior with scoops called a spoon tool and a heart and square tool. As soon as the mould is set up it has a cup placed at the in-gate to form a reservoir, so that the hollow pattern will get its proper supply of molten metal. The air, driven out from the hollow part when the metal pours in, goes through the sand. Great care is taken all the time with the boxes, and the final job to be done before the metal is run in, after the boxes have been placed in a convenient position close to the crucible, is to put weights on top to keep the whole lot firm; and even a piece of paper is placed on top of the in-gate, with a little piece of metal to keep it from blowing off, to prevent any small bits and pieces from falling down the channel and so spoiling the casting. The metal is prepared in a Morgan tipping crucible furnace, which in the Chatham foundry holds about 600 pounds of metal. When ready for casting, the metal is run into a shank held by two men. This shank consists of a metal ladle or bucket which has two handles, one shaped like a fork with two prongs and which facilitates turning, and the other a single-rod handle. A workman stands by when the metal is brought to the boxes, with a long scraper with which he scrapes off slag accumulating on top of the ladle. The mould is left to cool, which varies from an hour or so until up to twenty-four hours if necessary, and then taken out and sent to the hydro-blast machine. This is a combined sand and water blast which operates under pressure and cleans up the casting to a nice degree. It is done in a large steel box-like structure with doors on one side which can be closed when operating. A set of rails leads into it on which runs a bogie for taking in large amounts of castings and heavy ones. When ready to start work the operator dons a suit rather like a diver's and which has a small pipe of running water fitted to it to wash off any sand which may obscure the window of the head-dress. The actual job is done with a powerful hand-operated hose. When the cleaning process is taking place, outside observers can look in through a square window which is also cleaned by a jet of water. When the cleaning of the casting is completed it goes to the trimming shop, where the rough edges and the metal formed by the in-gate is cut off. Polishing up and painting is then to be done and the badge completed ready for setting up on the ship's bridge or quarterdeck. On the day I was privileged to see this process of badge-making it was interesting to note that the job being done was a set of badges previously mentioned, for the Royal Yacht H.M.S. *Britannia*.

Here, then, we have the whole process through which a badge has to go and details of the possible origins, etc. There can be little doubt that they made their appearance at a time when the figurehead and other bow decoration had gone from the ships, and when a desire arose for an emblem both for decoration and recognition purposes which would be a link between ship and crew, and which would help to instil pride in a ship and her achievements.

BATTLE HONOURS

There have been many histories written dealing with the part played by H.M. Ships in our island story, and I do not want to enlarge on what has already been done, but perhaps a brief reminder of those past naval battles will serve to help the reader to appreciate the way a ship of the present day has collected her battle honours. The battle honours displayed on board a vessel of the Royal Navy show where the ship herself or her forebears have served for the protection and honour of our country. This usually consists of a plaque with the badge of the ship carved thereon, with perhaps some other form of decoration and a list of the honours carved or painted where they can best be displayed. Lists of battle honours have been given throughout this book for individual vessels so that it will be easier to see what each ship has performed down the years. These are dated from 1588 to the 1939-45 war. The Korean phase may bring new campaign and battle honours to certain vessels of the Royal Navy and so help to swell the already imposing list.

Of all the important dates in history, I suppose 1588 is one of the most familiar, for it was in this year that the famous battle of the Spanish Armada was fought and which reflected so greatly to the credit of Britain's rising naval and commercial powers. Queen Elizabeth's fleet at that time consisted of 34 ships in all, and of this total only 24 could be collected together by Lord Howard of Effingham. Eventually the call to arms and the need for ships to repel the impending invasion by the Spaniards resulted in 197 vessels being gathered together. The Invincible Armada consisted of 132 ships, which, though less in numbers than ours, was much more powerful, the tonnage of the British ships being 29,744 and the Spaniards 59,120. Some of our ships were only 30 tons, but the smallest of the invading fleet was 300 tons. The Duke of Medina Sidonia, who was in command of this mighty fleet, suffered a great defeat, inflicted on him by Lord Howard of Effingham, Lord Henry Seymour, Sir Francis Drake, Frobisher, Hawkins and others. Fireships, storms and faulty navigation completed the indignity and humbled the might of Spain. Eleven Spanish standards were taken to St. Paul's and there hung for all to see.

In 1595 Sir Francis Drake died in the West Indies after a fruitless expedition, and with him perished also Sir John Hawkins.

It seemed that with the death of Drake, who had struck such terror into the hearts of the Spaniards, these worthies now thought that they could avenge their defeat and once more have a chance to invade England. They were doomed to disappointment, for Lord Howard of Effingham set out from Plymouth with a fleet to attack the Spaniards in Cadiz, where preparations for invasion were hurriedly going on. The result of this sudden attack by the British was the total destruction of the Spanish fleet. In the fleet used by Lord Howard were such familiar names as the following: *Ark Royal, Repulse, Warspite, Lion, Vanguard, Mary Rose, Dreadnought* and *Swiftsure*, names which have been used over and over again for vessels of the Royal Navy.

In 1652 a number of battles were fought between the Dutch and British, and in 1653 there was the battle of Portland. In this battle, Blake, General-at-Sea with his fleet and having with him Vice-Admiral Penn and Rear-Admiral John Lawson as his second and third in command, both very able professional sailors, and also his old colleagues Monk and Deane commanding a body of troops—stated to be the first time that soldiers of the line were employed on vessels of war—met up with Tromp as he was coming up the English Channel with a large fleet of merchant ships and 73 men-of-war. A running fight ensued in which many of the Dutch ships were taken in prizes and a number sunk. The General flew his flag in the *Triumph*, a familiar naval ship name. We also find in his fleet such names as *Vanguard, Victory* and *Lion*.

The Gabbard battle of 1653 was fought off Yarmouth and is described sometimes as the battle off Yarmouth or the Gober, and in this battle on 3rd June the English fleet under Monk and Deane met the Dutch under Tromp, de Ruyter and de Witt. Deane was killed in the early stages of the battle, the Dutch retired and then Blake joined up with more ships, with the fight being continued off Nieuport on the following day. In this battle Tromp made a very desperate effort to gain a victory and, attacking the *James* with Admiral Penn on board, he was very viciously repelled and driven back to his own ship, pursued in turn by the British who boarded his ship. The Dutch were driven below decks by the English sailors, and it is reported that Tromp himself fired the magazine in order to blow up the decks of his ship and rid himself of his unwelcome visitors.

Then followed the battle of Scheveningen or Camperdown, and this battle brought about the close of the first Dutch war; the Dutch admiral being defeated and killed.

The scene then shifts to Jamaica, which was taken by Admiral Penn in the latter end of 1654. Blake was sent by Cromwell to the Mediterranean, where he surprised Europe by his action against Tunis and Algiers which resulted in captive Christian slaves being released. He scored a great victory at Santa Cruz in the Canary Islands, and on the way home when entering Plymouth Sound he died. Cromwell died in 1658, and on 23rd May, 1660, Charles II embarked in Holland on board the *Royal Charles* (ex *Naseby*), once Admiral Blake's flagship. Then once more we were at war with the Dutch and a number of incidents led up to the battle of Lowestoft, won by H.R.H. The Duke of York on 3rd June, 1665. The Four Days' Fight of 1666 took place off Dunkirk, and on the British side the commanders were Rupert and Monk, the Earl of Albemarle, and the Dutch were under de Ruyter, Evertzen and Tromp (a son of the earlier Tromp). The French declared war on England and joined with the Dutch fleet. A very hard and bloodthirsty battle ensued which only ended when fog came down. The *Royal Prince*, the flagship of Sir George Ayscue, ran aground and the ship was set on fire by the enemy and her crew were taken prisoner. The *Swiftsure* and the *Essex* were captured by the enemy.

In the St. James's Day battle of 1666 more hard fighting took place, the Dutch being severely beaten and blockaded in their own ports. We lost the *Resolution*, which blew up. Ships which carried familiar names taking part in this engagement, amongst others, were the *Royal Sovereign, Victory, Defence, Mary Rose, Warspite* and *Bonaventure*. Lack of care over defences and neglect of the Royal Navy led the Dutch to attack us on our own doorstep, and they sailed up the Thames, burnt Sheerness and then sailed up as far as Upnor Castle. The *Royal Charles* was taken away by them to Holland, and her stern decoration is to be seen in the Museum at Amsterdam. A treaty was then concluded with Holland.

Later on in 1672 war was resumed and we had the third Dutch war beginning with Sole Bay or Southwold. The Duke of York commanded the English fleet and de Ruyter the Dutch. He had to leave his flagship the *Prince* and go to the *St. Michael* and then to the *London*. The Earl of Sandwich was lost with many of his men in the *Royal James*, which blew up after catching on fire. Following this came Schooneveld in 1673 and the Battle of the Texel, and this brought to a close the third Dutch war.

James, Duke of York, was sent to exile in Ireland and tried to regain his throne with Irish and French help, and from this came the battle of Bantry Bay in 1689. The British and the Dutch were together in the fight against the French, for England was now threatened with invasion. Lord Torrington and Sir George Rooke were now in command of the fleet and were soon engaged in the battle of Beachy Head (1690). In this the French beat the Dutch and chased our own ships back into the Thames. Lord Torrington was sent to the Tower, acquitted of the charges laid against him, but was relieved of his command and commission. Admiral Edward Russell now took over command and with the battle of Barfleur in 1692 the invasion threat was stopped. Then in 1693 came the delaying action at Lagos Bay, when Admiral Rooke and the Dutch were convoying a large fleet of merchantmen. The French attacked and many of the convoy's ships were captured or sunk.

With Queen Anne on the throne we were in conflict with Spain, and a great battle was fought in Vigo Bay, with many French and Spanish ships captured or set on fire; our forces being under the command of Sir George Rooke. Sir George Rooke captured Gibraltar on 23rd July, 1704, and with the Dutch to aid him he fought the Count de Toulouse off Malaga on 13th August, 1704. Rooke led the centre and Sir Cloudesley Shovel and Sir John Peake led the van. Sir George Byng later won a victory over the Spanish fleet off Messina in 1718 (Passero), and Vice-Admiral Vernon took Portobello on 22nd November, 1739.

Admiral Matthews fought actions with the French and Spanish fleets off Toulon in 1744, and there were the victories gained by Anson and Hawke off Finisterre in 1747. On the quarterdeck of the *Monarch*, Admiral Byng was shot after a court-martial on 14th March, 1756, following the affair off Minorca. On 10th September, 1759, came Admiral Pocock's action with the Comte d'Ache, and for this encounter the Admiral received the ribbon of the Order of the Bath.

There were successes in North America and expeditions against French ports. On 18th-19th August, 1759, Admiral

Boscawen fought the action with the French under de la Clue, and in the same year there was the decisive defeat of Conflans by Sir Edward Hawke on 20th-21st November. More widespread actions came: Basseterre in Guadaloupe reduced by Commodore Moore; the capture of Pondicherry, Belle Ile and Havana, Martinique and Grenada; then the war of American Independence, 1776-1783. There was Lord Howe's action in 1778 with the Count d'Estaing, and then Vice-Admiral Byron's action with the same opponent off Grenada on 6th July, 1779. On 16th January, 1780, there was Sir George Rodney's victorious battle off Cape St. Vincent, Sir Samuel Hood's engagement with the Comte de Grasse on 28th April, 1781, and an action between Sir Thomas Graves and the same enemy commander on 5th September, 1781. In the same year Admiral Sir Hyde Parker had a battle with the Dutch fleet, and in the following year Sir George Rodney scored a great victory over de Grasse on 12th April. Sir Edward Hughes fought a series of actions against de Suffren in the East Indies, and these were keenly contested and heavy battles. On 1st of June, 1794, we have Lord Howe's great victory, the Glorious 1st of June. A succession of famous and some not so famous but nevertheless interesting engagements followed on as the years rolled by. Vice-Admiral Hotham's engagement at Genoa in 1795 was not a very good one owing to poor handling of the vessels on both sides; Admiral Cornwallis fought a running battle and then at the critical moment the Channel fleet came up under Lord Bridport; and in 1797 came the great victory of Sir John Jervis at St. Vincent over the Spaniards when he was blockading Cadiz. In the battle Nelson showed the brilliance which was to distinguish him later on. Two more great events came in that year, the capture of Trinidad by Rear-Admiral Harvey from the Spaniards, and the defeat of the Dutch at Camperdown by Admiral Duncan. The next famous battle was that of the Nile in 1798, and this was Nelson's first command of a large fleet. This battle showed his genius, for not one of the French fleet escaped capture or destruction.

The opening of the nineteenth century found Great Britain attacking the Danish fleet to prevent it falling into enemy hands at Copenhagen; this was in 1801, the fleet being under the command of Admiral Sir Hyde Parker and with Nelson as second-in-command, whose plan of attack was the one carried out.

In 1805 we had Calder's action at Ferrol against the French and Spanish fleets, and then the memorable battle of Nelson's on the 21st October, 1805, where Nelson lost his life and Great Britain one of its most able and best loved Admirals. The next year Sir John Duckworth attacked the French off San Domingo and scored a resounding victory. In order to prevent the Danes letting their ships fall into Napoleon's hands, we again had to attack them, and this resulted in Copenhagen being bombarded, the surrender of the fleet and the destruction of vessels building, by Admiral Gambier. Napoleon was still triumphantly active in Europe and it was found necessary to send a fleet to the Dardanelles in 1807 under Sir John Duckworth; but although some ships of the Turks were destroyed or taken, the action was not as impressive as it was expected to be.

Captain Brisbane's action at Curacoa with the *Arethusa*, *Latona*, *Anson* and *Fisgard* in 1807 added more glory to the Royal Navy and a name which has been borne by one of our cruisers. This *Curacoa* served in the Second World War, but was, alas, sunk in convoy by collision with the *Queen Mary*. In 1809 the French were severely beaten at the Basque Roads by Admiral Gambier and Lord Cochrane. Captain William Hoste beat a combined French and Neapolitan fleet at the Island of Lissa in the Adriatic in 1811; and Lord Exmouth, in company with a Dutch Squadron, attacked Algiers in 1816 in order to make the Dey release Christian slaves, thereby doing what Blake did so many years before. Great destruction was done to the Algerian ruler's defences and ships.

Another spot of trouble arrived when the Greeks turned against the Turkish rule. The Turks joined up with the fleet of its Egyptian Dependency, and Britain, France and Russia were allied to stop the war against Greece. In the negotiations there was some treachery and fire was opened on some of our small craft. Sir Edward Codrington, who was in command, was forced to destroy the Turkish and Egyptian fleets at the Battle of Navarino, 1827.

The battles of Sidon and Acre were next and these came in 1840, and on this occasion Britain was helping Turkey to put down a rebellion of the Egyptians against the Turks.

The next war found Britain and France protecting Turkey against Russia, the Crimean War of 1854-5. A fleet was sent to the Black Sea under Vice-Admiral Dundas, and another to the

Baltic under Sir Charles Napier: 1855 saw the end of the war and peace negotiated. This war was probably the dividing line between the old and the new navy, for steam had now taken the place of sail. Indeed, it was the *Arethusa* which was the last H.M. vessel to go into action under sail alone.

Following incidents in Japan in trying to open up trade with that hitherto unknown country, British, French, American and Dutch vessels went to the Straits of Shimonoseki in 1864 under Admiral Kuper, resulting in more settled conditions.

The Great War of 1914-1918 found the Royal Navy playing a hard part and engaged in all kinds of work, convoys, battles and patrols. A sweep was made into Heligoland Bight on 28th August, 1914, to carry out a plan for engaging the German forces; the battle of Coronel, in which our forces under Admiral Sir Christopher Cradock were beaten by the Germans; then the battle of the Falkland Islands, which reversed the fortunes and it was now the German turn to be wiped out. Our forces were under Sir Doveton Sturdee and the enemy under Admiral Graf Spee.

After raids on our coasts, Admiral Beatty caught the Germans returning and the battle of the Dogger Bank resulted, the German battleship *Blucher* being sunk. An unsuccessful attempt was made to force the Dardanelles in 1915, making it a long drawn out affair with much loss in lives and in materials. The battle of Jutland on 31st May, 1916, caused the German fleet to retire, and they never came out again except to surrender on 21st November, 1918.

The Second World War brought a thrill with the battle of the River Plate, fought by the *Exeter*, *Ajax* and *Achilles* against the German pocket battleship *Admiral Graf Spee*, which ended with the German vessel going into Montevideo, then scuttling itself on orders from Germany, and the final episode of its commander, Captain Langsdorff, committing suicide. In this war the Royal Navy had a stupendous task: the operations in Norway; the submarine menace; the miracle of Dunkirk and the heroic story of the little ships and the merchant navy; the battles in the Mediterranean; the Russian convoys; the Malta convoys; the Battle of the Atlantic; the war in the Pacific; landings in North Africa; the attack on Italy by the landings at Sicily, Salerno and Anzio; the South of France; the D Day landing in Normandy and the great sweep into France and finally into the heart of Germany itself. Then came the final phases: the attacks on Japanese-held islands, the attack on Japan itself, Okinawa and the all-out American and British attacks, the dropping of the atom bombs on Nagasaki and Hiroshima, and then peace with a free world triumphant.

From these engagements and many others besides came the battle honours which so many ships proudly bear, from which comes the inspiration to the men who fight the ships, which represent Naval honour, tradition and service to the country. In the badges carried by ships of the Royal Navy we can see in symbolic form the achievements of the glorious past, and which are handed on with reverence to the future sailors of Great Britain and the Commonwealth.

Official details have been given for battle honours of H.M. Ships and F.A.A. Squadrons, and states that the award of such battle honours is to foster *esprit de corps* amongst officers and ships' companies.

Ships have displayed battle honours for a long time, but they are now to be awarded officially. The battle honours are dated from 1588 (Armada) onwards. They fall into the following headings:

(i) Fleet or squadron actions.
(ii) Single ship or boat service actions.
(iii) Major bombardments.
(iv) Combined operations (*i.e.*, with Army).
(v) Campaign awards.
(vi) Area awards.

The scrolls showing the battle honours are now to be carved from teak, and outside dimensions have been arranged for various classes of vessels. The badge of the ship is to be carved as an integral part of the scroll, and the letters normally displayed are to be BLOCK LETTERS. The manufacture of the scrolls is to be undertaken by the main dockyards—viz., Portsmouth, Devonport and Chatham. Fleet Air Arm squadrons are to be displayed flanking the scroll of the carriers in which they are borne.

Battle honours have been assessed for the ships and F.A.A. squadrons which are not in the post-war fleet, and particulars can be obtained from the Secretary of the Admiralty. A large number of the battle honours of such ships are recorded in this book.

F.A.A. badges and battle honours have not been given a place in this book as it is felt that they should be given a book to themselves (only a few could have been mentioned here), so that a more worthy account could be presented.

It is interesting to note who was on the throne at the time of a particular battle or when a certain ship was built, and so a list of rulers of our country since 1588 has been included for such a reference.

SHAPES OF BADGES

The early unofficial badges were of any shape as thought out by their designers, but when the badges were put on an official footing the shapes and laid down sizes were as under (1948):

Battleship: Ship's badge round, with naval crown. Size 2' 2½" high and 1' 10¾" across; approx. weight 80 lb. Large boat's badge, 7" diameter; approx. weight 8 lb. Small boat's badge, 5¼" diameter, approx. weight 5 lb.

Cruiser: Ship's badge pentagonal, with crown. Size 1' 8⅞" high and 1' 4¾" across; approx. weight 36 lb. Large boat's badge, 7⅝" high, 7⅝" across; approx. weight 8 lb. Small boat's badge, 5¼" high and 5¾" across; approx. weight 5 lb.

Auxiliary: Ship's badge, diamond shaped with crown. Size 1' 7⅛" high, 1' 5¾" across; approx. weight 36 lb. Large boat's badge, 8" high, 8" across; approx. weight 8 lb. Small boat's badge, 6¼" high, 6¼" across; approx. weight 5 lb.

Destroyer: Ship's badge shield shaped, with crown. Size 1' 3⅞" high, 10" across; approx. weight 33 lb. Large boat's badge, Nil. Small boat's badge, 5¼" high, 5" across; approx. weight 5 lb.

Standard Design. Ship's badge round, with crown. Size 1' 6¼" high, 1' 2⅛" across; weight 31-33 lb. No boat's badges.

RULERS OF GREAT BRITAIN, THE EMPIRE AND COMMONWEALTH SINCE 1588

1558-1603 Elizabeth I.
1603-1625 James I.
1625-1649 Charles I.
1649-1653 The Commonwealth.
1653-1658 The Protectorate.
1660-1685 Charles II.
1685-1688 James II.
1689-1694 William and Mary.
1694-1702 William III.
1702-1714 Anne.
1714-1727 George I.
1727-1760 George II.
1760-1820 George III.
1820-1830 George IV.
1830-1837 William IV.
1837-1901 Victoria.
1901-1910 Edward VII.
1910-1936 George V.
1936 (Jan. 20-Dec. 11) Edward VIII.
1936-1952 George VI.
1952 Elizabeth II.

H.M.S. ABERCROMBIE

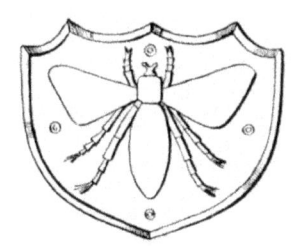

Unofficial Badge: No colours known.

Official Badge

FIELD: White.

BADGE: A boar's head erased blue in front of two swords in saltire proper.

MOTTO:

Badge derived from the Arms of General Abercromby.

BATTLE HONOURS

Guadeloupe	1810	February 5th.
Dardanelles	1915-16	February 19th—January 8th.
Sicily	1943	July 10th—August 17th.
Salerno	1943	September 9th—October 6th.
Mediterranean	1943	

A third-rate vessel of 74 guns was the first to carry the name, and she came into the Navy List in 1809 on 17th April. She was

H.M.S. ABERCROMBIE—*continued*

originally the French *Hautpoult* (74), taken by the *Pompee* (74), *Castor* (32) and *Recruit* (18) off Porto Rico on 18th April. This prize was taken over by Commander Charles Napier of the *Recruit*, and she was renamed *Abercrombie*. From 1811 to 1813 she saw service in the Channel Fleet, and on 30th April, 1817, she was sold for £3,810.

The next one was a monitor of 6,150 tons, carrying two 14-inch and two 6-inch guns, and with a speed of 6.5 knots. On 21st November, 1914, she was ordered from Harland and Wolff of Belfast and named *Farragut*, later being named *Admiral Farragut*. She was commissioned for the Mediterranean in 1915 and renamed *M.1* and then later renamed *Abercrombie*. At Mudros in 1916 and on 14th January was in action bombarding enemy positions and batteries until the withdrawal from Gallipoli. During the years 1916-1918 she was in the Eastern Mediterranean.

The present *Abercrombie* was until recently moored in the River Medway and is now being dismantled. This vessel was completed in May, 1943, and is of 7,850 tons, and carries the same armament as the *Roberts*. Her service in the Second World War can be seen from the battle honours.

H.M.S. ACHILLES

Description of Badge
FIELD: Red.
BADGE: The head of Achilles helmeted, all gold.
MOTTO: *Fortiter in Re* (Bravely in Action).

The badge is in allusion to Achilles, who was a Greek chieftain in the Trojan war. He was the son of Peleus and Thetis. Quite a number of marvellous myths are bound up in the childhood of Achilles, for his mother tried to make him invulnerable and to give him immortality. He was supposed to have been plunged into the Styx by his mother Thetis in order to achieve this, but in doing so she held him by the heel. From the legend we get the story of the "heel of Achilles," the one spot where Achilles might suffer a mortal blow.

BATTLE HONOURS

Belle Ile	1761	June 7th.
River Plate	1939	December 13th.
Guadalcanal	1942-3	August 1942—February 1943.
Okinawa	1945	March 26th—May 25th.
"Leopard"	1917	Single ship action.

The *Achilles* was a cruiser of the *Leander* class of 7,030 tons displacement, built by Cammell Laird and completed in 1933, and her armament was eight 6-inch and eight 4-inch A.A. guns. She took part in the famous River Plate action against the *Admiral Graf Spee*.

H.M.S. ACTAEON

Description of Badge

FIELD: Barry wavy of 14 white and blue.

BADGE: On a pomme demi-stag erect gold attacked by two hounds white.

MOTTO:

Actaeon was a hunter who was changed into a stag because he surprised Diana whilst she was bathing. His own dogs failed to recognize him and he was devoured by them.

BATTLE HONOURS

Belle Ile	1761	June 7th.
Martinique	1762	February 16th.
China	1856-60	

In 1757 the first *Actaeon*, a 28-gun frigate, was launched at Chatham, and she was of 585 tons. In 1761 she was commanded by Captain Paul Henry Ourry under Commodore the Hon. Augustus Keppel. The second *Actaeon* was built in 1775 at Woolwich Dockyard. She was sent to attack Charleston in South Carolina under Commodore Sir Peter Parker. Unfortunately she ran aground and could not be got off; she was therefore set on fire and abandoned. The Americans boarded her before she blew up and took away trophies.

The next *Actaeon* was a 44-gun frigate, launched in the Thames in 1778. Her tonnage was 887. She was sold in 1802.

A French vessel became the next *Actaeon* and was originally the French *Actaeon*, captured off Rochefort by the frigate

H.M.S. ACTAEON—*continued*

Egyptienne on 2nd October, 1805. This vessel was broken up in 1815.

The next *Actaeon* was a 26-gun ship, launched at Portsmouth in 1831. She was of 620 tons. She was commanded by Captain W. T. Bate at the bombardment of Canton in 1857, in 1860 was at the Taku Forts under Commander John Ward, and was sold in 1889.

Actaeon number six was formerly a 50-gun frigate, of 2,388 tons, and was launched in 1832 as the *Vernon*. She was later attached to a torpedo school at Portsmouth.

Then came an 8-gun screw corvette launched at Portsmouth in 1869 and of 1,760 tons. She was then the *Dido*, and was afterwards attached to the Torpedo School in Sheerness Harbour as the *Actaeon*.

The *Ariadne* which was launched in 1859 at Deptford was a vessel of 4,538 tons and was a 26-gun frigate. This vessel became the Torpedo School at Sheerness in 1905 and was renamed *Actaeon*.

The present *Actaeon* is a sloop of the modified *Black Swan* class, built by Thornycroft in 1945, the ninth of her name.

H.M.S. ADVENTURE

Description of Badge
FIELD: Black.

BADGE: An anchor silver between two shields bearing the cross of St. George and the Irish harp respectively.

MOTTO: Dare all.

The badge is derived from the *Adventure* medal awarded to Captain Wyard in 1650.

BATTLE HONOURS

Dover	1652	May 19th.
Portland	1653	February 18th—20th.
Gabbard	1653	June 2nd—3rd.
Lowestoft	1665	June 3rd.
Orfordness	1666	July 25th.
Sole Bay	1672	May 28th.
Barfleur	1692	May 19th—24th.
Belle Ile	1761	June 7th.
China	1855-60	
Malta Convoys	1942	
Normandy	1944	June 6th—July 3rd.
"Two Lions"	1681	Single ship action.

The *Adventure* was a special type of cruiser minelayer completed at Devonport in 1927. Her displacement was 6,740 tons and she carried four 4.7-inch A.A. and smaller guns.

H.M.S. AENEAS

Description of Badge
FIELD: Red.

BADGE: A demi-warrior in armour white, the armour and helmet garnished gold.

MOTTO: *Audentis Fortuna Juvat* (Fortune helps the daring).

A Trojan who after the fall of Troy settled in Italy. He was the hero of Virgil's "Aeneid."

No battle honours are recorded for this name.

The *Aeneas* is a submarine of the A class and was built by Cammell Laird. The tonnage of this class was 1,120/1,620 tons.

H.M.S. AFRICA

Description of Badge
BADGE: A gold lion on a brown mount having on it a red tablet on which is the name of the ship in black.

A badge which denotes both the name and the African Lion. This ship is known to have had a number of unofficial badges.

BATTLE HONOUR
Trafalgar   1805   October 21st.

A battleship of 16,350 tons and a speed of 18 knots, one of the *King Edward VII* class launched at Chatham in 1905. In 1916 she was in the British Adriatic Squadron and in 1917 was on convoy work on the West Coast of Africa.

H.M.S. AGAMEMNON

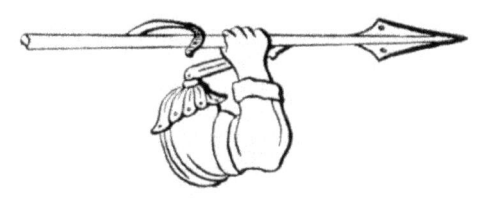

This vessel had an unofficial badge which became one of the first official badges, and also has a present type of badge.

Unofficial Badge: An arm holding a spear. No colours known.
First Official Badge: An arm proper, gold bracelet, green shoulder-robe, end of sleeve blue, gold edged. Scroll gold with the name H.M.S. AGAMEMNON black on it.
Official Badge: (As above but with standard surround.)
FIELD: Black.
BADGE: An arm, the hand grasping a spear, gold.
MOTTO: *Multa Tula Fecique* (I have borne much and done much).

The badge is from Greek mythology in allusion to the name. Agamemnon was the son of the King of the Mycenae, Atreus, and was a General-in-Chief of the Greeks during the Trojan war. He sacrificed his daughter Iphigenia to Artemis on the advice given him by Calchas in order to bring success to his enterprise. The arm holding the spear most likely comes from the story of Hector and Ajax, in which Hector keeps back the Trojans with his spear, holding it in the middle, and Agamemnon, realizing what he intended to do, did the same along the foremost ranks of the Greeks.

BATTLE HONOURS

Ushant	1781	December 12th.
The Saints	1782	April 12th.
Genoa	1795	March 14th.
Copenhagen	1801	April 2nd.
Trafalgar	1805	October 21st.
San Domingo	1806	February 6th.
Crimea	1854-5	
Dardanelles	1915-16	

H.M.S. AGAMEMNON—*continued*

The *Agamemnon* which carried this first unofficial badge was probably the steel turreted battleship launched at Chatham in 1879, but this cannot be certain and it may have belonged to the later *Agamemnon* of 1907. This vessel of 1879 was specially designed to go through the Suez Canal. On her first trip through in 1885 she ran aground and blocked the channel for several days; however, she got off and continued on to her Eastern duties and later returned to the Mediterranean.

The official badges belonged to the *Agamemnon* of 1907, which was built at Beardmore's. She was of 16,600 tons and belonged to the *Lord Nelson* class and was designed by Sir P. Watts. Her main armament was four 12-inch and ten 9.2-inch guns. Speed 18½ knots. This vessel served at the Dardanelles in 1915-16.

The first *Agamemnon* was perhaps the most notable. A 64-gun battleship, she was built at Buckler's Hard in 1781 and was the favourite ship of Nelson. The last *Agamemnon* was an auxiliary minelayer, purchased from the Blue Funnel Line in 1940 and converted. She was resold to her former owners in 1946.

H.M.S. AGINCOURT

Unofficial Badge: No colours known.

Official Badge
FIELD: Red.

BADGE: Within a wreath of palm gold a heraldic antelope statant, white collared and chained gold.

MOTTO:

Badge derived from one of the badges of Henry V, who was the Commander-in-Chief in the battle.

BATTLE HONOURS

Camperdown	1797	October 11th.
Egypt	1801	March 8th—September 2nd.
Jutland	1916	May 31st.

H.M.S. AGINCOURT—*continued*

The first *Agincourt* was a 64-gun ship of 1,416 tons, built on the River Thames by Mr. Perry. She was originally laid down as the *Earl Talbot*, an East India Company ship, but was bought for the Royal Navy whilst building. She was launched as the *Agincourt* on 23rd July, 1796. On 11th October, 1797, she was at the battle of Camperdown, for which there was a medal award. It is interesting to note, however, that the Commanding Officer of the *Agincourt*, Captain John Williamson, was sentenced by court-martial to be placed at the bottom of the Post Captain's list and rendered incapable of serving again.

During the years 1799 and 1800 she was on the Newfoundland station and was the flagship successively of Vice-Admiral Waldegrave and Vice-Admiral Sir Charles M. Pole. From 1800 to 1803 she was at the Egyptian campaign, for which there was a medal award. She conveyed General Grant and the 25th Regiment to Egypt and was at the occupation of Corfu, at the survey of the Maddalena Islands, and was renamed *Bristol* on 6th January, 1812.

The next *Agincourt*, third rate, of 1,747 tons and 74 guns, was launched at Plymouth on 19th March, 1817. From 1842 to 1846 she was the flagship of Rear-Admiral Sir Thomas Cochrane, Commander-in-Chief, East Indies and China, and during 1848-50 she was depot ship at Devonport, subsequently becoming a receiving hulk and renamed *Vigo* in April, 1865.

An ironclad battleship of 10,600 tons bore the name, launched at Laird's, Birkenhead, on 27th March, 1865. After being a flagship under Rear-Admiral Commerell at the Dardanelles, and under Rear-Admiral Sullivan when detached to Egypt, she became a tender to H.M.S. *Pembroke*, at Chatham, as depot for boys, in 1893. In 1898 she was tender to H.M.S. *Boscawen* at Portland, and renamed *Boscawen III*, in 1904.

Then came a battleship of 27,500 tons, originally built for Brazil by Armstrong Whitworth & Co. and then purchased by Turkey, and launched on 22nd January, 1913, as the *Sultan Osman I*. On the outbreak of war in August, 1914, she was taken over by the Admiralty and renamed *Agincourt*. She served at the battle of Jutland, and eventually was sold to Rosyth Shipbreaking Co. Ltd. on 19th December, 1922.

The present *Agincourt* is a *Battle* class destroyer and was built by Hawthorn Leslie in 1945.

H.M.S. AISNE

Description of Badge
FIELD: Red.

BADGE: Within a wreath of palm gold a dolphin embowed proper.

MOTTO: Armed I seek no enmity.

The badge is derived from the arms of Sir John French.

No battle honours are recorded for this name.

The *Aisne* is one of the *Battle* class of destroyers, and was built by Vickers-Armstrongs.

H.M.S. AJAX

Description of Badge
FIELD: Black.

BADGE: A Greek helmet gold, crested red.

MOTTO: *Nec Quisquam Nisi Ajax* (None but Ajax can overcome Ajax).

The name is derived from Greek mythology. There were two chieftains who bore this name, Ajax the Greater, the son of Telamon, and Ajax the Lesser, who was the son of Oileus, King of Locris. In the stories from these myths Hector of the Trojans fought Ajax of the Greeks; eventually they stopped fighting and parted in friendship, giving one another presents.

BATTLE HONOURS

St. Vincent	1780	January 16th.
St. Kitts	1782	January 25th—26th.
The Saints	1782	April 12th.
Egypt	1801	March 8th—September 2nd.
Trafalgar	1805	October 21st.
San Sebastian	1813	September 8th.
Baltic	1854-5	
Jutland	1916	May 31st.
River Plate	1939	December 13th.
Mediterranean	1940-41	
Malta Convoys	1941	
Matapan	1941	March 28th—29th.
Greece	1941	April 24th—29th.

H.M.S. AJAX—*continued*

Crete	1941	May 20th—June 1st.
Ægean	1944	
Normandy	1944	June 6th—July 3rd.
South France	1944	August 15th—27th.

The *Ajax* was a cruiser of the *Leander* class and was 6,985 tons displacement, built by Vickers-Armstrongs and completed in 1935. She carried as her main armament eight 6-inch and eight 4-inch A.A. guns. This vessel took part in the action against the *Admiral Graf Spee*.

H.M.S. ALAMEIN

Description of Badge
FIELD: Red.

BADGE: Within a wreath of palm gold a crescent moon in base white, a dexter arm mailed grasping a broken spear.

MOTTO: *Gardez Bien.*

Badge derived from the arms of Field-Marshal Lord Montgomery.

No battle honours are recorded for this name.

This vessel is one of the *Battle* class of destroyers. She was built by Hawthorn Leslie in 1945.

H.M.S. ALAUNIA

Description of Badge
FIELD: Blue.

BADGE: On a plate a horse's head erased black, collared gold.

MOTTO:

The badge is derived from the country of the Alanis, a horse-breeding and warlike race.

BATTLE HONOUR
Atlantic   1939-41

The *Alaunia* is an ex Cunard liner and was taken over by the Admiralty as an armed merchant cruiser in November, 1939, then converted into a repair ship. Her tonnage is about 14,000. Released in 1946.

H.M.S. ALBEMARLE

Description of Badge

A ducal coronet with green bonnet out of which comes a swan's head and neck. Underneath is a scroll green and red on which is the motto in black, *Ne Cede Malis* (Do not yield to misfortunes), and also the name of the ship in black.

Badge is from the Earl of Albemarle's crest.

BATTLE HONOUR
Barfleur   1692   May 19th—24th.

The *Albemarle* was a battleship of 14,000 tons and was armed with four 12-inch and twelve 6-inch guns. She was one of a class of five ships known as the *Duncan* class, and was launched at Chatham on 5th March, 1901, serving on various stations as a flagship. In 1916, from January to September, she served in the White Sea; May, 1917 to November, 1918 as overflow ship to the Royal Naval Barracks, Devonport; and on 19th November, 1919, she was sold.

H.M.S. ALBION

Description of Badge
FIELD: Blue.

BADGE: Issuant from water barry wavy in base proper a rock white, theron a lion sejant affronte gold.

MOTTO:
   Badge in allusion to the name.

	BATTLE HONOURS	
Algiers	1816	August 27th.
Navarino	1827	October 20th.
Crimea	1854-5	
Dardanelles	1915	

The first *Albion* was a 74-gun third rate built at Deptford and launched on 16th May, 1793. She was commissioned in 1770 by Captain (later Admiral) the Hon. Samuel Barrington, and in 1779 she took part in the battle off Grenada and in 1780 in the battle off Martinique. In 1794 she was converted into a floating battery and lost on the Swin in April, 1797.

There also appears in the Navy List a store ship *Albion* belonging to the Transport Office, and other hired armed vessels of the name.

Then comes another third rate of 74 guns, built on the River Thames and launched in 1802. In 1814 she was in the operations against Washington, in 1826 at the bombardment of Algiers, and in 1827 at the battle of Navarino. She was then fitted as a receiving

H.M.S. ALBION—*continued*

ship and served as a lazaretto at Leith from 1831 to 1835, being broken up at Deptford in 1836.

Following this vessel there came a second rate of 90 guns, built at Devonport and launched in 1842. This vessel served in the Crimea in 1854 and landed a naval brigade under Captain Stephen Lushington, and also took part in the bombardment of Sebastopol. She was converted into a screw line of battleship in 1861 and sold for breaking up in 1884.

The next ship which appears in the list is a twin-screw, first class armoured battleship of 12,950 tons, built on the Thames and launched at Blackwall on 21st June, 1898, by H.R.H. The Duchess of York (the late Queen Mary), serving on various stations as a flagship. On 1st August, 1914, she was the flagship of Rear-Admiral H. L. Tottenham; in 1915 served in the Dardanelles and at Salonica; and in 1919 she was sold to Thomas Ward Ltd. for breaking up.

The present *Albion* is an aircraft carrier of 18,300 tons displacement, and was begun in 1944 at Swan Hunter's.

H.M.S. ALBRIGHTON

Description of Badge
FIELD: Per fess wavy white and red.

BADGE: A stirrup with leather counterchanged.

MOTTO:

BATTLE HONOURS
Dieppe 1942 August 19th.
Normandy 1944 June 6th—July 3rd.
English Channel 1942-4
Biscay 1944
North Sea 1945

The *Albrighton* is a *Hunt* class destroyer built at Clydebank in 1941. Her tonnage is 1,050 and her main guns are four 4-inch.

H.M.S. AMBROSE

This vessel had an unofficial badge and an official one.

Unofficial Badge: A plaque showing St. Ambrose holding a model of a submarine. On the right side is a naval crown and round the figure are the words H.M.S. AMBROSE, SUBMARINE FLOTILLA. No colours known.

Official Badge
FIELD: Blue.

BADGE: A crozier gold rising out of three wavelets silver.

MOTTO: *De Profundis Adsumus* (Out of the depths we are here).

The vessel carries no battle honours.

H.M.S. AMBROSE—*continued*

The unofficial badge was designed by Major Dobb in 1918. It is derived from St. Ambrose, who is the patron saint of Milan in Italy, and was the son of a prefect of Gaul. Much against his will, after settling a controversy between the orthodox Catholics and the Arians by his eloquence, he was consecrated Bishop; however, he set to work to be worthy of his office. He insisted on the supremacy of the Church over civil power. There are various legends about this saint with regard to the healing of the sick and lame, for which reason, and for the obvious one of the name and the duties the ship performed, the badge was chosen. As St. Ambrose is often represented as a Bishop with a beehive at his feet, perhaps this is another reason for its adoption on the assumption that a submarine depot ship is as busy as a beehive and the submarines swarm round its sides.

The official badge is derived from the first, but has become simplified and is an allusion to the name by indicating the Bishop's office with a crozier.

H.M.S. *Ambrose* was a hired armed merchant cruiser built by Sir Raylton Dixon & Co. Ltd., Middlesbrough, for the Booth Line, Liverpool. Later on she was bought for the Royal Navy and fitted out as a submarine depot ship. She was of 6,480 tons gross. After doing duty in various services, on 1st June, 1938, she became T.B.D. depot at Rosyth *vice* H.M.S. *Greenwich*, and was renamed *Cochrane*.

H.M.S. AMETHYST

Description of Badge
FIELD: Blue.

BADGE: A winged anchor gold.

MOTTO:

Badge derived from the arms of Seymour, with reference to Sir Michael Seymour, who commanded the *Amethyst* with distinction in 1808.

BATTLE HONOURS

China	1856-60	
Ashantee	1873-4	June 9th—February 4th.
Heligoland	1914	August 28th.
Dardanelles	1915	
Atlantic	1945	
Korea	1951-2	
"Thetis"	1808	Single ship action.
"Cerbere"	1800	Boat service action.
"Niemen"	1809	Single ship action.

The first *Amethyst* was a fifth rate of 1,029 tons and 38 guns, captured from the French. The next *Amethyst* was on operations near Quiberon, in August in the expedition to Ferrol, and on 28th January, 1801, assisted in the capture of French 36-gun frigate *Dedaigneuse* off Cape Ortegal. She captured the French *General Brune* (14) on 9th April, 1801, and on 10th November, 1808, she captured the French *Thetis* (40) near L'Orient

H.M.S. AMETHYST—*continued*

after a two-hour fight. For this her captain, Michael Seymour, was knighted, and a medal granted for the action, with a gold medal for the captain. On 5th April, 1809, she engaged the French 40-gun frigate *Niemen* in the Bay of Biscay, and after the *Niemen* had ceased firing, the *Arethusa* (38) came up and fired a few shots at the already beaten ship, who then hauled down her colours. The captain, Sir Michael Seymour, was created a baronet and the action was included in the list for General Service Medal (1847). Her next exploit was the Scheldt expedition, and in 1811 on 15th or 16th February she was wrecked in Plymouth Sound.

The next was a sixth rate of 923 tons and 26 guns, built at Plymouth in 1844. In 1858 she was engaged in the operations in China, and in 1859 was employed in restoring order at San Blas and Mazatlan on the Pacific coast. At Mazatlan she cut out from the batteries an American brig which had been captured by the Mexicans. She was then lent to the Telegraph Construction Company and finally sold to them in 1869.

Following her was a sixth-rate screw corvette of 1,405 tons and 14 guns, built at Devonport in 1873. She served on various stations, and in 1873-4 she contributed a Naval Brigade in the Ashantee campaign. On 27th May, 1877, in company with the *Shah*, she was in an encounter with the Peruvian rebel vessel *Huascar*, and was sold in 1887.

There was a turbine cruiser which was in Cruiser Force "C" at Heligoland Bight and in 1915 at the Dardanelles, and was sold in October, 1920.

A trawler bore this name, too, and was one of twenty purchased in 1935. 1936, Haifa (clasp PALESTINE to the General Service Medal).

A sloop of this name was built under the 1941 programme and was one of the modified *Black Swan* class. On 16th January, 1945, in company with *Hart, Lock Craggie, Peacock* and *Starling*, sank German U482; on 20th February, 1945, she sank U-boat U1208 whilst escorting convoy H.X. 337; and on 30th July, 1949, she ran the gauntlet of the Chinese Communist shore batteries in the Yangtse from a little below Chinkiang, and rejoined the fleet on 31st July.

H.M.S. ANSON

Description of Badge

FIELD: Per fess wavy white and blue.

BADGE: Out of a ducal coronet gold a spear head proper.

MOTTO: *Nil Desperandum* (Never Despair).

The badge is derived from the crest of the Earl of Lichfield.

	BATTLE	HONOURS
The Saints	1782	April 12th.
Donegal	1798	October 12th.
Curacoa	1807	January 1st.
Arctic	1942-3	

The first vessel to bear this name was built at Bursledon as a 60-gun ship of 1,197 tons in 1747. Her successor was a 64-gun ship, launched at Plymouth in 1781, and this vessel shared in Rodney's victory of 12th April, 1782. She was then cut down to a 44-gun ship and was in the expedition to Quiberon in June, 1795. While still with the squadron she was present when a number of ships of a French convoy were captured. In 1797 she was in an attack on a French convoy which resulted in a 28-gun French corvette, the *Calliope*, being driven ashore on the Penmarc'h Rocks and cannonaded until she went to pieces, and later assisted at the capture of two large privateers. She also recaptured a 24-gun corvette which the French had taken earlier. In 1798 she took a late share in the action with Bompart off the Irish coast. On 18th October, 1798, she fell in with the 46-gun frigate

H.M.S. ANSON—*continued*

Loire, which had escaped from the previous engagement after having been badly beaten by the *Mermaid*, and this proved an easy capture. In 1800 she chased a French squadron of four vessels and captured a new vessel only thirty-three days off the stocks, the *Hardi*. On 29th July she captured the gunboat *Gibraltar* (10) off the famous rock. On 14th August, 1806, in company with the *Arethusa*, she attacked the Spanish 38-gun frigate *Pomona* and twelve gunboats off Havannah. The *Pomona* surrendered; the gunboats were destroyed and a fort silenced. On 15th September she attacked a French vessel of 84 guns, the *Foudroyant*, which had been dismasted in bad weather, but her opponent was a bit too heavy for her despite being handicapped.

On New Year's Day, 1807, in company with other vessels, she assisted at the capture of Curacoa, which has come to be one of the most brilliant engagements in the history of the Royal Navy. On 28th December she was attempting to make a port owing to a gale and ran ashore, losing 60 officers and men.

The next *Anson* was a 74-gun ship, launched at Hull in 1812, but she was not employed on any war service.

Another *Anson* was built at Woolwich in 1860 and was a 91-gun ship. This vessel as the *Algiers* did duty until 1904 as a guardship at Chatham.

Then came a battleship launched at Pembroke in 1886 of 10,300 tons.

The present battleship of 35,000 tons, built in 1941, perpetuates the name. Like her sisters, she saw service in the Second World War.

H.M.S. ANZAC

The badge is based on the General Service badge of the Australian Imperial Forces.

BATTLE HONOUR
Korea   1951-3

H.M.S. *Anzac* was a flotilla leader of the later *Marksman* type of 1,666 tons. Speed 34 knots. She was begun under the emergency war programme and completed on 24th April, 1917, being presented to Australia in 1919. After service she was paid off into reserve in 1931 to be scrapped. The latest *Anzac* was built for the Royal Australian Navy as a destroyer in 1948 at Williamstown, Victoria.

H.M.S. APOLLO

Description of Badge
FIELD: Blue.

BADGE: A sun in splendour gold.

MOTTO: *Arcu Semper Intento* (With bow always bent).

The badge is derived from Greek mythology, in which the sun is represented by Apollo, one of the principal gods in the Greek Pantheon. The source of inspiration, art, poetry and medicine.

BATTLE HONOURS
St. Vincent	1780	January 16th.
China	1842	
Crimea	1854	
Normandy	1944	June 6th—July 3rd.

The first *Apollo* was a hospital ship of 744 tons and carried 20 guns. She was added to the Royal Navy in 1747 as the *Apollo*, having been originally the French *Apollon*, taken by Lord Anson in the battle with de la Jonquiere off Finisterre. She served with Boscawen in the East Indies, and on 17th April, 1749, was wrecked in a hurricane off Fort St. David, Madras.

A fifth rate followed of 679 tons and 32 guns, launched by T. Hodgson in 1763 as the *Glory*. In 1774 she was renamed the *Apollo*. On 31st January, 1779, she captured the French *Oiseau* (32); in 1780 she was present at Rodney's action with Langara off Cape St. Vincent and at the subsequent relief of Gibraltar; on

H.M.S. APOLLO—*continued*

15th June, 1780, she engaged the French privateer *Stanislas* (26), which ran ashore to escape capture; and in 1786 she was broken up at Woolwich.

Another *Apollo* was launched on the River Thames by Perry & Sons on 18th March, 1794, a fifth rate of 994 tons and 38 guns. On 22nd June, 1796, in company with the *Doris* (36), she captured the French *Legere* (22) off Sicily; in 1798 captured the Spanish privateer *Aguilla* (22); and on 7th January, 1799, she was wrecked on the coast of Holland, her crew being saved.

The next was a fifth rate of 956 tons and 36 guns, launched on the River Thames on 16th August, 1799, built by Mr. Dudman. In 1800 she captured the Spanish vessel *Cantabro* (18) off Havana, captured and destroyed the Spanish vessel *Resolucion* (18) in the Gulf of Mexico; in 1801 she captured the French privateer *Vigilant* (14); in 1803 she captured the French cutter *Dart* in Bay of Biscay; and on 2nd April, 1804, while escorting an outward bound convoy, was lost on Cape Mondego, Portugal, with Captain J. W. Taylor Dixon and 60 men.

Then came another fifth rate of 1,080 tons and 38 guns, launched at Bursledon in 1805, having been built by Mr. Parsons. She served in the Egyptian operations of 1807 and landed a naval brigade at the capitulation of Alexandria. On 31st October, 1809, the boats of the squadron she was serving with captured and destroyed eleven armed French vessels under the batteries in Rosas Bay (Medal); on 13th February, 1812, captured the French frigate *Merinos* under the guns of the batteries at Cape Corse. In 1813, on 27th May, boats of *Apollo* and *Cerberus* took three out of eleven gunboats and four vessels under the fire of troops at Faro; 1822-1830 was converted and employed as a Royal Yacht under Captain the Honourable Sir Charles Paget. In 1838 she was converted for service as a troopship. On 21st July, 1842, she was at the China war and concerned in the capture of Chinkiang (Medal); 1854, service in the Black Sea in the Russian war (Medal); and in 1856 she was broken up at Portsmouth.

On 10th February, 1891, a twin-screw cruiser of 3,400 tons was launched at Chatham of this name, and was capable of a speed of 20 knots. She became a drill ship for the R.N.R. at Southampton during 1901-1904, and in 1908 was fitted for service as a

H.M.S. APOLLO—*continued*

minelayer. During 1914-1916 she was based on Sheerness; then in 1917 she was commissioned as depot ship for the 4th Flotilla at Devonport, being sold in 1920 to Messrs. Castle for breaking up.

The next *Apollo* was a cruiser of 7,000 tons and 32.5 knots, launched at Devonport on 9th October, 1934; and in 1938 she was transferred to the Royal Australian Navy and renamed *Hobart*.

The present vessel of the name was completed in 1944 as a minelayer of 2,650 tons.

H.M.S. ARCHER

Unofficial Badge: A bow and arrow gold, winged proper, naval crown gold, white sails red and green gems. Scroll yellow edged red, letters black. Name of ship black.

In allusion to the name.

Official Badge
FIELD: White.

BADGE: A demi-archer to the sinister clad in green and drawing bow proper.

MOTTO:

BATTLE HONOURS

Baltic	1854-5
Heligoland	1914 August 28th.
Atlantic	1943-4
Biscay	1943

H.M.S. ARCHER—*continued*

The fourth *Archer* was a torpedo boat destroyer of 775 tons and carried as her armament two 4-inch and two 12-pdr. guns and two torpedo tubes. She was launched in 1911 by Yarrow. From 1914 to 1916 she served with the Grand Fleet; October, 1916 to August, 1917 she was at Devonport; from September, 1917, to the end of the war was in the Mediterranean; and in 1921, on 17th May, she was sold.

The *Archer* of the Second World War was an escort aircraft carrier (ex *Mormacland*).

H.M.S. ARETHUSA

Description of Badge
FIELD: Green.

BADGE: A crescent moon gold over wavelets silver and blue.

MOTTO: *Celeriter Audax* (Swiftly Audacious).

The badge is derived from Greek mythology. Demeter (Ceres), daughter of Cronus and Rhea, and one of Zeus's many consorts, was goddess of agriculture and civilization. She had a daughter Persephone (Proserpina), the goddess of vegetation. This goddess used to go to the island of Sicily, where, attended by laughing girls, she gathered flowers on the slopes of Mount Aetna and danced on the plain Enna with the nymphs. Persephone was carried off by Pluto, King of the Underworld, who was struck by her beauty and who thought she would be an attractive adornment to his gloomy kingdom. Demeter searched for Persephone but could not find her, and so neglected her duties of looking after the world's crops. After a brief spell with the daughters of Celeus, King of Attica, Demeter returned to Sicily. Whilst wandering along the banks of the river one day she saw her daughter's girdle, which had been given to the nymph Cyane at the moment when Pluto's chariot was descending into the underworld. Demeter, convinced she was at last on her daughter's track, eventually sat down near a crystal fountain to rest. The fountain's murmuring grew in volume until Demeter fancied that she heard it speaking. The goddess was not mistaken for soon she could distinguish words, and the fountain begged her to listen

H.M.S. ARETHUSA—*continued*

if she wanted news of her child. The fountain then went on to tell her how she had not always been a mere stream but was once a nymph called Arethusa, and that she had been changed into this form by Diana, who had saved her from the attentions of the river god Alpheus. It was in her flight from Alpheus that she had passed through the underworld and seen Persephone.

BATTLE HONOURS

Ushant	1781	December 12th.
St. Lucia	1796	May 24th.
Curacoa	1807	January 1st.
Crimea	1854	
China	1900	Entitled to medal. Not eligible for battle honour.
Heligoland	1914	August 28th.
Dogger Bank	1915	January 24th.
Normandy	1944	June 6th—July 3rd.
Malta Convoys	1941-42	
Norway	1941	

During the Seven Years War a number of names appeared connected with mythology or with personalities mentioned by classical writers. From about this period comes such names as the *Arethusa*.

The first *Arethusa* was a fifth rate of 32 guns, taken from the French in 1759. She was the *L'Arethuse* and was captured by the 36-gun frigate *Venus*. Her name was changed to that of *Arethusa*, and later she fought the famous action with the *Belle Poule*. This vessel was wrecked in 1779.

Then another of the name was launched in 1781 and carrying 38 guns. This *Arethusa* played a very active part in the second Napoleonic wars, taking part in the Quiberon Expedition of 1795 and in the capture of Trinidad in 1797 when General Abercrombie landed with 4,000 soldiers. The Spaniards surrendered with one ship of the line and 100 pieces of artillery.

On 23rd August, 1806, H.M.S. *Arethusa* and H.M.S. *Anson* captured and brought out from under the guns of Morro Castle the Spanish ship *Pomona* of 36 guns, a medal being struck to commemorate this action. In the following year, 1807, the

H.M.S. ARETHUSA—continued

captain was knighted and received a gold medal for the capture of Curacoa. Broken up at Sheerness, May, 1814. The next *Arethusa* was a fifth rate of 1,085 tons and carried 46 guns. She was built at Pembroke and launched on 29th July, 1817. In 1836 she was allocated as a lazaretto at Liverpool and renamed *Bacchus* in 1844. She served as a coal depot at Devonport and was sold to Castle's in 1883. An *Arethusa*, fourth rate, was launched in 1849 at the Pembroke Yard, designed by Sir Wm. Symonds. She was armed with 50 guns. This vessel saw service in the Crimea during the Russian war of 1854-5 and was the last naval sailing vessel to go into action under sail alone. Leaving the service of the Navy, she became the training ship *Arethusa* moored in the River Thames at Greenhithe in 1874 until 1932, when she was broken up. All that remains of her now is the fine figurehead which is to be seen outside the Arethusa Swimming Baths at Lower Upnor on the River Medway.

Following this ship there was a second-class cruiser built in 1882, and she served on the China station during the Boxer rebellion of 1900.

Then came a light cruiser of the name launched in 1913. She was in the Harwich Force on 18th August, 1914, commanded by Commodore Tyrwhitt, and an action was fought in the Heligoland Bight which resulted in three German cruisers being sunk. In 1916, when returning from a sweep in the North Sea, the *Arethusa* was mined and sunk.

The last naval vessel to hold the name was a cruiser launched in 1934, and she had an eventful and distinguished career. She fought at Norway and in the Mediterranean and led the bombarding forces on D Day. In her war service she had been both torpedoed and mined. When His Majesty the late King George VI visited his forces in Normandy it was the *Arethusa* which took him over. The end of her days came when she was selected for tests of a scientific nature with relation to atomic rays and afterwards assigned for breaking up.

The name has now gone from the serving ships, but it is perpetuated in the famous training ship *Arethusa*. This fine vessel, the ex German four-masted barque *Peking*, has in her keeping the battle honour plaque of H.M.S. *Arethusa*. Most of the boys from this ship enter the Royal Navy on the completion of their training.

H.M.S. ARGONAUT

Description of Badge

FIELD: Red.

BADGE: Upon water in base barry wavy white and blue a lymphad gold, therein a demi-Greek warrior in armour gold, holding in the dexter hand a fleece also gold, and in the sinister hand his shield also gold.

MOTTO:

The badge is derived from Greek mythology, the Argonauts being Greek heroes who were sailors in the Argo and who went in search of the Golden Fleece under the command of Jason.

BATTLE HONOURS

North Africa	1942	
Mediterranean	1942	
Arctic	1942	
Ægean	1944	
Normandy	1944	June 6th—July 3rd.
South France	1944	August 15th—27th.
Okinawa	1945	March 26th—May 25th.

The first *Argonaut* was one of the ships captured by Sir S. Hood in the Mona Passage after the battle of the Saintes which was fought by Rodney. She was a third rate of 1,452 tons and 64 guns, being named the *Jason* and commissioned on the West Indies station under this name. An Admiralty order was given to change her name to *Argonaut* on 21st December, 1782, but her name was not changed until 20th January when she paid off at

H.M.S. ARGONAUT—*continued*

Plymouth. She was commissioned for the East Indies, but was recalled and sent to the Halifax station and then the West Indies. From 1797 to 1802 she was a hospital ship in the River Medway, and in 1804 was again on the same service. In 1822 she became a hospital ship at Chatham and in 1831 was taken to pieces.

In the battle of Trafalgar a Spanish vessel called the *Argonauta* was taken but sank after the battle, and there was also a French *Argonaute* which managed to escape.

There was a cruiser of 11,000 tons called the *Argonaut* launched at Fairfield's on 24th January, 1898. She carried sixteen 6-inch guns and had a speed of 20.75 knots. From 1900, when she commissioned for the China station, she had a very uneventful career and seemed to have spent most of her time with a nucleus crew. In August, 1914, she was commissioned for the 9th Cruiser Squadron to operate between Finisterre and the Canaries. She was sold in 1920 after having been accommodation ship at Portsmouth from 1916 to 1919.

The present *Argonaut* is a cruiser built under the 1939 programme, of 5,450 tons, and carries eight 5.25-inch guns. She was completed in 1942 and served in many operations during the Second World War. The *Argonaut* was very extensively damaged by submarine attack, and had to be repaired in the United States, which necessitated a lot of rebuilding.

H.M.S. ARGUS

Description of Badge
FIELD: Green.

BADGE: A peacock gold.

MOTTO: *Occuli Omnium* (The eyes of all).

Badge is derived from Greek mythology. Argus was the many-eyed monster which never closed more than two of its numerous eyes at any one time. (Juno) Hera was jealous of the maiden Io, who was the daughter of the river god Inachus, and Argus, being a servant of Hera's, was set to watch over Io when she was changed into a beautiful heifer. Zeus gave the task of freeing Io from the guardianship of the many-eyed monster to Hermes, who eventually slew it, having lulled it to sleep with a story. Hera, being very angry at the death of her servant, took the eyes of Argus to adorn her favourite bird, the peacock.

BATTLE HONOURS

Groix Island	1795	June 23rd.
Abyssinia	1868	April 13th. Took part but not eligible for honour.
Ashantee	1873-4	June 9th—February 4th.
Arctic	1941	
North Africa	1942	
Atlantic	1941-2	
Malta Convoys	1942	

H.M.S. ARGUS—*continued*

The *Argus* was begun as a liner, being built for the Lloyd Sabaudo Line of Italy, and her name was then the *Conte Rosso*. Work on her was stopped in 1914 and she was bought and converted into an aircraft carrier. Her displacement was 14,450 tons and she was built by William Beardmore & Co. Ltd. She was fitted as a *Queen Bee* tender in 1937 and later modified to do the service of an escort carrier. In 1947 she was broken up.

H.M.S. ARIADNE

Description of Badge
FIELD: Blue.

BADGE: Within a wreath of vine gold a celestial crown also gold with silver stars.

MOTTO: Swift and Fearless.

This badge comes from Greek mythology, the source of inspiration for the names of so many of our ships, and from which we can get so many lovely stories. Theseus sailed with the annual tribute of youths and maidens to the island of Crete, determined to slay the Minotaur for whom they were destined. He achieved his purpose by the aid of Ariadne, for she had fallen in love with him. Later at the island of Naxos, Theseus abandoned Ariadne and this lovely princess was found by Bacchus and they fell in love; his gift to her was a crown adorned with seven golden stars, this afterwards becoming the constellation known as Ariadne's Crown.

BATTLE HONOUR
St. Lucia   1778   December 15th.

Ariadne number one was a sixth rate of 432 tons and 20 guns; she was launched at Chatham on 27th December, 1776. In 1777 on 15th December she was at Cul de Sac, St. Lucia, in Barrington's Squadron, which beat off two attacks by D'Estaing; on 30th December at the capitulation of St. Lucia; as a repeating frigate in Byron's action with D'Estaing off Grenada on 6th July, 1779;

H.M.S. ARIADNE—*continued*

in an action with French privateers off Flamborough Head in 1780; on 13th July, 1795, in Hotham's action off Hyeres; on 19th May, 1798, in the combined expedition under Captain Home Popham and Major-General Sir Eyre Coote to destroy the lock gates at Ostend; on 17th July, 1805, with consorts engaged a division of Napoleon's invasion flotilla off Ostend; and in 1814 she was sold.

The next *Ariadne* was a sixth rate of 511 tons and 20 guns, being launched at Pembroke on 10th February, 1816. In the month of January, 1820, she was made into a 26-gun ship, and from 1822 to 1828 she was at the Cape of Good Hope and the Mediterranean. Following this she was fitted with 28 guns, and from November, 1828 to 1830 she was engaged in special service in the Atlantic searching for reported islands and shoals. During this commission her captain, Fred Marryat, wrote his first sea novels. From 1830 to 1834 she was in the West Indies; in 1837 she was a coal depot at Alexandria; and on 23rd July, 1841, she was sold.

Then came a screw frigate of 3,214 tons and 26 guns, launched at Deptford on 4th June, 1859. In 1860 she was escort to the *Hero*, which took the Prince of Wales out and home on his visit to Canada. From 1871 to 1873 she was a training ship for cadets, in 1876 a tender to the Vernon Torpedo School, and in 1905 she was renamed *Actaeon* on becoming Torpedo School at Sheerness.

A first-class cruiser (protected) of 11,000 tons and carrying sixteen 6-inch guns also bore the name of *Ariadne*. She was launched at Clydebank on 22nd April, 1898. In 1902 she was the flagship of Vice-Admiral Sir A. L. Douglas on the North America and West Indies stations. From December, 1902 to February, 1903 she was concerned in the Venezuelan blockade; in 1904 was the North America and West Indies station flagship under Vice-Admiral D. H. Bosanquet; in 1914 training ship for stokers at Portsmouth; in 1916 overflow ship at Devonport; in April, 1917, she was in the Humber completing for service as a minelayer; and on 26th July she was sunk by a submarine in the Channel on passage from the Humber to Portsmouth.

The present *Ariadne* is a fast minelayer of 2,650 tons and was completed in 1943.

H.M.S. ARIEL

Description of Badge
FIELD: Blue.

BADGE: Within a chaplet of honeysuckle gold a winged boy white.

MOTTO: *Invisibilis Quaero* (Unseen I seek).

Badge in allusion to Shakespeare's Ariel.

BATTLE HONOURS
Heligoland	1914	August 28th.
Belgian Coast	1914	
Dogger Bank	1915	January 24th.
Jutland	1916	May 31st.

The first *Ariel* was a sixth rate of 455 tons and 20 guns, built on the River Thames by Perry & Co., and launched on 7th July, 1777. On 10th September, 1779, off South Carolina she was captured by the French *Amazone* of 26 guns after an action lasting about an hour and a half, in which *Ariel* lost one of her masts.

The next to bear the name was a sloop built at Liverpool of 319 tons and 16 guns, launched on 18th October, 1781. She served on the East Indies station, and was paid off at Portsmouth in 1792, being sold in 1802.

Then came a sloop of 367 tons and 20 guns built at Yarmouth, and launched on 19th April, 1800. She was sold at Deptford on 12th July, 1816.

H.M.S. ARIEL—*continued*

The brig sloop *Ariel* of 236 tons and 10 guns was built at Deptford, and launched on 28th July, 1820. She foundered with the loss of all hands in a hurricane near Sable Island in 1828.

One of the Post Office packets called the *Arrow* of 149 tons was transferred to the Admiralty on 1st April, 1837, and renamed *Ariel*. This vessel was sold at Woolwich on 17th May, 1850.

A screw steam sloop of 486 tons called the *Ariel* was built at Pembroke, and launched on 11th July, 1854. She saw service at the Baltic in 1855, and in the years between 1857 and 1861 was employed in the repression of piracy in the Persian Gulf. From 1862 to 1864 she was on anti-slavery operations on the east coast of Africa, and was sold at Portsmouth on 23rd May, 1865.

The next *Ariel* was a screw composite gunboat of 406 tons, built at Chatham, and launched on 11th February, 1873. She sailed for the Cape of Good Hope and West Coast of Africa stations, and in 1875 was engaged in a punitive expedition against native pirates in the Congo river. In the year 1876 she was employed in operations in the lower reaches of the River Niger and in the blockade of Dahomey, returning in December and paying off at Chatham. On 26th November, 1877, she recommissioned for coastguard service at Hull, and was eventually sold in August, 1889.

Messrs. Thornycroft built a T.B.D. at Chiswick of 310 tons and she was called *Ariel*. This vessel was launched on 5th March, 1897, and was eventually wrecked by striking Ricasoli breakwater at Malta while testing harbour defences on 19th April, 1907.

The next *Ariel* was also a T.B.D., built at Woolston, Southampton, by Messrs. Thornycroft, and launched on 26th September, 1911. She served at the action off Heligoland and in the Dogger Bank action. On 10th March, 1915, she rammed and sank the German submarine U12 in the North Sea, was at the battle of Jutland, and was sunk by mine in the North Sea on 2nd August, 1918.

Ariel is now a shore establishment.

H.M.S. ARK ROYAL

Description of Badge
FIELD: Blue.

BADGE: An ark silver, crowned gold, upon three wavelets gold.

MOTTO: *Desire n'a pas repos* (Desire has no rest).

The badge is in allusion to the name.

BATTLE HONOURS

Armada	1588	July 21st—29th.
Cadiz	1596	June 21st.
Dardanelles	1915	
Norway	1940	
Spartivento	1940	November 27th.
"Bismarck"	1941	
Mediterranean	1940-1	
Malta Convoys	1941	

The motto mentioned in the description of the badge was that of Lord Howard of Effingham, the Lord High Admiral, who commanded the first ship of the name against the Spanish Armada. This vessel was built as the *Ark Raleigh* for Sir Walter Raleigh at Deptford in 1587 and sold to Queen Elizabeth for £5,000. She was rated as 800 tons, but as built was a vessel of 692 tons. Her complement was 268 mariners, 32 gunners and 100 soldiers, and she carried 55 guns. In 1588 at the famous Armada battle she was the flagship of Lord Howard of Effingham. Later on in 1596, in company with thirteen other vessels, she made an attack

H.M.S. ARK ROYAL—continued

on Cadiz resulting in the total destruction of the Spanish fleet at that port. 1608 gave her a further change of name on being rebuilt and she became the *Anne Royal*, named after Anne of Denmark, James I's queen. During a shift of berth in the Medway she was bilged on her own anchor and sunk and, although she was later refloated, it was decided not to repair her and so she was broken up.

The second *Ark Royal* was purchased whilst building at the Blyth Shipbuilding Company's yard in 1914 and became a seaplane carrier of 7,400 tons. After commissioning she saw service in the Mediterranean, Dardanelles, Black Sea and China stations; then from 1922 to 1932 she was in the Nore Command, and in 1935 became the *Pegasus*.

The third *Ark Royal* was an aircraft carrier laid down by Cammell Laird on 16th September, 1935, and launched on 13th April, 1937. She was 22,000 tons and her complement was 1,575. During the war of 1939-45 she took part in several Malta Convoys, and was in the *Bismarck* operations of 1941. The first U-boat to be destroyed was the U39 after she had made an attack on the *Ark Royal* 150 miles west of the Hebrides. During the month of December, 1939, she was patrolling the waters south of Cape of Good Hope to intercept raiders, and then served with the fleet which had the task of immobilizing the Oran squadron. *Ark Royal's* aircraft made a torpedo attack on the dam at Lake Tirso, Sardinia, and then bombed Leghorn and Pisa; her aircraft also shadowed the *Bismarck* and later made an attack which severely damaged the German vessel. The German wireless frequently "sank" the *Ark Royal*, but she was actually torpedoed by a German submarine 150 miles east of Gibraltar and foundered when she was being towed on 14th November, 1941.

The present aircraft carrier (No. 4 of the name) was launched on 3rd May, 1950, at Cammell Laird's, her original name being *Irresistible*, and is one of the largest British aircraft carriers.

H.M.S. ARMADA

Description of Badge
FIELD: Blue.

BADGE: A lion statant gardant within a chaplet of laurel, all gold.

MOTTO:

This badge is derived from the crest of Charles, Lord Howard of Effingham.

There are no battle honours recorded for this name.

The *Armada* is one of the *Battle* class of destroyers, and was built by Hawthorn Leslie in 1943.

H.M.S. ARROGANT

Description of Badge

A fighting cock proper on a gold and black wreath. Above is a naval crown gold, white sails, red and blue gems. Below is a scroll in allusion to the name.

	BATTLE HONOURS	
The Saints	1782	April 12th.
Baltic	1854-5	

The seventh ship was a *Ram* cruiser of 5,750 tons fitted with double rudders; very small turning circle, and reputed to be an excellent ship for steaming in fine weather. She was built in 1898 and was a depot ship of sorts. Was a tender to *Dolphin* for submarines at Blockhouse. Sold in 1923.

H.M.S. ARTEMIS

Description of Badge
FIELD: Blue.

BADGE: A quiver with arrows and a bow in saltire both gold surmounted by a crescent white.

MOTTO:

Derived from Greek mythology. The name *Artemis* is the Greek name for *Diana*. She is the goddess of the moon and the chase. She was the twin sister of Apollo, daughter of Zeus and Latona.

There are no battle honours listed for this vessel.

The *Artemis* is a submarine of the "A" class, built at Scott's. Displacement of this class was 1,120/1,620 tons.

H.M.S. ATHERSTONE

Description of Badge

FIELD: Red.

BADGE: Upon a white roundel a fox's mask within a mascle also red.

MOTTO:

Badge derived from the pack colours of a red and white collar and the mascle from the arms of Osbaldeston, a master of the pack.

BATTLE HONOURS

English Channel	1940-2	
North Sea	1942-3	
St. Nazaire	1942	March 28th.
Mediterranean	1943	
Sicily	1943	July 10th—August 17th.
Salerno	1943	September 9th—October 6th.
Atlantic	1943	
Adriatic	1944	
South France	1944	August 15th—27th.

The *Atherstone* is a *Hunt* class destroyer of 1,000 tons and four 4-inch guns. She was built by Cammell Laird, designed for escort duties. Her long list of honours for the Second World War gives a good indication of the service they were called upon to perform. It will be noted that she took part in that very fine episode of St. Nazaire.

H.M.S. AURORA

Unofficial Badge: This badge was carried by H.M.S. *Aurora*, a light cruiser of 3,520 tons. Aurora, sea and sky in proper colours white horses, gold chariot.

Official Badge
FIELD: Party per fesse barry of silver and black.

BADGE: In chief red a rising sun gold.

MOTTO: *Post Tenebras Lux* (After darkness light).

The badge is from Greek mythology and refers to Aurora, goddess of the dawn, the daughter of Hyperion and sister of Selene and Helios. Aurora's work was to open the gates of the east for the sun. She had a star on her forehead and rode in a rosy chariot drawn by white horses.

H.M.S. AURORA—*continued*

BATTLE HONOURS

St. Lucia	1778	December 15th.
Minorca	1798	November 15th.
Guadeloupe	1810	February 5th.
China	1900	June 10th—December 31st.
Dogger Bank	1915	January 24th.
Norway	1940	
Malta Convoys	1941	
"Bismarck"	1941	May 23rd—27th.
Mediterranean	1941-2-3	
North Africa	1942-3	
Sicily	1943	July 10th—August 17th.
Salerno	1943	September 9th—October 6th.
Ægean	1943	
South France	1944	August 15th—27th.

The last *Aurora* was a cruiser of 5,270 tons and was completed at Portsmouth in 1937. Her armament consisted of six 6-inch and eight 4-inch A.A. guns. Her service in the Second World War was very widespread and she had some exciting moments in company with the *Penelope* in the Mediterranean. After the war she was transferred to the Chinese Navy.

H.M.S. AUSONIA

Description of Badge
FIELD: Red.

BADGE: In front of an axe and a sledgehammer in saltire proper a lion's mask gold.

MOTTO:

The badge is in allusion to the work it does as a repair ship, and the lion's mask to represent the Cunard Company, from whom the ship was obtained.

BATTLE HONOUR
Atlantic   1939-41

The *Ausonia* is an ex Cunard liner and was taken over by the Admiralty for service as an armed merchant cruiser and converted into a repair ship. Her tonnage is about 14,000.

H.M.S. BARFLEUR

Description of Badge
FIELD: Blue.

BADGE: A goat statant white within a chaplet of laurel gold.

Badge is derived from the crest of Admiral Russell, later Earl of Orford.

BATTLE HONOURS
Vigo	1702	October 12th.
Velez Malaga	1704	August 13th.
Passero	1718	July 31st.
St. Kitts	1782	January 25th—26th.
The Saints	1782	April 12th.
First of June	1794	June 1st (and May 28th—29th).
Groix Island	1795	June 23rd.
St. Vincent	1797	February 14th.
China	1900	June 10th—December 31st.

The first *Barfleur* was built at Deptford in 1697 of 1,476 tons and of 90 guns, and was named to commemorate Admiral Russell's victory off Cape Barfleur on 22nd May, 1692. In October, 1702, she was at the capture and destruction of a French squadron and several Spanish galleons in the harbour of Vigo. The enemy lost seventeen ships of war, including ten sail of the line. While she was still off Vigo the *Barfleur* made a prize of the *Dartmouth*, a 50-gun ship which had previously been taken by the French in February, 1695. The *Barfleur* carried the flag of Admiral Sir Cloudesley Shovel in the great battle off Malaga on 13th October,

H.M.S. BARFLEUR—continued

1704, when Admiral Sir George Rooke defeated the Count de Thoulouse, High Admiral of France. She was rebuilt at Deptford in 1713 and in 1718 she carried the flag of Admiral Sir George Byng when he totally defeated the inferior but large fleet of Vice-Admiral Don Castenata off Syracuse on 11th August. He captured or destroyed eighteen ships of war, including seven sail of the line. She bore the flag of Rear-Admiral Rowley under Admiral Matthews on 11th February, 1744, in a very poorly supported attack on the French fleet off Toulon; the *Barfleur*, however, against general censure, received and merited universal praise. On 20th September, 1757, she assisted in the attack on the Isle D'Aix, the defences of which were destroyed.

In 1768 a new *Barfleur* was launched at Chatham of 1,947 tons and carrying 98 guns. Under the flag of Rear-Admiral Sir S. Hood and accompanied by eighteen ships of the line an attack was made on the Comte de Grasse with twenty-six sail of the line off Martinique. In the same year she operated in an attack on the French off the Chesapeake, and in the following January he dispossessed the Comte de Grasse of the anchorage at St. Kitts and defeated the many attacks made on him by twenty-nine sail of the line. In 1782, on 9th and 12th April, the *Barfleur* greatly distinguished herself when de Grasse was attacked by Admiral Sir George E. Rodney at Guadeloupe. When the great French war began the *Barfleur* was commanded by Captain Collingwood and bore the flag of Rear-Admiral Bowyer at Ushant on the 1st June, 1794. It was on this date that Admiral Lord Howe defeated the French fleet with a loss to the French of seven ships of the line. She was one of the squadron of Admiral Lord Bridport on 23rd June, 1795, when he defeated a strong squadron off L'Orient and captured three sail of the line. On 14th February, 1797, she carried the flag of Vice-Admiral Waldegrave at the great victory off St. Vincent by Admiral Sir John Jervis. She was blockading the Spanish fleet at Cadiz on the following July, and on the 3rd July her boats were present when Sir Horatio Nelson personally engaged the ships of the enemy and put the lot to flight. The *Barfleur* was also in Vice-Admiral Sir R. Calder's squadron at his victory over a superior enemy fleet at Ferrol on 22nd July, 1805. This ship had a narrow escape from destruction when commanded by Sir Edward Berry in the Mediterranean,

H.M.S. BARFLEUR—continued

being struck by lightning and having her fore top-gallant mast shattered; it reached the magazine door and tore up the lead outside the powder room.

Another *Barfleur* was a first-class twin-screw battleship, launched at Chatham on 10th August, 1892, of 10,500 tons and carrying 14 guns. She was Rear-Admiral Bruce's flagship on the China station during the outbreak of 1900. The only seaman killed in the storming of the forts of Pei Ho was an ordinary seaman from the *Barfleur*. She was in the operations for the relief of Admiral Seymour at Tientsin and in the fighting leading up to the relief of the legation at Peking. Eight officers of the *Barfleur* received promotion or decoration, and Midshipman Basil J. D. Guy was awarded the V.C.

The present *Barfleur* is a *Battle* class destroyer built by Swan Hunter in 1943.

H.M.S. BARROSA

Description of Badge
FIELD: Red.

BADGE: Within a wreath of palm gold a dapple-grey horse's head erased regardant proper, gorged with a band of black charged with a rose between two escallops gold.

MOTTO:

Badge derived from the arms and supporters of Lieutenant-General Thomas Graham, the victor of Barrosa.

BATTLE HONOURS
Benin   1897   February 8th—28th.
South Africa   1899-1900

The first *Barrosa* was a fifth rate of 947 tons and 36 guns, launched at Deptford in 1812, and in October she was commissioned for the North America station, where she served until the end of the war with the United States. From 1823 to 1840 she was on harbour service at Portsmouth, and in 1841 was sold for £1,830.

The next was a corvette of 1,700 tons and 20 guns, and was launched at Woolwich on 10th March, 1860, serving on the East Indies and China stations. In 1864 she was at the forcing of the Straits of Shimonoseki, Japan; in 1867 her armament was reduced to 17 guns, and in 1877 she was broken up.

There was a *Barrosa* cruiser, third class, and of 1,580 tons and armed with six 4.7-inch guns. She was launched at Portsmouth

H.M.S. BARROSA—*continued*

on 16th April, 1889. In 1892 she commissioned for naval manœuvres and served on the Cape of Good Hope and West Coast of Africa stations. In 1895 she was engaged in the Brass River Expedition, and on 17th August was at the capture of H'Weli. Then came the Benin Expedition in 1897 and service in the South African war from 1899 to 1901, where she landed a naval brigade. She was sold in 1905.

The present *Barrosa* is a destroyer of the *Battle* class, and was built at Clydebank.

H.M.S. BATTLE-AXE

Description of Badge
FIELD: Blue.

BADGE: A battle-axe gold.

MOTTO:

In allusion to the name.

No battle honours are recorded for this vessel.

This vessel is one of the *Weapon* class of destroyers.

H.M.S BELFAST

Description of Badge
FIELD: Blue.

BADGE: Upon waves in base white and blue a seahorse gorged with a mural crown proper.

MOTTO:

The badge has been derived from the crest of the city of Belfast.

	BATTLE HONOURS	
North Cape	1943	December 26th.
Normandy	1944	June 6th—July 3rd.
Arctic	1943	
Korea	1950-2	

The *Belfast* is a vessel of the improved *Southampton* class of cruisers. She was built by Harland and Wolff under the 1936 estimates. Her displacement tonnage is 10,000, and she carries twelve 6-inch and eight 4-inch A.A. guns as her main armament. In the Second World War she was heavily damaged by a mine and had to have a large amount of rebuilding done to her. She served from the Arctic to Normandy, and has done a large amount of service in the Korean theatre of war.

H.M.S. BELLEROPHON

Unofficial Badge: Horse and wings white; sea, sun, sky and figure in proper colour. Scroll light blue with dark blue letters. Gold edges and ends to scroll.

Official Badge

FIELD: Barry wavy ten, white and blue.

BADGE: Demi-griffin rampant erased gold around and tongued red.

MOTTO:

From Greek mythology, Bellerophon had the task of slaying the Chimæra, which he did on the winged horse Pegasus, given to him by Pallas.

BATTLE HONOURS

First of June 1794 June 1st (and May 28th—29th).
Cornwallis's Retreat 1795 June 17th.

H.M.S. BELLEROPHON—continued

Nile	1798	August 1st.
Trafalgar	1805	October 21st.
Syria	1840	September 10th–December 9th.
Crimea	1854	
Jutland	1916	May 31st.

The first *Bellerophon* was launched at Frindsbury in October, 1786, and was a third rate of 1,613 tons and armed with 74 guns. She was at Howe's victory of the 1st of June, 1794, at Cornwallis's Retreat in 1795, and in 1798 at the battle of the Nile. In company with the *Elephant* (74), *Theseus* (74), *Vanguard* (74), *Aeolus* (36) and *Tartar* (28), captured the French *Duquesne* (74) and *Oiseau* (16) in the West Indies on 26th July, 1803; on 23rd November in the same year, in company with the *Elephant* (74), *Blanche* (36), and *Desiree* (36), captured the French *La Decoverte* (6); and in December with *Elephant* (74), *Hercule* (74), *Vanguard* (74), *Desiree* (36) and *Pique* (36) captured the French *Surveillante* (40), *Clorinde* (40), *La Vertu* (40) and *Cheri* (12). She was at Trafalgar on 21st October, 1805, and in this battle her captain J. Cooke was killed. On 8th July, 1809, she captured seven Russian gunboats off Hango, on the coast of Finland, in company with the *Implacable* (74), *Melpomene* (38) and *Prometheus* (18); on 19th December, 1813, she captured the French privateer *Genie* (16); in July, 1815, Napoleon surrendered on board in the Basque Roads; in October, 1815, she was converted into a convict hulk, and in 1824 was renamed *Captivity*. She was sold in 1836 for £4,030.

On 6th October, 1818, the *Waterloo* was launched at Portsmouth as a second rate of 2,056 tons and 80 guns. In 1824 this vessel was renamed the *Bellerophon*. In 1840 she served at the bombardment of Acre, and in 1854 at the bombardment of Sebastopol, being sold in 1892.

The next *Bellerophon* was a broadside ironclad of 4,270 tons and 15 guns, launched at Chatham on 15th April, 1865. From 1866 she served on various stations until in 1892 she became the port guard ship at Pembroke. In 1906 she was the workshop for artificers at Devonport and known as *Indus III*. On 27th July, 1907, the battleship *Bellerophon* of 18,600 tons and 26 guns was launched at Portsmouth and served with the Home and Grand Fleets, being at the battle of Jutland in 1916. The name is now held by the Reserve Fleet.

H.M.S. BELLONA

Description of Badge

FIELD: Blue.

BADGE: A shield and trophy of classic weapons gold.

MOTTO:

The badge is derived from Bellona, the Roman goddess of fury in war—the one who inspired the war spirit.

	BATTLE HONOURS	
Copenhagen	1801	April 2nd.
Basque Roads	1809	April 11th.
Jutland	1916	May 31st.
Norway	1944-5	
Normandy	1944	June 6th—July 3rd.
Biscay	1944	
Arctic	1944-5	
"Courageux"	1761	Single ship action.

The *Bellona* is a cruiser of the later *Dido* class, and was built by Fairfield and completed in 1943. The displacement of the ships of this class is from 5,700 to 5,770 tons. They carry eight 5.25-inch dual-purpose and numerous other smaller guns. She has been loaned to the New Zealand Government.

H.M.S. BERMUDA

Description of Badge
FIELD: White.

BADGE: A demi-lion affronte erased red holding in the dexter paw a trident also red.

MOTTO:

The badge has been derived from the arms of Bermuda.

	BATTLE HONOURS
North Africa	1942
Atlantic	1943
Arctic	1943

This ship is a cruiser of the *Fiji* class of 8,000 tons and armed with twelve 6-inch and eight 4-inch A.A. guns, and was completed in 1942. She served, as her battle honours show, at North Africa, in the Atlantic and in the Arctic.

H.M.S. BERWICK

Description of Badge
FIELD: White.

BADGE: On a mount green a bear black, chained gold, in front of a tree proper.

MOTTO: *Victoriae Gloria Merces* (Glory is the reward for victory).

Badge from the arms of Berwick.

	BATTLE HONOURS	
Barfleur	1692	May 19th—24th.
Vigo	1702	October 12th.
Gibraltar	1704	July 24th.
Velez Malaga	1704	August 13th.
Dogger Bank	1781	August 5th
Atlantic	1939	
Norway	1940	
Spartivento	1940	November 27th.
Arctic	1941-2-3-4	

The *Berwick* was a cruiser of the *Kent* class and was completed by Fairfield in 1928. This class of ship were all reconstructed during the years 1935 to 1938.

H.M.S. BIRMINGHAM

Description of Badge
FIELD: White.
BADGE: An arm proper holding a hammer proper, issuant from a mural crown gold.
MOTTO: Forward.

The badge is derived from the crest and motto of the City of Birmingham.

BATTLE HONOURS
Heligoland	1914	August 28th.
Dogger Bank	1915	January 24th.
Jutland	1916	May 31st.
Norway	1940	
Korea	1952-3	

The first *Birmingham* was a light cruiser of 5,440 tons and carried nine 6-inch guns, built by Messrs. Armstrong Whitworth and launched on 7th May, 1913. On 9th August, 1914, she rammed and sank the German submarine U15, and on 28th August, 1914, she was at the Heligoland Bight. In the same year, on 15th-16th December, she was in action against enemy ships raiding the coast of Yorkshire. In 1915, on 28th January she was at the Dogger Bank, and in August was engaged in the hunt for the German minelayer *Meteor* which resulted in the scuttling of that vessel by her C.O. She also served at the battle of Jutland, and on 5th February, 1931, was sold to Messrs. T. W. Ward & Co.

The present *Birmingham* is a cruiser of 9,100 tons, built at Devonport and completed in 1937. She carries nine 6-inch and eight 4-inch A.A. guns as her main armament.

H.M.S. BLACK PRINCE

Unofficial Badge: Black shield showing the three feathers of the Black Prince in white with gold labels. Above is a naval crown gold, white sails, red and green gems. Below a scroll white on which is the name of the ship in black.

Official Badge
FIELD: Blue.

BADGE: The head of the Black Prince in armour white.

MOTTO: With high courage.

BATTLE HONOURS
Jutland	1916	May 31st.
English Channel	1944	
Arctic	1944	
Ægean	1944	
Normandy	1944	June 6th—July 3rd.

H.M.S. BLACK PRINCE—*continued*

| South France | 1944 | August 15th—27th. |
| Okinawa | 1945 | March 26th—May 25th. |

Launched on 8th November, 1904, at Blackwall, the fourth *Black Prince* was an armoured cruiser of 13,550 tons of the *Duke of Edinburgh* class. She was armed with six 9.2-inch and ten 6-inch guns, and had a speed of 23 knots. She served in various squadrons, and in 1914 during August to November she was in the Red Sea; then on 26th November, 1914, she was with the Grand Fleet. On 31st May, 1916, she was at the battle of Jutland, where she was sunk in action.

The present *Black Prince* served with the Royal New Zealand Navy, and was one of the ships which had the honour of escorting Her Majesty The Queen and H.R.H. The Duke of Edinburgh on their Royal Tour in the *Gothic*.

H.M.S. BLACK SWAN

Description of Badge
FIELD: White.

BADGE: Upon water in base barry wavy blue and white a black swan proper.

MOTTO:

Badge in allusion to the name.

	BATTLE HONOURS
Norway	1940
Atlantic	1941-3
North Sea	1940
Korea	1950-1

The *Black Swan* of the present day is the first ship of the name and gives this name to the class of sloops used as escort vessels. She is of 1,250 tons and carries eight 4-inch A.A. guns. She was built by Yarrow in 1939.

H.M.S. BLAKE

Unofficial Badge: An initial letter B in which a broom and whip are entwined. It is surrounded by cabling and at the base is a small scroll on which is written H.M.S. BLAKE. No colours are known.

Official Badge
FIELD: Blue.

BADGE: Within a chain gold a martlet white.

MOTTO:

The chain is taken from that granted to the Admiral for the campaign of 1653. The martlet comes from his crest.

No battle honours are recorded for this vessel.

The unofficial badge refers to the part played by Robert Blake, General-at-Sea, in his battles with Tromp. Tromp is reputed to

H.M.S. BLAKE—*continued*

have carried a broom at the masthead to indicate that he had swept the seas. With the defeat of the Dutch, Blake is supposed to have carried a whip indicating that he had whipped them. This badge is from the first-class cruiser of 9,000 tons, launched at Chatham on 23rd November, 1889. She carried two 9.2-inch and ten 6-inch guns and had a speed of 20 knots. After her launch she performed various services, and in 1907 was fitted as a destroyer depot ship; on 31st July, 1914, she accompanied the Grand Fleet to Scapa, serving there in the same capacity throughout the war, being moved occasionally for short periods to Invergordon and Rosyth. On 9th June, 1922, she was sold. The badge shown is that of the new cruiser laid down as one of the *Tiger* class and which was begun by Fairfield in 1944.

H.M.S. BONAVENTURE

Unofficial Badge: Shows the representation of a ship's wheel, yellow with gold spokes. In the centre an Elizabethan vessel proper. The name of the ship and the dates in black. Above is a naval crown gold, white sails, red and blue gems. Underneath is a scroll blue with gold lettering.

In allusion to the name and to the early ship of the name.

Official Badge
FIELD: Barry wavy of six white and blue.

BADGE: Within a horseshoe inverted gold a griffin red.

MOTTO:

The horseshoe symbolizes the name, the griffin recalls Drake's association with the ship.

H.M.S. BONAVENTURE—*continued*

BATTLE HONOURS

Lowestoft	1665	June 3rd.
Four Days' Battle	1666	June 1st—4th.
Orfordness	1666	July 25th.
Sole Bay	1672	May 28th.
Schooneveld	1673	May 28th and June 4th.
Texel	1673	August 11th.
Barfleur	1692	May 19th—24th.
China	1900	Entitled to medal but not honour.
Malta Convoys	1941	

First badge: This ship was a second-class cruiser of 4,360 tons and had a speed of 20 knots. She served on various stations and in 1907 she was a seagoing base for submarines. During the Great War years she saw service as a submarine depot ship in Home waters and the Mediterranean. On 12th April, 1920, she was sold for breaking up. There was a light cruiser built in 1939 and sunk 1941, and a submarine depot ship of this name which was sold to the Clan Line in 1946.

Present vessel belongs to R.C.N., an aircraft carrier, ex *Powerful*, launched 1945.

H.M.S. BOXER

Description of Badge
FIELD: Red.

BADGE: A boxing glove apaumee white laced and edged gold.

MOTTO: *Praemonitus Praemunitus*.

The badge is in allusion to the name.

BATTLE HONOURS
Crimea	1855	
Sicily	1943	July 10th—August 17th.
Salerno	1943	September 9th—October 6th.
Anzio	1944	January 22nd—31st.

The *Boxer* is a radar training ship and her displacement is 5,970 tons; built by Harland & Wolff. She was fitted and used as a landing ship with her sisters *Bruiser* and *Thruster*; then she became a fighter direction ship, and her present work is for seagoing radar training attached to the Navigation School.

H.M.S. BRECON

Description of Badge

FIELD: Barry wavy of four blue and white.

BADGE: A cape red lined and collared ermine and laced with a cord knotted gold.

MOTTO: By luck and good guidance.

Badge derived from the seal of Brecon.

BATTLE HONOURS

English Channel	1943	
Sicily	1943	July 10th—August 17th.
Salerno	1943	September 9th—October 6th.
Ægean	1944	
South France	1944	August 15th—27th.
Mediterranean	1944	
Atlantic	1945	

The *Brecon* is a *Hunt* class destroyer of 1,175 tons, and was built by Thornycroft. Her main armament is six 4-inch guns. The battle honours show the extent of her service during the Second World War. The writer has cause to remember her, for he had to enlist her aid to tow L.S.T. 368 from a bed of soft mud inside Salerno harbour whilst being shelled by a battery on the top of Monte el Ceste.

H.M.S. BRITANNIA

H.M.S. BRITANNIA

Unofficial Badge: There have been a number of variations of design for badges of this ship name. The one shown came from H.M.S. *Britannia*, a battleship (pre-*Dreadnought*) of 16,350 tons. Britannia is dressed in white with gold helmet and trident. Shield bearing the national colours. Scroll blue, with motto *Pro Gloria* in black letters.

Official Badge:
BADGE: Royal Coat of Arms.

MOTTO:

BATTLE HONOURS

Barfleur	1692	May 19th—24th.
Ushant	1781	December 12th.
Genoa	1795	March 14th.

H.M.S. BRITANNIA—*continued*

St. Vincent	1797	February 14th.
Trafalgar	1805	October 21st.
Crimea	1854	

The first *Britannia* was a first rate of 1,703 tons and 100 guns, built at Chatham in 1682 by Phineas Pett. In 1692, on 19th May, she fought at the battle of Barfleur and was the flagship of Admiral Sir Edward Russell. During the years 1714-1719 she was rebuilt at Woolwich, and broken up at Chatham in 1749.

There was an armed store ship of 535 tons and 20 guns of this name purchased in 1781, and this vessel was wrecked on the Kentish Knock in 1782.

Another first rate of the name was built in 1762 at Portsmouth, of 2,091 tons and 100 guns, and launched on 19th October. In 1781 on 12th December she was in Kempenfelt's attack on a French convoy under de Guichen off Ushant. In 1793 she was the flagship of Vice-Admiral Wm. Hotham at Toulon with Vice-Admiral Lord Hood; in 1795 she was at the action with the French off Genoa on 13th-14th March, which resulted in the award of a medal, and in the same year on 13th July she was at the action off Hyeres. On 14th February, 1797, she was at the battle off Cape St. Vincent, for which a medal was awarded, under the flag of Vice-Admiral Charles Thompson; and was at the famous battle of Trafalgar in 1805 as the flagship of Rear-Admiral the Earl of Northesk, and her Captain was Charles Bullen. This vessel was renamed *St. George* in 1812.

The next one to carry the name was a first rate of 2,616 tons and 120 guns, launched at Plymouth on 20th October, 1820. In 1854 she was at the Crimea in the Russian war in the bombardment of Sebastopol and was the flagship of Vice-Admiral J. W. D. Dundas; in 1858 on 21st December she was commissioned for service as a cadet's training ship to replace H.M.S. *Illustrious*. On 10th August, 1869, she was paid off at Devonport and replaced by the *Prince of Wales*. Her destination then was the breakers' yard.

The *Prince of Wales* was a screw ship of the line of 3,994 tons and 115 guns, launched at Portsmouth on 25th January, 1860, by the Princess of Leiningen. She was originally laid down as a sailing ship, but was converted to screw whilst building and was renamed *Britannia*, replacing the previous vessel as a cadets'

H.M.S. BRITANNIA—*continued*

training ship. Her end came in 1914 when she was sold to Messrs. J. B. Garnham & Sons and then to Messrs. Hughes Bolckow. Towed away from Dartmouth in July, 1916.

The next vessel to carry this name was the battleship *Britannia* of 16,350 tons and carrying four 12-inch and four 9.2-inch guns. She was launched at Portsmouth on 10th December, 1904, and during the Great War of 1914-18 she saw service with the 3rd Battle Squadron and the 9th Cruiser Squadron. She was sunk by a submarine off Cape Trafalgar on 9th November, 1918.

H.M.S. *Britannia's* name was also given to the Royal Naval College Dartmouth.

The present *Britannia* is the Royal Yacht which has been built to serve a dual purpose, Royal Yacht and Hospital Ship. She took the Royal children out to Tobruk to meet their parents, Her Majesty Queen Elizabeth II and H.R.H. The Duke of Edinburgh, on their return to this country, right to the Pool of London for a most triumphant Welcome Home after their round the world tour.

H.M.S. BROADSWORD

Description of Badge

FIELD: Barry wavy of eight white and blue.

BADGE: In front of a rondel red a broadsword in pale point downwards proper, pommel and hilt gold.

MOTTO:

In allusion to the name.

No battle honours are recorded for this vessel.

This vessel is one of the *Weapon* class of destroyers, and was built in 1946 by Yarrow.

H.M.S. BRUCE

Unofficial Badge: Shield with a gold field, red cross in saltire, a chief red on which is a battleaxe gold. Above is a bonnet in black, red, grey and yellow, and an arm in which is held a crowned sceptre. Below is a scroll blue, gold edged with the inscription FUIMUS in gold.

Official Badge
FIELD: Gold.
BADGE: A saltire red charged with a spider gold.
MOTTO: *Tentata attingo* (By attempt I attain).

The badge is in allusion to the story of Bruce and the spider and from the arms of Bruce.

There are no battle honours recorded for H.M.S. *Bruce*.

The vessel which carried the badges was a destroyer of 1,530 tons, built and launched by Cammell Laird on the 26th February, 1918. She carried five 4.7-inch and one 3-inch A.A. guns and six 21-inch torpedo tubes.

H.M.S. BULWARK

Unofficial Badge: This badge was carried by a former *Bulwark* and was designed as a boat's badge by Lady Scott. Colours not known.

Official Badge

FIELD: Barry wavy of ten white and blue.

BADGE: A sword erect proper the blade enfiled with a crown palisado gold.

MOTTO:

Badge is in allusion to the name.

No battle honours are recorded for this vessel.

The first *Bulwark* was a third rate of 74 guns, and was ordered to be built at Portsmouth on 11th June, 1778, and registered at Portsmouth on the list of the Navy by Admiralty order. The building of the ship was not proceeded with and her name was removed from the list.

H.M.S. BULWARK—*continued*

In 1804 there began building at Portsmouth a third rate of 74 guns under the name *Scipio*, but she was renamed *Bulwark* in 1806 and was launched on 23rd April, 1807. In 1814 she was in the American war expedition up the Penobscot river, and in 1826 was broken up at Portsmouth.

Then came a screw line of battleship of 3,716 tons which began building at Chatham in 1859; work was, however, suspended on her in 1862, and an Admiralty order of 1872 directed that she be taken down, this being completed on 18th March, 1873.

Once again a screw line of battleship was ordered, and this one was of 6,557 tons, built at Pembroke as the *Howe* and launched on 7th March, 1860. She was never completed for sea and was ordered to be fitted up for service as a training ship for boys to replace the *Impregnable* and was renamed *Bulwark*. In 1886 she was again renamed *Impregnable*.

No. 5 was a battleship of 15,000 tons, carrying four 12-inch guns, built at Devonport and launched on 18th October, 1899. She was lost off Sheerness by an internal explosion on the 26th November, 1914.

The latest *Bulwark* is an aircraft carrier of 18,300 tons, begun at Harland and Wolff's and completed in 1954.

H.M.S. CADIZ

Description of Badge
FIELD: Blue.

BADGE: Within a wreath of laurel and palm gold a Talbot's head erased white, eared red, in front of two cross crosslets fitchee in saltire also white.

MOTTO: *Ad Omnia Paratus* (Ready for anything).

The badge is derived from the laurel and palm for a combined operation, the cross crosslets for Howard, the Lord High Admiral, and the Talbot's head for Essex, the military Commander-in-Chief.

There are no battle honours recorded for this name, but the *Cadiz Merchant* has a battle honour for Barfleur 1692.

The *Cadiz* is one of the *Battle* class of destroyers built by Fairfield in 1944.

H.M.S. CAMPANIA

Description of Badge
FIELD: Red.
BADGE: A demi-lion rampant gold.
MOTTO: Of One Company.

The badge based on the Cunard Company's badge of a lion; the motto was the ship's own suggestion.

BATTLE HONOURS
Norway	1944-5
Atlantic	1944
Arctic	1944-5

H.M.S. *Campania* was purchased at the end of 1914 by the Admiralty, and was commissioned as an aircraft carrier in April, 1915, doing service with the Grand Fleet. She was fitted with a flying-off deck forward and storage for nine large seaplanes. These could be hoisted out into the water or flown off the deck. In September, 1915, she was altered to carry and tow a kite balloon. When serving with the Grand Fleet she was employed continuously in reconnaissance and patrol work off the Orkneys. On 5th November, 1918, she was sunk in Burntisland Roads.

The present *Campania*, an escort (ferry carrier), was launched in June, 1943, and was converted from the hull of a 12,000 ton cargo vessel laid down for the Shaw Savill and Albion Line. During the Festival of Britain she was loaned by the Admiralty for use as a floating exhibition ship for the 1951 Festival of Britain. After this service she was reduced to the reserve, but was later used for taking men and materials to the Monte Bello Islands off the coast of Australia for atomic explosion experiments.

H.M.S. CAMPERDOWN

Description of Badge
FIELD: Blue.

BADGE: A bugle-horn stringed white within a chaplet of laurel gold.

MOTTO:

Badge derived from the arms of Admiral Duncan, the Earl of Camperdown.

No battle honours are recorded for this name.

The *Camperdown* is one of the *Battle* class destroyers and was built by Fairfield. She carries four 4.5-inch guns.

H.M.S. CENTAUR

Official Badge: (Superseded).
FIELD: Blue.
BADGE: A man seahorse gold blowing a shell trumpet silver
MOTTO: *Celeriter Ferox* (Swiftly Fierce).

Official Badge
FIELD: Green.
BADGE: A centaur drawing a bow white.
MOTTO: *Celeriter Ferox* (Swiftly Fierce).
 In allusion to the name.

BATTLE HONOURS
Havana	1762	August 13th.
St. Kitts	1782	June 25th—26th.
The Saints	1782	April 12th.
Minorca	1798	November 15th.

H.M.S. CENTAUR—continued

Baltic	1855	
China	1860	
Belgian Coast	1916-17	
"Curieux"	1804	February 2nd. Single ship action.
"Sevolod"	1808	August 26th. Single ship action.

Derivation of badge is, of course, from mythology, the Centaurs being a race of savage half-men half-horses living between Pelion and Ossa in Thessaly, the progeny of Centaurus, son of Ixion, and the cloud, their mothers being mares. They are treated as embodying the relation between spiritual and animal in man and nature.

The first vessel of the name was a sixth rate of 504 tons and carrying 24 guns. She was built at Hull by Mr. Hugh Blades and launched on 11th June, 1746. In 1753 she was commissioned by Captain Henry Cosby. This vessel was sold out of the service on 30th January, 1761.

During Boscawen's action off Lagos on 18th August, 1759, the French *Centaure* (74) was taken, and in 1760 she was purchased for H.M. service and registered as *Centaur*. Whilst on the Jamaica station under Captain Forrest on 5th June, 1761, she captured the French *St. Anne* (64), and in 1762 she was at the reduction of Havana. On 27th July, 1778, she was at the battle of Ushant; 29th April, 1781, at Sir Samuel Hood's action with the Comte de Grasse off Martinique; Rear-Admiral Graves's action off the Chesapeake, 25th January, 1782; Sir Samuel Hood's action with the Comte de Grasse off St. Kitts, 12th April, 1782, at the battle of the Saintes; and on the way home from Jamaica in 1782 she foundered in a hurricane. Only Captain Inglefield and 11 others were saved.

Then came a third rate of 74 guns and 1,842 tons, launched at Woolwich on 14th March, 1797. In November, 1798, she was at the capture of Minorca; 16th March, 1799, assisted by the *Cormorant* (20), drove ashore and destroyed the Spanish *Guadeloupe* (34) near Cape Oropesa; 19th November, 1799, assisted in the capture of a French Squadron of men-of-war bound to Toulon from Jaffa off Cape Sicie; June, 1803, at the reduction of St. Lucia and Tobago; January, 1804, seizure of the Diamond Rock; 4th February, 1804, her boats cut out the French gun

H.M.S. CENTAUR—*continued*

brig *Curieux* at Fort Royal, Martinique (Bar to Naval General Service Medal). During April and May of 1804 she was at the capture of Surinam, and on 16th July, 1806, her boats assisted at the cutting out of the French *Cesar* (16) in the Gironde (Bar to Naval General Service Medal).

On 25th September she assisted at the capture of the French 40-gun frigates *Gloire, Indefatigable, Minerve* and *Armide* off Rochefort. In this action Commodore Sir S. Hood was seriously wounded and suffered the loss of his right arm. In 1807 she was at Copenhagen, and on 24th December of the same year she was at the occupation of Madeira. On 26th August, 1808, in action with the Russian Fleet in the Baltic and at the capture of the *Sevolod* (74) (Bar to Naval General Service Medal). In 1819 she was broken up at Plymouth.

Then came a paddle-wheel steam frigate of 6 guns built at Portsmouth and launched on 6th October, 1845. In 1849 to 1854 she was flagship on the West Coast of Africa and East Coast of South America stations. In 1855 at the Russian war in the Baltic (Medal); in 1860 in China (Medal). She was broken up in 1864 at Devonport.

Armstrong Whitworths built a cruiser of 3,750 tons which was launched on 6th January, 1916, and called the *Centaur*. In 1916 to 1918 she served with the Harwich Force, and was succeeded in 1932 as Commodore "D" ship in the Home Fleet by the *Cairo*. As she had reached the age limit of sixteen years she was sold in 1934. It is interesting to note that the King of Sweden in 1930 and the King of Denmark in 1931 and 1932 hoisted their flags as Honorary Admirals of the Fleet in this ship.

In April, 1947, the Duchess of Kent launched the light aircraft carrier *Centaur* at Belfast. She is of 18,300 tons and incorporates the new arrangement of angle-deck landing, and she proceeded on her acceptance trials on 22nd September, 1953.

H.M.S. CENTURION

Unofficial Badge: This badge was carried by H.M.S. *Centurion*, a battleship (super-*Dreadnought*) of 23,000 tons. Yellow field, centurion proper, black edge round the plaque.

Official Badge
FIELD: Red.

BADGE: The Roman Centurion's standard gold.

MOTTO: One in a hundred.

Badge in allusion to the name.

	BATTLE HONOURS	
Armada	1588	July 21st—29th. Merchant ship of the City of London.
Cadiz	1596	June 21st.
Dover	1652	May 19th.

H.M.S. CENTURION—*continued*

Portland	1653	February 18th—20th.
Gabbard	1653	June 2nd—3rd.
Santa Cruz	1657	April 20th.
Lowestoft	1665	June 3rd.
Orfordness	1666	July 25th.
Barfleur	1692	May 19th—24th.
Velez Malaga	1704	August 13th.
Finisterre	1747	May 3rd.
Louisburg	1758	July 26th.
Quebec	1759	September 13th.
Havana	1762	August 13th.
St. Lucia	1778	December 15th.
China	1900	June 10th—December 31st.
Jutland	1916	May 31st.
Normandy	1944	June 6th—July 3rd. Block ship.
"N.S. de Covadonga"	1743	Single ship action (under consideration)

The last *Centurion* was a battleship of 25,395 tons and employed as a radio-controlled target ship. During the Second World War she was made up to represent a heavier unit in Eastern waters, and was sunk as part of the Mulberry Harbour, 9th June, 1944.

H.M.S. CERES

Description of Badge
FIELD: Green.

BADGE: Five ears, two barley, three wheat, gold.

MOTTO: Harvest betimes.

LATER MOTTO: *Tu ne cede malis* (Do not yield to evil).

The badge is derived from Greek mythology and refers to Ceres, the goddess of the harvest.

BATTLE HONOURS

St. Lucia	1778	December 15th.
Egypt	1801	March 8th—September 2nd.
Atlantic	1939	
Normandy	1944	June 6th—July 3rd.

The first *Ceres* was a sloop of 361 tons and 18 guns. She was launched at Woolwich on 25th November, 1777, and on 9th March, 1778, in company with the *Ariadne* (24), she captured the American cruiser *Alfred* (24) in the West Indies. On 17th December, 1778, she was captured by the French frigate *Iphigenie* (32) off St. Lucia when commanded by Captain Richard Dacres, but on 19th April, 1782, she was recaptured by a part of Rodney's fleet under Sir Samuel Hood. On 4th July of the same year she was renamed *Raven* by Admiralty Order.

The next *Ceres* was a fifth rate of 689 tons and 32 guns, launched at Liverpool on 19th September, 1781. In 1794 she was at the capture of Martinique, and in April of the same year, in company with the *Quebec* (32), the *Rose* (28) and a sloop, carried the works

H.M.S. CERES—*continued*

on the Saintes. She was at the June attack on Guadaloupe in 1794; at the operations against San Domingo in March, 1796; in 1803 a receiving ship at Sheerness; in 1816 a victualling depot; and in 1830 she was taken to pieces. (In 1814 the *Niger* (38) and *Tagus* (36) captured the French 40-gun ship *Ceres*).

In September, 1830, a buoy boat of 25 tons was purchased at Devonport for use as a tender, and on 9th October, 1871, she was attached to the training ship *Ganges* at Falmouth. She then became a tender to *Jackal* on the coast of Scotland in 1874, and in 1877 was sold by auction at Greenock for £133 9s. 10d.

A light cruiser of 4,190 tons and carrying five 6-inch guns was launched at Clydebank on 24th March, 1917, and commissioned later for the 6th Light Cruiser Squadron. She was at the Heligoland Bight action on 17th November, 1917, and on 26th November sailed for the Baltic and the Gulf of Finland. In 1941 she was in operation against Italian possessions in Eritrea, Abyssinia and Eastern Somaliland. She was sold in 1946 for breaking up.

Establishment.—On 1st October, 1946, *Demetrius*, the R.N. Supply and Secretariat School, Wetherby, Yorkshire, was renamed *Ceres* as soon as the name became available.

H.M.S. CEYLON

Description of Badge
FIELD: White.

BADGE: On a mount green between two groves of palm trees proper an elephant affronte also proper.

MOTTO:

The badge is derived from the arms of Ceylon.

	BATTLE HONOURS	
Sabang	1944	July 25th.
Burma	1945	
Korea	1950-2	

The first *Ceylon* was a fifth rate of 672 tons and 32 guns. In 1806 she was the *Bombay*, an East Indiaman bought in India and made into a frigate. On 1st July, 1808, she had her name changed to *Ceylon*, and on 18th September, 1810, she was captured by the French *Venus* (40) and *Victor* (16), but was recaptured the same day by the *Boadicea* (38). In 1817 she was converted into a troopship, in 1832 she was fitted as a receiving ship at Malta, and in June, 1875, she was sold at Malta for £900.

The second *Ceylon* was a yacht of 311 tons, built in 1891. She saw service in the Mediterranean and Dardanelles from June, 1915, to May, 1916.

The present *Ceylon* was built by Stephen & Co. in 1938, and is a cruiser of 8,000 tons, carrying twelve 6-inch and eight 4-inch A.A. guns, and was completed in 1943. Her battle honours show where she served in the Second World War.

H.M.S. CHALLENGER

Unofficial Badges: A circular badge in which is shown a bounding kangaroo and the words KIA ORA, meaning Good Luck. Another shows a fighting cock with spurs displayed surrounded by a belt on which is the name of the ship. The fighting cock represents the name "Challenger." No colours are shown.

Official Badge
FIELD: Blue.

BADGE: A stag statant on a mount proper.

MOTTO: *Depugnare Superbos* (To fight the proud).

The badge is taken from Landseer's picture "The Challenger."

BATTLE HONOURS
San Sebastian	1813	September 8th.
Cameroons	1914	

H.M.S. CHALLENGER—*continued*

The sixth ship was a second-class cruiser of 5,880 tons and with a speed of 21.3 knots, and she carried eleven 6-inch guns. She was launched at Chatham on 27th May, 1902, and in 1914-15 she was at the Cameroons, 1915-18 at German East Africa and Zanzibar, and on 31st May, 1920, she was sold to Messrs. T. W. Ward Ltd. There have been eight of the name, and the work done by the survey vessels which have carried the name will be long remembered. The latest was built at Chatham in 1931, being originally designed to investigate new fishing grounds, and was made a hydrographic survey vessel. Now withdrawn from service.

H.M.S. CHATHAM

Description of Badge

The arms of Chatham. Chief light blue charged with two lymphads, fess chequy gold and red, base dark blue charged with a wreath green and swords in saltire. Helmet gold, crest a naval crown, green wreath and gold trident. Mantling blue and gold. Underneath a scroll red with motto in black and the name of the ship in black.

From the arms of Chatham.

BATTLE HONOURS
Barfleur	1692	May 19th—24th.
Quiberon Bay	1759	November 20th.
Dardanelles	1915-16	February 19th—January 8th.

This vessel was a light cruiser of 5,400 tons, and her armament was eight 6-inch guns and four 3-pdrs. She was launched at Chatham on 9th November, 1911, and in 1914 she was the escort of the Indian Expeditionary Force. In 1914-15 she was in at the destruction of the German *Königsberg* in the Rufigi river; in 1915 at the Dardanelles, where she flew the flag of Rear-Admiral Wemyss at the evacuation; in 1916 with the Grand Fleet; 1920-24 with the New Zealand Navy; in 1924-5 flagship of the East Indies Squadron; and in 1926 she was sold.

H.M. DOCKYARD CHATHAM

Description of Badge
FIELD: White.

BADGE: On a cross couped red a sword fess-wise to the dexter white, pommel and hilt surmounted by a trident palewise all gold.

MOTTO:

This badge is derived from parts of the arms of the boroughs of Chatham and Gillingham. Designed by the late Sir Arthur Cochrane, K.C.V.O., Clarenceux King of Arms, Admiralty Adviser on Heraldry.

Chatham has the distinction of being the first of the Royal Dockyards to be granted an Official Badge.

H.M.S. CLEOPATRA

Description of Badge
FIELD: Black.

BADGE: Cleopatra's head proper, crowned gold.

MOTTO: *Invicta ut Olim* (Unconquered as ever).

The badge is derived from the famous Cleopatra, Queen of Egypt, distinguished for her beauty and her love affairs, who fascinated Caesar. She finally killed herself by the bite of an asp, self-applied.

BATTLE HONOURS

Dogger Bank	1781	August 5th.
Martinique	1809	February 24th.
Burma	1853	
Belgian Coast	1916	
Malta Convoys	1942	
Sirte	1942	March 22nd.
Sicily	1943	July 10th—August 17th.

The first of the name was built at Bristol by J. H. Hillhouse, of 689 tons and 32 guns, being launched on 26th November, 1779. On 5th August, 1781, she was at the action of Hyde Parker with the Dutch off the Dogger Bank; in April, 1796, she captured the French *Aurore* (10) on the America station; on 22nd March, 1801, her boats with those of the *Andromache* cut out a Spanish gunboat from Levita Bay, Cuba; and on 17th February, 1805, she was captured by the French vessel *Ville de Milan* (46) off Bermuda after an action of five hours, being recaptured by the *Leander* later. In

H.M.S. CLEOPATRA—*continued*

1809, on 22nd January, she captured the French frigate *Topaze* (40) from under the battery near Pointe Noire, Guadaloupe, being assisted by the *Jason* (38) and the *Hazard* (18). She was also at the capture of Martinique in February, 1809, and was taken to pieces at Deptford in 1814.

Then came a sixth rate of 918 tons and 28 guns, launched at Pembroke on 28th April, 1835. On 27th January, 1841, this vessel captured the Spanish slaver *Segundo Rosario* with 284 slaves on board in the West Indies, and in 1862 was sold at Chatham.

Following her was a third-class cruiser of 2,380 tons and 14 guns, launched at Glasgow on 1st August, 1878. In February, 1894, she was at the Intervention at Bluefields, Nacarugua, in 1905 attached to *Defiance* torpedo school as overflow ship, and as *Defiance III* was sold for breaking up in June, 1931.

A light cruiser of this name was launched on 14th January, 1915, at H.M. Dockyard, Devonport, of 3,750 tons and four 6-inch guns. On 6th July, 1915, she joined the 5th Light Cruiser Squadron at Harwich. She took part in the search for the German minelayer *Meteor*, rammed and cut in half the German destroyer G.194, engaged enemy ships after the raid on Lowestoft, off the Schouwen Bank and off Terschelling, and in November, 1918, was present at the surrender of the German High Seas Fleet. She was sold on 26th June, 1931, at Sheerness for breaking up.

The present *Cleopatra* is one of the *Dido* class of 5,540 tons displacement. During the Second World War she served with distinction in the Mediterranean.

H.M.S. COCHRANE

Unofficial Badge: Shield white, red chevron and three boars' heads blue, supported by two greyhounds collared and chained gold. Above, an earl's coronet. The crest a horse passant silver. Underneath is a scroll blue with the name of the ship in white.

Derived from the arms of the Cochrane family.

Official Badge

FIELD: Barry wavy of six blue and white.

BADGE: In front of three anchors, one erect and two in saltire gold, a torteau charged with a horse passant white. Crest from the arms of the Cochrane family.

BATTLE HONOUR

Jutland   1916   May 31st.

The *Cochrane* was an armoured cruiser of 13,550 tons, one of the *Warrior* class. Her main armament consisted of two 9.2-inch

H.M.S. COCHRANE—*continued*

and four 7.5-inch guns, and her speed was 23 knots. She was launched on 20th May, 1905, at Govan; built by Fairfield. The 31st May, 1916, found her at the battle of Jutland, and in 1917 she was engaged in North Atlantic Convoy duties. From 7th March to 30th October, 1918, she was detached for duties at Murmansk in the defence of Northern Russia. She served at the operations at Pechonga, and on 14th November, 1918, she grounded in the River Mersey and became a total loss. Now a shore establishment.

H.M.S. COLLINGWOOD

Unofficial Badge: This badge is still used by H.M.S. *Collingwood* at Fareham. Field blue, red chief, lion and stags' heads gold, chevron gold. Word TRAFALGAR in gold. The battleship *Collingwood* also carried it but with supporters at crest.

Official Badge

FIELD: Barry wavy of four white and blue.

BADGE: In front of a holly tree couped proper the attires of a stag conjoined black, within the attires a motto scroll red with the word TRAFALGAR in gold letters.

MOTTO: *Ferar Unus Et Idem* (I shall carry on regardless).

BATTLE HONOURS
Jutland	1916	May 31st.
Atlantic	1941-4	

H.M.S. COLLINGWOOD—*continued*

The first *Collingwood* was a second rate of 2,584 tons and armed with 80 guns. She was launched at Pembroke on 17th August, 1841. In 1844 she was flagship of Rear-Admiral Sir George Seymour on the Pacific station, and in 1860 was reduced to a third rate of 68 guns. This ship was then taken in hand at Sheerness to be converted into a screw vessel, and in 1867 she was sold to Messrs. Castle.

Then came an armour-plated barbette ship of 10 guns and 9,150 tons, launched at Pembroke on 22nd November, 1882. She was on the Mediterranean station for a number of years and then became coastguard ship at Bantry Bay from 1897 to 1903. In 1909 she was sold.

The next was a battleship of 19,250 tons and armed with ten 12-inch and eighteen 4-inch guns, launched at Devonport on 7th November, 1908. She was at the battle of Jutland, and in 1919 became gunnery drill ship at Devonport, being re-commissioned on 1st October, 1919, as a tender to *Vivid*. In 1921 she was a boys' training ship at Portland and tender to *Colossus*, then sold at Portsmouth in 1922. H.M.S. *Collingwood* is now a shore training establishment.

H.M.S. COLOSSUS

Unofficial Badge: A shield on which is placed a Maltese cross. Four animals are also shown, but the original sketch does not give clear details and they are most likely lions and unicorns, badge derived from the Knights of St. John.

Official Badge
FIELD: Blue.

BADGE: A giant's head affronte couped at the shoulders white, his head rayonne gold.

MOTTO:

This badge was taken from the Colossus of Rhodes, a giant bronze figure of Apollo, 120 feet high, which was placed astride the harbour of Rhodes. This was one of the seven wonders of the world, but was destroyed in 224 B.C. by an earthquake. A long time afterwards it was sold to a Jew for old metal.

H.M.S. COLOSSUS—*continued*

BATTLE HONOURS

Groix Island	1795	June 23rd.
St. Vincent	1797	February 14th.
Trafalgar	1805	October 21st.
Baltic	1855	
Jutland	1916	May 31st.

This ship was a battleship of 20,500 tons, and her main armament was composed of ten 12-inch and twelve 4-inch guns, and she had a speed of 21 knots. She was launched at Scott's Shipbuilding and Engineering Company at Greenock on 9th April, 1910. From 1911 she served in various squadrons, and in 1916, on 31st May, she was at the battle of Jutland, where she led the 5th Division of the Battle Fleet. In this battle she was hit twice, but fortunately without serious damage. In 1921 she became a boy's training ship and in 1928 she was sold.

The last vessel to bear the name *Colossus* was launched as a light fleet carrier, giving her name to the class. She was turned over to the French Navy and became the *Arromanches*.

H.M.S. COMMONWEALTH

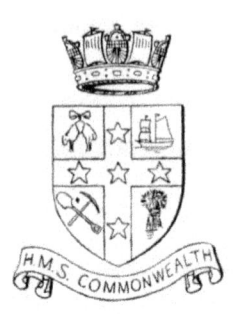

Description of Badge

A shield having a field blue, on which is a red cross charged with five gold stars. First quarter, a lamb gold; fourth quarter, a wheatsheaf or garb gold; second quarter, a sailing ship proper; third quarter, a pickaxe and shovel in saltire gold. Above is a naval crown gold with white sails, red and blue gems. Underneath is a scroll white, red edged, with the name of the ship in black.

The badge is representative of the Commonwealth of Australia.

No battle honours are recorded for this vessel.

The *Commonwealth* was a battleship of the *King Edward* class, 16,350 tons, and carried four 12-inch and four 9.2-inch guns. She was built by the Fairfield Shipbuilding and Engineering Company at Govan and launched on 13th May, 1903. During the years 1905-1918 she served with the Atlantic, Channel, Home and Grand Fleets. In 1921 she was sold for breaking up.

H.M.S. CONQUEROR

Description of Badge

The figure of Father Time and a scroll white on which is the motto TEMPUS OMNIA VINCIT (Time conquers all things) red. Underneath in letters of black the name of the ship.

Badge in allusion to the name.

BATTLE HONOURS
Lagos	1759	August 17th.
The Saints	1782	April 12th.
Trafalgar	1805	October 21st.
Jutland	1916	May 31st.
North Sea	1942-3	
Biscay	1944	
Atlantic	1944-5	
English Channel	1943-4-5	

This vessel was a battleship of 22,500 tons and carried 26 guns. She was launched on 1st May, 1911, at Dalmuir and later served in the 1914-18 war, where she was in the Jutland engagement. On 19th December, 1922, she was sold to the Upnor Shipbreaking Company Ltd.

H.M.S. CORNWALL

Unofficial Badge: This badge was the one carried by H.M.S. *Cornwall*, an armoured cruiser of 9,800 tons. The field of the shield is black and the fifteen bezants are gold. The edge of the shield is also gold. Above is a naval crown. The scroll is white with the motto ONE AND ALL in black.

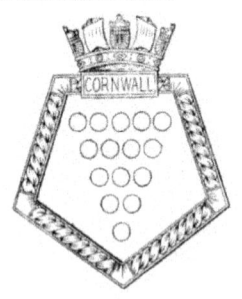

Official Badge
FIELD: Black.
BADGE: Fifteen bezants gold.
MOTTO: One and All.

BATTLE HONOURS
Barfleur	1692	May 19th—24th.
Falkland Islands	1914	
Dardanelles	1915	

Badges from the arms of Cornwall.

H.M.S. CORNWALL—*continued*

H.M.S. *Cornwall* (1902—9,800 tons) served at the Falkland Islands in 1914 and in 1915 was engaged in bombardments in the Eastern Mediterranean. From 1908 to 1914 she was a training ship for cadets. She was sold in 1921.

The last H.M.S. *Cornwall* was a cruiser of 10,000 tons and was sunk in the Second World War by Japanese dive-bombers in the Indian Ocean.

H.M.S. CORUNNA

Description of Badge
FIELD: Red.

BADGE: Within a wreath of palm gold on a mullet white a Moor's head proper.

MOTTO:

The badge is derived from the arms of Lieutenant-General Sir John Moore, Commander-in-Chief.

No battle honours are recorded for this name.

The *Corunna* is a destroyer of the *Battle* class, built at Swan Hunter's in 1945.

H.M.S. COSSACK

Description of Badge
FIELD: Blue.

BADGE: Riding in water barry wavy white and blue a mounted Cossack proper.

MOTTO:

The badge is in allusion to the name.

BATTLE HONOURS

Baltic	1855
Belgian Coast	1914-16
Narvik	1940
Norway	1940
"Bismarck"	1941 May 23rd—27th.
Atlantic	1940-1
Malta Convoys	1941
Korea	1950-3

The *Cossack* is a destroyer of the "C" class and is of 1,710 tons and was built by Vickers-Armstrongs in 1944. The main guns carried are four 4.5-inch.

The *Cossack* is a name which will live for ever in the naval history of our country for her exploits in connection with the rescue of merchant seamen from the *Altmark* in a Norwegian fiord. This *Cossack* of 1,870 tons foundered after being torpedoed by a U-boat west of Gibraltar. She was built in 1937.

H.M.S. COURAGEOUS

Description of Badge
FIELD: Black.

BADGE: A right arm proper, the hand grasping a serpent green.

MOTTO: *Fortiter In Angustis* (Bravely in difficulties).

In allusion to the name.

BATTLE HONOURS
The battle honours given here are those of the *Courageux*.

Ushant	1781	December 12th.
Genoa	1795	March 14th.
Bay of Biscay	1805	November 4th.

The *Courageous* was an aircraft carrier originally designed as cruiser for shallow draught operations, and completed her conversion at Devonport in 1928. Armstrongs completed her as a cruiser in 1917. This vessel was sunk by a U-boat off the west coast of Ireland whilst on anti-submarine patrol.

H.M.S. CROSSBOW

Description of Badge
FIELD: Blue.

BADGE: A crossbow gold with a quarrel in chief red over a base barry wavy of four white and blue.

MOTTO:

Badge in allusion to the name.

No battle honours are recorded for this vessel.

This vessel is one of the *Weapon* class of destroyers. She was built in 1945 at Woolston by Thornycroft.

H.M.S. CRUSADER

Unofficial Badge: A crusader white, red cross on chest, blue sash, carrying a gold shield with a red cross, stockings red with green criss-cross pattern, and the words DEUS VULT in black. Scroll white and blue, gold edged, with name in black.

Official Badge
FIELD: Black.

BADGE: A shield silver, thereon a cross red.

MOTTO: *Non Nobis Domine* (Not under us, Lord).

Badge in allusion to name.

BATTLE HONOURS
Belgian Coast. 1914-16
Korea 1952-3

H.M.S. CRUSADER—*continued*

Whites of Cowes launched the *Crusader* on 20th March, 1909, and she was a torpedo boat destroyer of 1,045 tons, and her armament was two 4-inch guns and two 18-inch torpedo tubes, and she could do 34 knots. During the Great War she served in the 6th Destroyer Flotilla, Dover Patrol. In 1914 from 20th October to 8th November she took part in the bombardment of the Flemish coast by the Dover Force, Rear-Admiral the Honourable Horace Hood hoisting his flag in her at intervals. From August to October, 1915, she was escorting and screening monitors bombarding the Flemish Coast. On 20th June, 1920, she was sold.

The present *Crusader* belongs to R.C.N. and is a destroyer of 1,710 tons built in 1944 at Cowes.

H.M.S. CUMBERLAND

Description of Badge
FIELD: Red.

BADGE: A rose gold with red and gold centre.

MOTTO: *Justitiae tenax* (Tenacious of Justice).

The badge is derived from part of the county arms and the motto of Cumberland.

	BATTLE	HONOURS
Sadras	1758	April 29th.
Negapatam	1758	August 3rd.
Porto Novo	1759	September 10th.
St. Vincent	1780	January 16th.
Baltic	1854	
Cameroons	1914	
North Africa	1942	
Arctic	1942-3	
Sabang	1944	July 25th.
Burma	1945	

The first *Cumberland* was a third rate of 1,220 tons, and was built at Bursledon in 1695. In 1707 she was captured by a French squadron under Du Guay Trouin.

There was a third rate of 1,308 tons and 80 guns built at Deptford in 1710 of this name, and she was taken to pieces in 1732.

Another third rate followed and she was of 1,401 tons and 66 guns, built at Woolwich in 1739 when she had 80 guns, these being cut down to 66 in 1748. She saw action in the West Indies

H.M.S. CUMBERLAND—*continued*

in 1741; in the East Indies in 1756, where she took part in the destruction of the pirate *Angria*; in 1758 at the action off Negapatam; in 1759 at the action off Pondicherry; and in 1760 she sank at anchor off Goa.

A bomb vessel of 181 tons and 8 guns also had the name of *Cumberland* and was purchased in 1739. In 1740-1 she was in the attack on Cartagena and Chagres and in 1742 was broken up.

Another third rate of the name was built at Deptford in 1774. She was of 1,674 tons and she carried 74 guns. This vessel served at the battle of Ushant in 1778, in the action off Finisterre in 1780, at the relief of Gibraltar in 1781, in 1783 at the action off Cuddalore, and in 1804 she was broken up.

There was a schooner *Cumberland* of 29 tons bought in 1803, being used by Flinders in his survey of Australia.

In 1807 the 1,718-ton third-rate vessel of 74 guns was built at Northfleet and was called the *Cumberland*. She was in an attack on a French convoy near Toulon in 1809 and in the destruction of armed ships and part of a convoy in Rosas Bay in the same year. In 1830 she was made into a convict hulk, in 1833 was renamed *Fortitude*, and in 1870 was sold.

The last of the third rates of this name appeared in 1842 when she was built at Chatham. This vessel was of 2,214 tons and had 70 guns. In 1854 she was at the attack on Bomarsund, converted into a training ship in 1869, and in 1889 was burned on the Clyde.

It is interesting to note that Sir Provo Wallis, of Chesapeake and Shannon fame, did his last sea service on the *Cumberland* (70) and was with this ship on the south-east coast of America as Commander-in-Chief, having hoisted his flag in her on 1st April, 1857.

The first cruiser of the name was of 9,800 tons and had 14 guns. She was built at Glasgow in 1902, taking part in operations in the Cameroons and the surrender of Duala. She captured many enemy merchant ships. Sold in 1921.

The *Kent* class cruiser named *Cumberland* was completed in 1928 by Vickers and is of 10,000 tons with eight 8-inch and eight 4-inch A.A. guns. In the Second World War she served in theatres of operations as far apart as the Arctic and Sabang. She is now being used for experimental purposes with radar and radio. She is also fitted with Denny Brown fin stabilizers.

H.M.S. CURACOA

Description of Badge
FIELD: Black.

BADGE: A stork's head white, in his beak a snake green.

MOTTO: *Certamine Summo* (In the midst of battle).

The badge is from the crest and motto of Rear-Admiral Sir C. Brisbane (1769-1829), the conqueror of Curacoa in 1807.

BATTLE HONOURS

Crimea	1855
New Zealand	1863-6
Norway	1940
Atlantic	1940
North Sea	1940-1-2
Arctic	1942

The *Curacoa* was a cruiser of the *Ceres* class and her tonnage was 4,290. She was completed by Pembroke Dockyard in 1918 and carried five 6-inch and two 3-inch A.A. guns. She was mined in 1919 and then refitted. During the Second World War she was sunk in a collision with the *Queen Mary* in the North-West Approaches.

H.M.S. CYCLOPS

Unofficial Badge: The figure of Cyclops proper, background in proper colours. Gold blue scroll with black and white letters.

Official Badge
FIELD: Black.

BADGE: A sixteen-pointed star red, bordered gold, within which an eye proper.

MOTTO: With Eye and Hand.

From Greek mythology. There were three classes of Cyclops in these stories. One of them was a set of one-eyed giants who infested the coasts of Sicily, preying on human flesh; then there were the Brontes, Steropes and Arges, which were elemental powers subject to Zeus; and lastly there was a people of Thrace, who were well known for their skill in building.

H.M.S. CYCLOPS—*continued*

BATTLE HONOURS

Egypt	1801	March 8th—September 2nd.
Syria	1840	September 10th—December 9th.
Crimea	1854-5	

The fourth *Cyclops* was a repair ship of 11,300 tons and was purchased in 1905 while building. She was launched on 27th October, 1905, by James Laing and Son. Her original name was *Indrabarah*.

H.M.S. CYGNET

Description of Badge
FIELD: Black.

BADGE: A cygnet silver on wavelets gold and blue.

MOTTO: *Inter Pares Insignis* (Notable among her fellows).

Badge in allusion to the name.

BATTLE HONOURS

Armada	1588	July 21st—29th.
Portland	1653	February 18th—20th.
Havana	1762	August 13th.
Guadeloupe	1810	February 5th.
Alexandria	1882	July 11th.
Sicily	1943	July 10th—August 17th.
Atlantic	1943-4	
Arctic	1944-5	

The first *Cygnet* was a pinnace of 30 tons and 3 guns, built in 1585. In 1587 she was in Drake's expedition to Cadiz (singeing the King of Spain's beard), commanded by John Sherrif; under Lord Henry Seymour she was in the battle of the Armada, 1588; in 1598 in the Channel squadron; and in 1603 she was apparently condemned.

There was a vessel of 233 tons and armed with 20 guns of the name of *Cygnet*, which was bought at Dunkirk in 1643. She served on guard duties and was at the battle of the Kentish Knock and the battle off Portland, being sold in 1654.

H.M.S. CYGNET—continued

Then came a sixth rate of the name of 60 tons and 6 guns. She was built at Chatham in 1657. In the second Dutch war she was employed on convoy work and cruising. She appears to have been sold soon after 1667.

There was a fireship called the *Cygnet* of 100 tons and 8 guns, bought in August, 1688, which was captured by two French privateers off Cape Clear whilst with convoy from Barbados on 20th September, 1693. Her captain, John Perry, was dismissed the service by court-martial.

Following this ship was a sloop of 386 tons and 18 guns, and she came into the service by capture and was originally the French *Guirlande*, taken in 1758 and renamed *Cygnet*. She was at the capture of Havana in 1762 under the command of Captain the Hon. Charles Napier. In 1768 she was sold at South Carolina.

The next to bear the name was a ship sloop of 301 tons and 16 guns, launched at Portsmouth on 24th January, 1776. In the years 1776 to 1783 she saw service in the war of American independence, and in 1798 to 1801 service in the French revolutionary war, being sold in August, 1802.

After this ship came another ship sloop of 365 tons and 18 guns, launched on 4th September, 1804, at Messrs. Palmers at Yarmouth. In 1806 this vessel captured the French *Imperiale* (3) off Dominica. She assisted at the destruction of the *Loire* and *Seine* (frigates *en flute*) on 17th-18th December, 1809, and a medal was awarded for this action. She was at the capture of Guadeloupe in 1810, and on 7th March, 1815, she was wrecked on the coast of French New Guinea.

Another *Cygnet* was a brig sloop of 237 tons and 10 guns, launched on 11th May, 1819, at Portsmouth, and sold on 6th August, 1835.

On 6th April, 1840, a 359-ton vessel was launched at Woolwich and in 1844 fitted as a packet sloop. This *Cygnet* was transferred to the coastguards as watch vessel No. 30, stationed at Chichester Harbour in 1857, and in 1877 she was broken up at Portsmouth.

The next to bear the name was a gun vessel second class of 428 tons and 5 guns. She was launched in 1860 by Messrs. Wigram and Son, Northam, and she was broken up at Portsmouth in 1868.

A gunboat first class was the next *Cygnet*, and she was of 455 tons and carried 4 guns. She was launched on 30th May, 1874,

H.M.S. CYGNET—*continued*

by Doxford, Sunderland. In 1876 she was on the Niger expedition, and she served at Alexandria, the Egyptian campaign, at Suakin, and in 1889 was sold.

The destroyer *Cygnet* of 355 tons and 6 guns was built in 1898 by Thornycroft. From 1914 to 1918 she served in the Local Defence Flotilla at the Nore, and was sold in 1920.

There was a minesweeper called the *Cygnet* of 300 tons which served in the 4th M.S. Flotilla during the 1914-18 war.

The destroyer *St. Laurent* transferred to the R.C.N. in 1937 was originally the *Cygnet*. She was of 1,375 tons and carried four 4-inch guns, and was built in 1931.

The present *Cygnet* is a sloop built by Cammell Laird at Birkenhead. Modified *Black Swan* class, and built in 1942.

H.M.S. DAINTY

Description of Badge
FIELD: Blue.
BADGE: A fan white and gold.
MOTTO: *Dulce Quod Utile* (It is pleasant if it is useful).

The badge has been derived from a fan on a portrait of Queen Elizabeth I.

BATTLE HONOURS
Calabria	1940	July 9th.
Libya	1940-1	
Atlantic	1940	
Mediterranean	1940-1	
Malta Convoys	1941	

The first *Dainty* was a vessel of 350 tons, built on the River Thames for Sir Richard Hawkins in 1588. In 1593 she sailed on Hawkins' voyage of discovery and exploration to the South Seas, and in 1594 attacked shipping and warehouses at Valparaiso. She was brought to action on 20th June, 1594, by a squadron of Spanish ships off San Mateo Bay, Equador. Her adversaries consisted of three ships with complements totalling some 1,300 men. She fought this overwhelming force for three days, but with all her crew wounded or killed the *Dainty* was forced to surrender. Her total crew numbered 75.

The next was a twin screw tug employed at Pembroke and later on at Queenstown from 1920 to 1923, and was afterwards transferred to the Irish Free State.

H.M.S. DAINTY—*continued*

In 1932 Fairfield's launched the destroyer *Dainty* at Govan, and she was of 1,375 tons and carried four 4.7-inch guns. From 1933 to the outbreak of the war she served on the China and Mediterranean stations. On 21st June, 1940, she was engaged in bombarding Bardia, and a week later, in company with H.M.S. *Ilex*, sank two Italian submarines, the *Console Generale Liuzzi* and *Vebi-Scebelli*, in an anti-submarine sweep off Crete. On 9th July she was at the battle of Calabria, then in 1941 engaged in Malta convoys, and was finally sunk off Tobruk by aircraft on 24th February, 1942.

The present *Dainty* is a vessel of the *Daring* class.

H.M.S. DARING

Description of Badge
FIELD: Black.

BADGE: An arm and hand in a cresset of fire all proper.

MOTTO: *Splendide Audax* (Finely daring).

The badge is derived from the story of Mucius Scaevola, who, when taken prisoner by Tarquin, put his hand into a fire to show that the Roman courage was unbroken.

No battle honours are recorded for this name.

The first to bear the name in the Navy List was a gun brig of 178 tons and which carried twelve 18-pounder carronades. She was built at Ipswich by Mr. Bailey and launched in 1804. She was run ashore and blown up on the West Coast of Africa to avoid capture by two French frigates in February, 1813. Following this vessel was a sloop of 426 tons and 12 guns, launched at Portsmouth in 1844. She served mainly on the North American and West Indies stations, and was broken up by Messrs. Castle and Beach in 1864. A screw composite sloop was the next of 894 tons, and carried 4 guns, built by Messrs. Wigram at Blackwall and launched in 1874. She served on the Pacific and China stations, and was sold to Mr. J. Cohen in August, 1889. Messrs. Thornycroft launched a vessel of this name at Chiswick in November, 1893, and she was a twin-screw T.B.D. of 260 tons.

The name *Daring* was allocated to one of the destroyers being built in 1912, but on the introduction of the system of classifying

H.M.S. DARING—*continued*

destroyers of the same year's building programme by their bearing names beginning with the same initials, this vessel was named *Lance* in October, 1913.

The *Daring* launched on 7th April, 1932, by Messrs. Thornycroft at Southampton was of 1,375 tons. She was sunk by U-boat off Duncansby Head on 18th February, 1940.

The present *Daring* gives her name to a new class of vessels, and was launched in 1950 at Wallsend by Swan Hunter.

H.M.S. DARTMOUTH

Description of Badge

The first official badge appeared to be an initial letter D; this was blue. Above was a naval crown gold with white sails and red and green gems. Beneath was a white scroll with a red edging. The words H.M.S. DARTMOUTH in red.

BATTLE HONOURS
Sole Bay	1762	May 28th.
Navarino	1827	October 20th.
Dardanelles	1915	

The first *Dartmouth* was a vessel of 306 tons and 32 guns, built in 1655 and probably named after the town of Dartmouth, which was taken by the Parliamentarians under General Fairfax in 1646. She assisted at the capture of three armed Dutch merchant vessels off the Irish coast in April, 1666, and in 1689 she was at the battle of Bantry Bay, operations on Lough Swilly, and at the relief of Londonderry. In 1690 she was lost off the Isle of Mull.

Then came a fourth rate of the name, built at Rotherhithe in 1693, of 600 tons and carrying 48 guns. On 4th February, 1695, after a six hours' action, she was forced to surrender to two French vessels of equal force to her own; and in 1702 she was recaptured at Vigo, being restored to the Navy, but this time under the name *Vigo*. Eventually she was lost in the Great Storm of 1703.

The next vessel to bear the name was a fourth rate of 681 tons and 50 guns, built at Southampton in 1697, subsequently being rebuilt at Woolwich in 1716 and again in 1741, and having her

152

H.M.S. DARTMOUTH—*continued*

tonnage increased to 856. She captured two privateers off the Start in 1709, and in April of the same year was at the capture of *Glorieux* (44) and the recapture of the *Bristol*, at the taking of Cette, the attack on Hyeres, capture of a French warship, and in 1710 at the capture of three French ships in the Straits.

During October, 1711, she drove on shore a French 16-gun vessel in the Channel, and in October, 1747, was blown up off Cape St. Vincent while engaged with the Spanish 74-gun ship *Glorioso*.

A fifth rate called the *Dartmouth* was built at Dartmouth in 1813 and was a frigate of 952 tons. She was at first armed with 36 guns, but this number was increased to 45. In 1827 she served at the battle of Navarino, and from about 1830 to 1853 she served as a lazaretto at Leith and then later as a receiving ship at Sheerness.

There was a fourth-rate frigate of 36 guns of this name which appears to have been commenced at Woolwich, but was taken down again in 1863.

A light cruiser of 5,252 tons and eight 6-inch guns named *Dartmouth* was commissioned in 1913 and served in 1914 in the Indian Ocean and the South Atlantic, then at the Dardanelles and in the British Adriatic Squadron, also being present at the bombardment of Durazzo in 1918.

H.M.S. DECOY

Description of Badge
FIELD: Green.

BADGE: A hawk's lure gold.

MOTTO: *Cave Quod Celo* (Beware what I hide).

BATTLE HONOURS

Ashantee	1873-4	
Alexandria	1882	July 11th.
Calabria	1940	July 9th.
Mediterranean	1940	
Greece	1941	April 24th—29th.
Crete	1941	May 20th—June 1st.
Libya	1941-2	
Atlantic	1942	
Malta Convoys	1941-2	

Badge derived from the decoy used for decoying the hawk from its quarry.

The first *Decoy* was a cutter of 10 guns, launched at Fishbourne in 1810, and in 1814 she was captured by the French after having grounded near Calais. The next was a screw gunboat of 212 tons and 2 guns. Launched at Pembroke in 1856 and taken to pieces at Haslar in 1869. Following her was another screw gunboat, this time of 408 tons and 4 guns, launched at Pembroke in 1871.

1873 Ashantee War (medal and clasp).
1879 Suppressed a rising on the Coanza River.
1882 Bombardment of Alexandria (medal and clasp).

H.M.S. DECOY—*continued*

1883 Blockade of the Nile.
1884-5 Egypt and Sudan (medal).
1885 Sold at Malta.

Then came a T.B.D. of 260 tons, launched at Chiswick in 1894. This vessel was lost in 1904 after a collision off the Scilly Isles; followed by a T.B.D. of 1,375 tons carrying four 4.7-inch guns, launched in 1932 at Thornycroft's, transferred to the Royal Canadian Navy and renamed H.M.S. *Kootenay* in 1943; and the latest *Decoy* is one of the *Daring* class.

H.M.S. DEFENCE

Unofficial Badge: Circular belt blue, gold edged and with the name of the ship in gold, buckle gold. In the centre a shield showing the national flag device, behind which are weapons proper, a royal crown above. Below is a scroll on which is the motto NOLI ME TANGERE above two cannons in base.

In allusion to name.

Official Badge.
FIELD: Blue.

BADGE: Two sea-axes in saltire white enfiled by a mural crown gold.

MOTTO:

Badge in allusion to the name.

H.M.S. DEFENCE—*continued*

BATTLE HONOURS

St. Vincent	1780	January 16th.
First of June	1794	June 1st (and May 28–29).
Nile	1798	August 1st.
Copenhagen	1801	April 2nd (support ship, not engaged.)
Trafalgar	1805	October 21st.
Jutland	1916	May 31st.

Armoured cruiser of 14,600 tons, four 9.2-inch, ten 7.5-inch and sixteen 12-pounder guns. She was launched at Pembroke on 27th April, 1907, and from 1911 to 1912 she was with the detached squadron escorting the King to India for the Delhi Coronation Durbar. In 1913 and 1914 she flew the flag of Rear-Admiral E. C. T. Troubridge in the Mediterranean Fleet. She was sunk at the battle of Jutland on 31st May, 1916.

This name is held by an 8,000-ton cruiser begun at Scott's in 1943 and completed in 1946. Work on her was suspended in July, 1946.

H.M.S. DEFENDER

Description of Badge
FIELD: Red.

BADGE: A fencing buckler and rapier silver and gold.

MOTTO: *Defendendo vince* (By defence I conquer).

The badge is in allusion to the name.

BATTLE HONOURS
Heligoland	1914	August 28th.
Dogger Bank	1915	January 24th.
Jutland	1916	May 31st.
Calabria	1940	July 9th.
Spartivento	1940	November 27th.
Greece	1941	April 24th—29th.
Crete	1941	May 20th—June 1st.
Libya	1941	
Malta Convoys	1941	

A gunboat of 168 tons and 12 guns was the first to carry the name of *Defender*, and she was built on the River Thames by Hill & Company and launched on 21st May, 1797. On 6th October her boats assisted at the cutting out of Dutch gunboats off the coast of Holland. She was sold in 1802. Following her was a gun brig of 179 tons and 12 guns, built at Chester by Mr. Courtney and launched on 28th July, 1804. In June, 1807, in company with the *Uranie* (38) off Cherbourg, she chased the French *Departements de la Manche* (40) and *Cygne* (16), which retired to

H.M.S. DEFENDER—*continued*

harbour. She was wrecked on Cob Point near Folkestone on 14th December, 1809. Then came an armed lugger of 81 tons and 8 guns. She was originally the French *Bear Marseillais*, taken by the *Royalist* (18) in 1809, and was sold in 1814.

A T.B.D. of 762 tons built on the Clyde by Denny and launched in August, 1911, was the next *Defender*. She served at Heligoland, the Dogger Bank and at the battle of Jutland, where, although herself damaged, she took on tow the crippled destroyer *Onslow*, both vessels arriving safely at Aberdeen on 2nd June, 1916. In 1917 and 1918 she served in the Channel and the Mediterranean, and in 1921 she was sold to Mr. Edgar Rees. Vickers-Armstrongs launched the next *Defender* in April, 1932, and she was a destroyer of 1,375 tons. In 1940 she was at Calabria and Spartivento, in 1941 at Matapan, Greece, Crete, Malta Convoys and Libya. On 11th July, 1941, she was sunk off Sidi Barrani by enemy aircraft.

The present *Defender* is a vessel of the *Daring* class, and was commissioned at Govan at the end of December, 1952, having been built by Alex Stephens & Sons Ltd. Was sent to Korea, but arrived in Eastern waters after the truce was made.

H.M.S. DEFIANCE

Description of Badge
FIELD: Black.

BADGE: A dexter hand couped at the wrist white grasping three streaks of lighning in bend sinister gold.

MOTTO: *Scientia Fiducia Plena Provocare* (With knowledge and confidence to defy).

Badge in allusion to the name.

BATTLE HONOURS

Orfordness	1666	July 25th.
Barfleur	1692	May 19th—24th.
Finisterre	1747	May 3rd.
Ushant	1747	October 14th.
Louisburg	1758	July 26th.
Quiberon Bay	1759	November 20th.
Havana	1762	August 13th.
Copenhagen	1801	April 2nd.
Trafalgar	1805	October 21st.

As H.M.S. *Defiance* is made up of vessels of the past, three others are coupled with the name: *Andromeda*, *Vulcan* and *Inconstant*. They are now to be scrapped.

The changes of name are rather confusing, but the following has been taken from official sources. *Andromeda*: *Defiance I* (late *Impregnable II*, late *Powerful II*, late *Andromeda*).

H.M.S. DEFIANCE—continued

The first *Defiance* was a 500-ton vessel of 32 guns, built in 1590. In 1591 she was at the Azores, in 1595 at the West Indies with Francis Drake, at the action off the Isle of Pines in 1596, rebuilt in 1612, and in 1650 she was sold.

There was a third rate which carried this name of 890 tons and armed with 66 guns, built at Deptford in 1666. On 1st-4th June of this same year she was in the Four Days' Battle, in July at the St. James's Day fight, and in 1668 on 6th December she was burnt by accident at Chatham.

Then came another third rate of the name and she was of 902 tons and carried 64 guns, built at Chatham by the famous Phineas Pett in 1675. She served at Bantry Bay in 1689, at Beachy Head in 1690, at Barfleur in 1692, and in 1695 was rebuilt at Woolwich. In 1702 she was with Vice-Admiral Benbow's squadron in the West Indies, under the command of Richard Kirby. Captain Richard Kirby was ordered to be shot after a court-martial for deserting Benbow. On rebuilding at Deptford in 1707 she had her tonnage increased to 949 and was reduced to a fourth rate of 50 guns. After this she served in the Mediterranean, Baltic squadron, operations against Sweden, at Santa Marta and at Cartagena. She then served as a hulk at Sheerness and in 1749 was broken up at Chatham.

The next *Defiance* was a fourth rate of 1,136 tons and 60 guns, launched at Deptford on 12th October, 1744. In 1746 she captured the French 40-gun ship *Embuscade*, and in 1747 was in Anson's victory off Finisterre. On 14th October, 1747, she was at Hawke's victory off Finisterre; on 8th June, 1755, captured the *Lys*; in 1756 at Byng's action off Minorca; in 1759 at Quiberon Bay; at the reduction of Havana in 1762; and in 1762 on 28th May she captured the Spanish *Marte* (18) and the Spanish *Venganza* (24). She was sold on 10th April, 1766.

In 1766 a vessel called *Defiance* was built for the Bombay Marine.

A *Defiance*, third rate, of 1,369 tons and 64 guns, was launched at Woolwich in 1769, serving at Ushant on 27th July, 1778, and in 1780 she was wrecked.

There was a hired merchantman of 18 guns called the *Defiance* which in 1782 captured a Dutch brig in the North Sea.

H.M.S. DEFIANCE—*continued*

Then a third rate of 1,645 tons and 74 guns was launched at Rotherhithe in 1783 bearing this name. In 1797 she was at the Mutiny at Spithead; in 1801 at Copenhagen; on 22nd July at Vice-Admiral Calder's action off Ferrol; in 1805 at the famous battle of Trafalgar; in 1808 at the blockade of Rochefort; on 24th February, 1808, at the destruction of French frigates off Sables d'Olonne; and in 1809 at the Basque Roads. In 1814 she became a prison ship and in 1817 she was broken up.

A gunboat of four guns of this name was bought in 1794 and sold in 1797.

Then came a second-rate single-screw vessel of 5,270 tons, which was to be fitted with 91 guns, but they were never installed. She was launched on 27th March, 1861, at Pembroke. On 13th December, 1884, she was first commissioned as a torpedo school ship at Devonport, and on 26th June, 1931, she was sold for breaking up. At the same time the *Spartan* (*Defiance II*) and *Cleopatra* (*Defiance III*) were also sold.

The new *Defiance* consisted of *Andromeda*, *Inconstant* and *Vulcan*, and these came under the command of Sir Lionel Sturdee.

These vessels (1953) are now to be scrapped.

H.M.S. DELIGHT

Description of Badge
FIELD: Green.

BADGE: Pan's Pipe gold and silver.

MOTTO: *Duris delectat virtus* (Valour delighteth in difficulties).

Badge in allusion to the name.

BATTLE HONOURS
Armada	1588	July 21st—29th. Merchant ship under Drake.
Cadiz	1596	June 21st.
Norway	1940	

The first *Delight* appeared in 1583 and was of 120 tons. She sailed in Sir Humphrey Gilbert's Newfoundland Expedition, and was wrecked on Isle of Sables on 29th August, 1583. A merchant ship bore this name in 1588 and fought against the Armada. She was of 50 tons and belonged to Sir William Wynter and was in the Squadron under Sir Francis Drake. Her commanding officer, Captain William Coxe, was killed in action. Then followed a merchant ship of Bristol, which in 1589 was commanded by Captain Merick and was in Chudleigh's Magellan expedition. She was wrecked on the French coast when returning in August, 1590. The next was a merchant ship of London, and in 1596 she took part in the expedition to Cadiz under Lord Howard of Effingham and the Earl of Essex.

H.M.S. DELIGHT—*continued*

A variety of vessels bearing this name then came. There was a hoy of 100 tons built in 1680 and sold at Portsmouth in 1714; a sixth rate of 163 tons and 14 guns, built at Woolwich and launched on 18th October, 1709, and sold in 1713; a sloop of 306 tons and 14 guns, built on the River Thames by Edward Greaves and launched in 1778. In January, 1781, this vessel was at the occupation of Wilmington. On 3rd September, 1781, she sailed from Spithead for North America with despatches and was never heard of again. Lord Keith captured a sloop of 336 tons and 18 guns called the *Sans Pareil* and she was commissioned under the name of *Delight* and registered on the List of the Navy. There was a brig of 284 tons and 16 guns built in Devonshire by Mr. Thorn and launched in 1806. She ran ashore on the coast of Calabria on 30th January, 1808, and was captured.

The Italian brig sloop of 340 tons and 14 guns called the *Friedland* was launched at Venice in 1807 and was captured by H.M. Ships *Standard* and *Active* in 1808, and registered on the List of the Navy as the *Delight*, but was sold in 1814. A brig sloop launched at Portsmouth on 10th May, 1819, of 237 tons and 10 guns carried the name. In February, 1824, she foundered with all hands in a cyclone off Mauritius. The next *Delight* was also a brig sloop of 233 tons and 10 guns launched at Chatham on 27th November, 1829, and from 1830 to 1843 she was engaged in packet service, being sold in 1844. Now we change over to steam and so we have a steam gunboat of 236 tons and 2 guns to continue the name. She was built by Messrs. Wigram at Blackwell in 1856 and sold at Halifax in 1867.

The *Skylark*, a coastguard cruiser of 70 tons launched in 1868, was renamed *Delight* in 1884 and sold in 1905.

Fairfield built the destroyer *Delight* on the Clyde in 1932. She was of 1,375 tons, and in 1940 she was engaged in operations off Norway at the evacuation of Narvik. On 29th July, 1940, she was sunk off Portland by German aircraft.

The present *Delight* was built in 1950 by Fairfield and is of the *Daring* class. Originally named *Ypres* and then *Disdain*.

H.M.S. DESPATCH

Description of Badge

FIELD: Blue.

BADGE: A caduceus gold.

MOTTO: *Festina Non Lente* (Hasten not slowly).

The badge is derived from the winged staff of Mercury, the messenger of the gods. Despatch signifying "with all despatch," as fast as possible.

BATTLE HONOURS

San Sebastian	1813	September 8th.
Atlantic	1939	
Spartivento	1940	November 27th.
Normandy	1844	June 6th—July 3rd.

The *Despatch* was a cruiser of the "D" class and was completed in 1922. She was built by Fairfield, but was towed round to Chatham for completion. She was of 4,850 tons and carried six 6-inch and three 4-inch A.A. guns as her main armament, and was sold in 1947.

H.M.S. DEVONSHIRE

Unofficial Badge: This badge was carried by the armoured cruiser H.M.S. *Devonshire* of 10,850 tons. Gold castle, naval crown, croll in light blue with dark blue letters, H.M.S. DEVONSHIRE.

Official Badge
FIELD: Silver.

BADGE: A lion rampant red, crowned gold.

MOTTO: *Auxilio Divino* (By the help of God).

The badge is derived from part of the arms and the motto of the Devonshire County Council.

BATTLE HONOURS
Barfleur	1692	May 19th—24th.
Finisterre	1747	May 3rd.
Ushant	1747	October 14th.

H.M.S. DEVONSHIRE—continued

Quebec	1759	September 13th.
Martinique	1762	February 16th.
Havana	1762	August 13th.
Louisburg	1758	July 26th.
Norway	1940	
Arctic	1941	
Diego Suarez	1942	May 5th—7th.

The first of the name was a second rate of 1,220 tons and 80 guns, built by W. Wyatt at Bursledon and launched on 6th May, 1692. In the same year she was at the battle of Cape Barfleur and the battle of La Hogue; in 1697, on 14th August, she was in Harlow's action with de Pointis, and in 1704 she was rebuilt at Woolwich. On 10th October, 1707, she was in Commodore Edward's engagement with French men-of-war under the famous Du Guay Trouin, and after she had made a running fight with five enemy ships until well into the evening, finally blew up and only two of her crew were saved.

The next of the name was a second rate of 1,304 tons and 80 guns. She was built at Woolwich and launched on 12th December, 1710. In 1711 this vessel was engaged in escorting store ships in connection with Rear-Admiral Hovenden Walker's unsuccessful expedition to Quebec. As she was too big a ship to navigate the St. Lawrence she was sent home. During the year 1717 she was engaged in operations in the Baltic; in October, 1740, she was made a hulk at Woolwich, and sold in October, 1760.

There was a *Devonshire* built at Woolwich and launched on 19th July, 1745, and she was a third rate of 1,471 tons and 66 guns, having been cut down from an 80-gun ship soon after launching. She had some interesting actions in 1747 and was in that of Anson's with de la Jonquiere off Finisterre; she captured the *Serieux* (60), which was carrying Jonquiere's flag, and as Hawke's flagship in the action with de l'Etenduere off Ushant she compelled two French ships to strike their flags and captured the *Terrible*.

In 1759 she was at the capture of Quebec; in 1760 at the operations in the St. Lawrence, including the capture of Montreal; in 1762 at the capture of Martinique and the capture of Havana; finally was broken up at Portsmouth in 1772.

H.M.S. DEVONSHIRE—*continued*

Messrs. Barnard & Co. built a *Devonshire* on the River Thames, launching her on 23rd September, 1812, and she was a third rate of 1,742 tons and 74 guns. In 1849 she became a temporary hospital for merchant seamen at Greenwich when the *Dreadnought* was under repair; in 1854 on 21st June she was commissioned as a prison ship for Russian prisoners of war at Sheerness; from 1857 to 1868 she was a school ship for steam reserve at Sheerness, and was broken up at that base in 1869.

Following her the next *Devonshire* was a twin-screw cruiser of 10,850 tons and 10 guns. She was built at H.M. Dockyard, Chatham, and was launched on 30th April, 1904. During the 1914-1918 war she served in the 3rd Cruiser Squadron with the Grand Fleet, in the raids on Yorkshire coast by the enemy, in the Dogger Bank action, and on the North America and West Indies stations. Her final end was the shipbreakers and she was sold to Messrs. T. W. Ward Ltd. on 9th May, 1921.

The present *Devonshire*, which has now been paid off, is a cruiser of 9,850 tons displacement, and originally carried six 8-inch and eight 4-inch A.A. guns, but she was stripped down, leaving only a turret when she became a cadet training ship and classrooms, etc., being built on her. She was completed at Devonport in 1929. During the war she was at the attack on Madagascar and served at Norway and in the Arctic.

H.M.S. DIADEM

Description of Badge
FIELD: Blue.

BADGE: A circlet of estoiles white.

MOTTO:

The badge is in allusion to the name.

BATTLE HONOURS
Genoa	1795	March 14th.
St. Vincent	1797	February 14th.
Egypt	1801	March 8th—September 2nd.
Cape of Good Hope	1806	January 18th.
Normandy	1944	June 6th—July 3rd.
Biscay	1944	
Arctic	1944-5	
Norway	1945	

The first *Diadem* was a third-rate vessel of 1,869 tons and 64 guns, built at Chatham in 1781. From 1783 to 1786 she was serving as the guard ship at Plymouth, and in 1793 during August and December she was at Toulon with Lord Hood. On 13th March, 1795, she was at Hotham's action off Genoa, and on 13th July she was at the action off Hyeres but was not engaged. She was at St. Vincent on 14th February, 1797, and in 1806 she was the flagship of Commodore Sir Home Popham at the capture of the Cape of Good Hope, where she landed a naval brigade. In June

H.M.S. DIADEM—*continued*

she was at Sir Home Popham's operations in the River Plate and in October at the capture and loss of Buenos Aires. In January, 1807, she was the flagship of Rear-Admiral Chas. Stirling; she was at the siege and capture of Montevideo, where she landed a naval brigade in February, and during June and July she was at the attack on Buenos Aires, the defeat and surrender of the army and the final withdrawal of the squadron. Her next service was *en flute* trooping to Spain in 1810 to 1813. She then became a receiving ship at Plymouth, and in 1832 she was taken to pieces.

Then came a fourth-rate screw frigate of 32 guns and 2,483 tons; later her guns were cut down to 24. This vessel was launched at Pembroke on 14th October, 1856, and then served on various stations until she was sold to Messrs. Castle & Sons in 1875.

The next *Diadem* was a first-class protected cruiser of 11,000 tons and carrying sixteen 6-inch guns. She was launched on 21st October, 1896, and served on various stations. On 31st December, 1914, she was a training ship for stokers at Portsmouth, and was sold in 1921.

The present vessel of the name is a cruiser of the *Dido* class and is of 5,700 tons. She carries eight 5.25-inch guns. She was built by Hawthorn Leslie and completed in 1944 in time to serve in the closing stages of the Second World War.

H.M.S. DIAMOND

Description of Badge
FIELD: Red.
BADGE: A diamond silver.
MOTTO: *Honor clarissima gemma* (Honour is the brightest Jewel).

The badge is in allusion to the name.

BATTLE HONOURS

Armada	1588	*Diamond* of Dartmouth under Drake. Merchant ship.
Kentish Knock	1652	September 28th.
Portland	1653	February 18th—20th.
Gabbard	1653	June 2nd—3rd.
Scheveningen	1653	July 31st.
Lowestoft	1665	June 3rd.
Orfordness	1666	July 25th.
Sole Bay	1672	May 28th.
Schooneveld	1673	May 28th—June 4th.
Texel	1673	August 11th.
Crimea	1854-5	
Spartivento	1940	November 27th.
Greece	1941	April 24th—29th.
Mediterranean	1941	
Malta Convoys	1941	

The first *Diamond* was a vessel of 60 tons and was one of the ships under Drake at the defeat of the Spanish Armada in 1588. Then came a fourth rate of 548 tons and carrying 48 guns, built

H.M.S. DIAMOND—*continued*

at Deptford by Peter Pett, senior, and launched in 1651. This vessel had quite an exciting career and was at the following battles: Kentish Knock, Portland, Gabbard, Blakes's attack on Porto Farina, battle of Lowestoft, on the last day of the Four Days' Fight, on the third and last day of Sir Robert Holmes's attack on the Dutch Smyrna Fleet off the Isle of Wight, battle of Sole Bay, Schooneveld, second battle of Schooneveld, Texel, and the battle of Bantry Bay in 1689; and on 20th September, 1693, she was taken by two French privateers off Cape Clear whilst escorting a homeward bound Barbadoes convoy. There was another fifth rate of 537 tons, built at Blackwall and launched in 1708. Her service included the blockade of Porto Bello with Admiral Hosier in 1726, Vernon's bombardment and capture of Chagres in 1740, a battle off Toulon on 11th February, 1744; and on 18th December, 1744, she was sold. Following her were two fifth rates, one of 697 tons and 44 guns built at Limehousf and launched on 30th October, 1741, sold in 1756, and another oe 710 tons, 32 guns, built and launched at Hull on 28th May, 1774; and she was sold on the 30th December, 1784.

The next *Diamond* had some exciting service and was launched on the River Thames on 17th March, 1794, and on 23rd August of this same year drove ashore and destroyed the French *Volontaire* near Penmarc'h Point. On 9th May, 1795, her boats assisted in capturing ten sail of a French convoy driven ashore near Cape Carteret, Normandy, and on 17th March, 1796, she assisted at the destruction of the French *Etourdie*, several other vessels and a battery at Port Erqui on the north coast of France. In 1800 she was at combined operations with military and French Royalists at Quiberon, and on 21st August, 1801, her boats, with those of the *Fisgard* and *Boadicea*, cut out the Spanish *Neptuno*, a gunboat and a merchant vessel at Corunna. In 1804 she captured the Spanish *Infanta Don Carlos* of 16 guns, and she was broken up at Sheerness in 1812. Another fifth rate of 1,076 tons and 46 guns was built at Chatham and launched on 11th January, 1816, and she was accidentally burnt at Portsmouth on 18th April, 1827. Another *Diamond* was built at Sheerness and launched on 29th August, 1848, and was a sixth rate of 1,055 tons and 28 guns. This vessel was at the Russian war of 1854-5 and landed a naval brigade for service at the siege of Sebastopol. She was then loaned as a

H.M.S. DIAMOND—*continued*

mission ship for service on the Tyne in 1866, and was renamed *Joseph Straker* in 1868, finally being sold to Castle's in 1885.

A third-class cruiser of 1,405 tons and 14 guns was launched at Sheerness on 26th September, 1874, and bore the name of *Diamond*. She served on the East Indies, China and Australian stations from 1875 to 1889, and was sold out of the service in August, 1889. Then came a third-class protected cruiser built by Messrs. Laird at Birkenhead and launched on 6th January, 1904. On 31st December, 1914, she rescued the survivors of H.M.S. *Formidable*, torpedoed by enemy submarine, and she was sold for breaking up in May, 1921.

On 8th April, 1932, Vickers-Armstrongs launched at Wallsend the destroyer *Diamond* of 1,375 tons and four 4.7-inch guns. In 1940, on 24th August, she was engaged in the bombardment of seaplane base at Bomba; in 1941 in January she served as an escort of a convoy to the relief of Malta; in April of the same year she was sunk by aircraft off Crete.

The present *Diamond* is a vessel of the *Daring* class. During exercises in 1953 she was in collision with H.M.S. *Swiftsure*. She was launched in 1950 at John Brown's at Clydebank.

H.M.S. DIANA

Unofficial Badge: No colour known.

Official Badge
FIELD: Blue.
BADGE: A crescent moon silver.
MOTTO: *Certo Dirigo ictu* (I aim with sure blow).

The name is derived from Greek mythology and refers to Diana or Artemis, Phœbe, Selene, Cynthia, goddess of the moon and chase, daughter of Zeus and Latona, twin sister of Apollo. A new badge has been suggested as this is not a very good example.

BATTLE HONOURS

Armada	1588	July 21st—29th. Merchant ship from City of London.
Louisburg	1758	July 26th.
Quebec	1759	September 13th.

H.M.S. DIANA—continued

Burma	1824-6	March 5th — February 24th. Hired steamer.
Norway	1940	
"Zefier"	1809	September 9th. Single ship action.

There have been a number of *Dianas*, and the first was a merchantman of 80 tons which fought against the Spanish Armada and was one of the ships provided at the charge of the City of London. Then came a fifth rate of 668 tons and 32 guns, built at Limehouse by Messrs. Batson, and launched on 30th August, 1757. She served at the capture of Louisburg and Quebec and made a successful attack on a French flotilla in the St. Lawrence. She was at Johnstone's action with Suffren at Porto Praya in 1781 and was sold at Deptford in 1793.

There was an armed schooner of 6 guns named *Diana* which was employed during the American War of Independence, but she was abandoned and burnt in face of the Colonists near Boston in 1776. Messrs. Randall built a fifth rate of 998 tons and 38 guns on the River Thames, and she received the name of *Diana*. This was in 1794, and in August of the same year she was concerned in the destruction of the French *Volontaire* (38) near the Penmarc'h Rocks. In 1804 with the *Pique* in company she took the Spanish vessel *Diligencia* (28) off Altavela. During the year 1810 with the *Niobe* (38) she attacked the French 40-gun frigates *Amazone* and *Eliza*, which resulted in the *Eliza* being driven ashore and later destroyed by the *Diana's* boats. On 24th August, 1811, with the *Semiramis* (38) she attacked a French convoy in the River Gironde and destroyed the *Teaser* (12), which had previously been taken by the French. Four years later she was sold to the Dutch Government.

A cutter of 10 guns also carried this name, having been taken up on the East Indies station. In 1807 this vessel captured the American pirate schooner *Topaze* near Macao; in August, 1808, she captured a Dutch brig of 6 guns and carrying a number of brass guns with which it was intended to strengthen the defences at Sourabaya; on 11th September, 1809, she captured the Dutch brig *Zefier* (14) near the Celebes, and for his gallantry in this action her captain, Lieutenant Wm. Kempthorne, was promoted to Commander and a medal was awarded; and in May, 1810, she was condemned by survey at the island of Rodriguez.

H.M.S. DIANA—*continued*

In 1824 a paddle-steamer named *Diana* was purchased in India and performed important services in the first Burmese war, where she was commanded by Midshipman (afterwards Commander) George Winsor.

The next one completed fitting out for the ordinary at Chatham, but was never commissioned. She was a fifth rate of 1,083 tons and 42 guns, launched in 1822. In 1868 she was lent to the contractors of the Bermuda Floating Dock for the accommodation of their workers, and removed from the Navy Lists in 1874, being broken up at Chatham.

Fairfield's of Glasgow built a second-class cruiser of this name at Glasgow, and she was launched on 5th December, 1895. In 1897 she commissioned for the Diamond Jubilee Review. In 1900 she was engaged in carrying relief crews to the Australian station. On 7th August, 1908, she relieved H.M.S. *Arrogant* as parent ship for T.B.Ds. in the Mediterranean, 1914 in the 12th Cruiser Squadron, then on the China and East Indies station, and in 1920 was sold to Mr. Sidney Castle for breaking up at Plymouth.

The next *Diana* was a destroyer of 1,375 tons, built by Palmers Shipbuilding Co., and launched on 16th June, 1932. In 1940 she served in operations in Norway and was then transferred to the Royal Canadian Navy and renamed *Margaree*. This vessel was lost whilst escorting a North Atlantic convoy, being involved in a collision. The present *Diana* is a vessel of the *Daring* class, ex *Druid*, launched in 1952 at Scotstoun.

H.M.S. DIDO

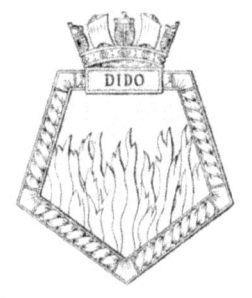

Description of Badge
FIELD: Blue.
BADGE: Issuant from the base flames proper.
MOTTO: Steadfast.

The badge is derived from Virgil's story of Dido, who killed and burnt herself when she was forsaken by Æneas.

BATTLE HONOURS

Egypt	1801	March 8th—September 2nd.
Syria	1840	September 10th—December 9th.
China	1842	
China	1900	June 10th—December 31st. Entitled to medal but not to battle honour; did not land a naval brigade, nor did they take part in the capture of Taku Forts.
Crete	1941	May 20th—June 1st.
Sirte	1942	March 22nd.
Malta Convoys	1942	
Sicily	1943	July 10th—August 17th.
Salerno	1943	September 9th—October 6th.
Ægean	1943	
Anzio	1944	January 22nd—31st.
South France	1944	August 15th—27th.
Mediterranean	1942-4	
Arctic	1944	
"Minerve"	24/6/1795. Single ship action.	

H.M.S. DIDO—*continued*

The first vessel to bear the name was a sixth rate of 595 tons and 28 guns, built at Sandgate by Messrs. Stewart and Hall, and launched on 27th November, 1784. In 1793 she was at Hood's occupation of Toulon; in 1795 during the month of May she captured the French *Temeraire* (20), in June was in action with the French *Minerve*. During the Egyptian campaign in 1801 she was with Keith and Abercromby. In 1804 she was fitted out as an army prison ship, and was sold in 1817.

Then came a sloop of 734 tons and 18 guns, built at Pembroke and launched on 13th June, 1831. This vessel served at the Syrian blockade in 1840, in 1842 in the first China war, in the suppression of piracy in Malayan waters during 1843-4, and in 1855 she was at Petropavlovski. In 1856 she was converted into a coal hulk at Sheerness, being scuttled in 1874 after catching on fire, but later on she was raised and found capable of further service, but was sold on 3rd March, 1903.

The name of *Dido* was allocated to a covered deck corvette screw vessel of 1,857 tons and 22 guns. This vessel was begun at Deptford in January, 1861, but her construction was discontinued in December, 1863.

The vessel that followed with this name was a first-class sloop of 1,277 tons and 6 guns, built at Portsmouth and launched in 1869. In 1871 she was at the Niger River, 1873-4 at Fiji, and in 1881 a naval brigade from her was present at Laing's Nek and Majuba.

From 1886 to 1906 she was lent to the War Department as a S./M. mining hulk in the River Forth and attached to H.M.S. *Vernon*, and renamed *Actaeon* in 1906.

The next to carry the name was a second-class protected cruiser of 5,600 tons and she carried eleven 6-inch guns. She was built at Govan by the London & Glasgow Co. and launched on 20th March, 1896. From 1913 to 1926 she was a destroyer depot ship, and on 16th December, 1926, she was sold to Messrs. Hay & Butch Ltd.

The present vessel with the name of *Dido* gives her name to this class of cruiser and was completed in 1940 by Cammell Laird. She carries as her main armament ten 5.25-inch guns. Her displacement is 5,450 tons. Her battle honours show how big a part she played in the Second World War.

H.M.S. DOMINION

Description of Badge

The shield of the arms of Canada, naval crown above. Below, a scroll white with red letters.

In allusion to the Dominion of Canada.

No battle honours are recorded for this ship.

The 23rd August, 1903, was the date which saw the launching of this 16,350 ton battleship of the *King Edward VII* class at Vickers by H.R.H. Princess Louise. She was armed with four 12-inch and four 9.2-inch guns. On the outbreak of war the *Dominion* joined the Grand Fleet, but in April, 1918, she became the accommodation ship at Chatham and served in that capacity until 1919, being sold to Wards for breaking up in 1921.

Canada became the Dominion in 1867 when the provinces of Ontario (formerly Upper Canada), Quebec (Lower Canada), Nova Scotia and New Brunswick federated. Manitoba joined in 1870 and Saskatchewan and Alberta in 1905, British Columbia in 1871, and Prince Edward Island in 1873. Newfoundland joined in 1949. For many years Canada was the only British Dominion. The arms, which were the quartering of the arms of the first four provinces, were granted in 1868, and despite the fact that other provinces later joined, the original arms were retained as being sufficiently complicated until 1921, when a newer coat of arms was granted. This in turn has been replaced in 1954 by a simplified coat. H.M.S. *Dominion*, built in 1903, adopted the Dominion arms shown as her badge, though on boats she also used a plain maple leaf.

H.M.S. DORSETSHIRE

Description of Badge
FIELD: Red.

BADGE: A lion passant gold.

MOTTO: *Pro Patria et Comitatu* (For country and county).

The badge is derived from the seal which is used by the county. The county has no arms and the seal used is that of the three lions of England.

BATTLE HONOURS

Gibraltar	1704	July 24th.
Velez Malaga	1704	August 13th.
Passero	1718	July 31st.
Quiberon Bay	1759	November 20th.
"Bismarck"	1941	May 23rd—27th.
Atlantic	1941	
"Raisonnable"	1758	Single ship action.

The *Dorsetshire* was a cruiser of 9,900 tons and armed with eight 8-inch and four 4-inch guns, being designed by Sir William Berry and completed in 1930. This vessel was in the famous seeking-out of the *Bismarck*, and was sunk by Japanese divebombers in the Indian Ocean when on the way to the Maldive Islands from Colombo, in company with the *Cornwall*.

H.M.S. DRAKE

H.M.S. DRAKE

Unofficial Badge: This badge was carried by H.M.S. *Drake*, an armoured cruiser of 14,100 tons. World in proper colours, ship black and orange bars, black masts, white sails, flags white with red cross. Hand, clouds and rope proper.

Official Badge
FIELD: Blue.

BADGE: On a plate a wyvern passant red, armed and tongued blue.

MOTTO: *Sic Parvis Magna* (thus from small things to great things).

BATTLE HONOURS
Lowestoft	1665	June 3rd.
Baltic	1855	
China	1856-60	

H.M.S. DRAKE—*continued*

The first *Drake* was a sixth rate built at Deptford in 1652 and was cast from the service after survey at Jamaica in 1690. There was a sixth rate bearing the name built at Redrith (Rotherhithe) and added to the Royal Navy in September, 1694. She was presumed lost on passage to Ireland in 1694-5. A yacht held the name built at Plymouth in 1705 and sold possibly in 1747. A sloop of the name built at Woolwich was added in 1705. Another sloop of the name was launched at Deptford in 1729. There was a *Drake* launched for the Bombay Marine in 1736 and twenty years later was fitted as a bomb ship. There was a vessel bearing the name launched at Wapping in 1740 and wrecked in Gibraltar Bay in November, 1742.

Then came a sloop launched at Deptford in 1743 and sold in 1748. A vessel of the name of *Drake* was received into the service and fitted as a sloop at Deptford; her name, however, was changed to *Resolution*. Another sloop of the name was surrendered at Belfast in 1778 to the American *Ranger*. A brig sloop launched at Dover in 1779 and paid off in Jamaica in 1800. A sloop captured from the French as the *Tigre* in 1799 and added as the *Drake*. This vessel was wrecked at Nevis in the West Indies in 1804. A brig sloop launched at Ipswich in 1808 had this name. She captured the French ship *Tilsit* in April, 1810, and was wrecked off Newfoundland on 20th June, 1822. A *Drake* was launched at Portsmouth in 1834 and fitted as a mortar vessel and renamed *Sheppey*. A gunboat was launched at Pembroke in 1856 named *Drake* and sold at Hong Kong in 1869. Then there came a gunboat which was used as a drill ship for R.N. Artillery Volunteers on the Clyde in 1891. The *Drake*, a twin-screw armoured cruiser of 14,100 tons, was launched at Pembroke in 1901 and was sunk by submarine in the North Channel off the coast of Ireland in October, 1917.

Drake, name of the Plymouth Barracks and Naval Establishment at Devonport, 1934.

H.M.S. DREADNOUGHT

Description of Badge

A bulldog's head proper, having above it a crown gold with white sails, red and green gems in crown. A blue scroll below with name in black.

An obvious allusion indicating the fearless British bulldog.

BATTLE HONOURS

Armada	1588	July 21st—29th.
Cadiz	1596	June 21st.
Lowestoft	1665	June 3rd.
Four Days' Battle	1666	June 1st—4th.
Orfordness	1666	July 25th.
Sole Bay	1672	May 28th.
Schooneveld	1673	May 28th and June 4th.
Texel	1673	August 11th.
Barfleur	1692	May 19th—24th.
Passero	1718	July 31st.
Cape Francois	1757	October 21st.
Trafalgar	1805	October 21st.

This vessel was a 10-gun turbine battleship, launched at Portsmouth in 1906, having a tonnage of 17,900 and a speed of 22 knots. This was the first fighting ship of the twentieth century to embody the all big gun principles as well as to be fitted with turbine machinery. On 5th August, 1907, King Edward VII and Queen Alexandra and other members of the Royal Family visited the ship at Spithead. She was broken up in 1921.

H.M.S. DRYAD

Official Badge: (Superseded).
FIELD: Red.
BADGE: A pair of dividers over a sprig of oak proper, the acorns gold.
MOTTO: *Nobis Tutissimus Ibis* (You will go safely with us).

Badge and motto in allusion to the name and the navigational training of H.M.S. *Dryad*.

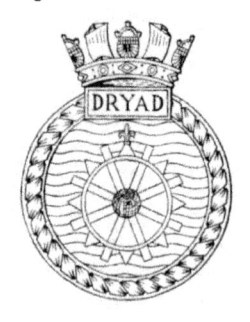

Official Badge
FIELD: Barry wavy white and blue.
BADGE: A globe surrounded by a ship's wheel with the points of a compass between the spokes.
MOTTO: *Nobis Tutissimus Ibis* (You will go safely with us).

H.M.S. DRYAD—*continued*

Badge and motto in allusion to the navigational training given by *Dryad*. The Dryads, however, were nymphs of the forest, hence the oak and acorns of the earlier badge. They were conceived as born to the tree they were attached to and also dying with it. Their revels were held among themselves, which they broke off and departed on the approach of human beings.

BATTLE HONOURS
Abyssinia	1868	April 13th.
"Proserpine"	1796	Single ship action.

The first *Dryad* was a fifth rate of 924 tons and 36 guns, launched on the River Thames on 4th June, 1795. She captured the French corvette *Abeille* off the Lizard on 2nd May, 1796, and in the same year on 13th June she captured the French frigate *Proserpine* (40) off Cape Clear. For this action a medal was granted in 1849. In 1809 she was with Lord William Stuart's frigate squadron in the operations to try and force the mouth of the Scheldt, the Walcheren Expedition. She drove a French brig, the *Isle d'Yeu*, ashore on 12th December, 1812, in company with the *Achates* (16), she came up on an engagement between the *Eurotas* (38) and the French *Clorinde* near Ushant, and was able to bring about the surrender of the French ship. In 1832 she became a receiving ship at Portsmouth, and in 1860 she was broken up.

Then came a screw sloop of 1,086 tons and 9 guns, built at Devonport in 1866. In 1868 she was engaged in landing parties during the Abyssinian war, and in 1868-9 was in operations against slavery whilst on the East Indies station. In July, 1883, she was serving in the protection of British interests at Tamatave during the bombardment by Rear-Admiral Pierre; in 1884 she landed a naval brigade in the Egyptian war, and in 1885 she was sold.

Following on was a twin-screw gunboat of 1,070 tons and 2 guns which was launched at Chatham in 1893, and in 1906 she became the Navigation School ship at Portsmouth.

Dryad is now the Navigation School shore establishment.

H.M.S. DUBLIN

Unofficial Badge: A shield blue edged gold, three castles gold with flames issuing from them proper. Name in black, white edged.

Official Badge
FIELD: Blue.

BADGE: A castle silver with flames issuing therefrom.

MOTTO: *Est Obedientia Felicitas* (Obedience is happiness).

The badge is part of the arms of Dublin.

BATTLE HONOURS
Louisburg	1758	July 26th.
Quebec	1759	September 13th.
Martinique	1762	February 16th.

H.M.S. DUBLIN—*continued*

Havana	1762	August 13th
Dardanelles	1915	February 19th—January 8th.
Jutland	1916	May 31st.

The *Dublin* was a second-class protected cruiser of 5,400 tons, and was built by Messrs. Beardmore & Co., Dalmuir, being launched on 30th April, 1912. During her service in the Great War she served at the Dardanelles and at Jutland. In 1916 she was operating in the North Sea, and in July, 1926, she was sold for breaking up.

H.M.S. DUCHESS

Description of Badge
FIELD: Blue.

BADGE: A duchess's coronet proper over a terrestrial globe silver.

MOTTO: *Duci non trahi* (To be led but not dragged).

The badge is derived from a voyage made round the world by a former vessel bearing the name *Duchess*. It was under the command of Stephen Courtney.

BATTLE HONOURS
Portland	1653	February 18th—20th.
Gabbard	1653	June 2nd—3rd.
Scheveningen	1653	July 31st.
Barfleur	1692	May 19th—24th.

The first to bear the name was a 24-gun ship captured in 1652. This vessel served at the battle of the Gabbard in 1653 and was sold in 1654. The next was a second rate of 1,546 tons and carried 90 guns. She was built at Deptford and launched in 1679. On 30th June, 1690, she was at Beachy Head as the flagship of Rear-Admiral Rooke; in 1692 on 19th May she was at Barfleur; on 31st December, 1701, she was renamed *Princess Anne*, and later changed her name to *Windsor Castle* and later *Blenheim*.

The Bristol ship *Duchess* of 260 tons was commanded by Stephen Courtney and with the *Duke*, commanded by Woodes Rogers, made a memorable privateering voyage round the world in 1708-1711, during which she rescued Alexander Selkirk, the

H.M.S. DUCHESS—*continued*

original Robinson Crusoe, who had been marooned on Juan Fernandez.

Then came a destroyer of the *Defender* class of 1,375 tons and armed with four 4.7-inch guns. She was built at Palmer's yard, and on 12th December, 1939, she was sunk in collision on the West coast of Scotland.

The present *Duchess* is a vessel of the *Daring* class of 2,610 tons, and was completed at Thornycroft's in January, 1952.

H.M.S. DUKE OF EDINBURGH

Description of Badge

This badge shows a cypher, the letters A E A entwined gold, above which is a ducal coronet. Underneath is a scroll yellow on which is the name of the ship in red.

Named after Alfred, Duke of Edinburgh.

BATTLE HONOUR
Jutland   1916   May 31st.

This ship was a 16-gun twin-screw cruiser, launched at Pembroke in 1904, and capable of a speed of 23 knots. Her tonnage was 13,500, and she was sold in 1920.

H.M.S. DUKE OF YORK

Description of Badge
FIELD: Dark Blue.

BADGE: The white rose of York upon a plate surrounded by the collar of the Order of the Garter and ensigned with a Royal Ducal Crown proper.

The badge is that of King George VI when he was the Duke of York, and was adopted by His Majesty's order.

BATTLE HONOURS
North Africa	1942	
Arctic	1942-3	
North Cape	1943	December 26th.

The first *Duke of York* was a cutter of 53½ tons, and carried as its armament four carronades and eight swivels, its complement being 24 men. It was purchased in 1763 and named after Edward Duke of York. She was sold at Sheerness on 1st July, 1766, for £40.

There was a hired armed vessel named *Duke of York* in service from 1795 to 1799 and also from 1804 to 1810, named after Frederick Augustus, second son of George III.

The *Duke of York*, the present battleship of 35,000 tons, was originally *Anson*, and was completed in 1941. The name was given to the ship in commemoration of the fact that King George VI bore this title.

The *Duke* of 1682 was named after the Duke of York, and the three-deckers that succeeded her were so named as well.

H.M.S. DUNKIRK

Description of Badge
FIELD: Blue.

BADGE: A unicorn's head erased white, maned and armed gold.

MOTTO:

Badge derived from the crest of Admiral Sir Bertram Ramsay.

BATTLE HONOURS
Lowestoft	1665	June 3rd.
Orfordness	1666	July 25th.
Sole Bay	1672	May 28th.
Schooneveld	1673	May 28th—June 4th.
Texel	1673	August 11th.
Passero	1718	July 31st.
Quiberon Bay	1759	November 20th.

There was a *Dunkirk*, originally the *Worcester* of 1651, a ship of 629 tons and carrying 48 guns. In 1660 and the following year she carried the flag of the Earl of Marlborough on taking over possession of Bombay. She was at the battle off the Texel in 1673, where her captain, Francis Courtnay, was killed. In 1693 she was one of Wheeler's squadron at the West Indies, and on 17th June, 1694, she assisted in the capture of the French 54-gun ship *Invincible*. She assisted at the bombardment of Fort Fornelle in Minorca, which surrendered on 9th September, 1708.

The *Dunkirk* which followed her was a 60-gun ship which was at the battle off Cape Passero in 1718; in 1741 at the attack

H.M.S. DUNKIRK—*continued*

on Cartagena; in the battle of Toulon in 1744; under the command of Captain the Hon. Richard Howe. The next *Dunkirk* on 8th June, 1755, assisted by the *Torbay* (14), captured the French *Alcide* (64). In 1756 she was in the expedition to the Chausey Islands off Granville and at the destruction of the French fortification there. Then in 1757, whilst in company with H.M.S. *Lancaster*, she captured the French vessel *Comte de Grammont* (36), and also recaptured a ship which had been taken by the French in April, 1757, the *Merlin* (10). Then on 29th December, 1758, she was present at the capture of Goree and at Hawke's victory of 1759 in Quiberon Bay. She then became a receiving ship, then a convict ship, finally being sold at Plymouth in 1792.

There was also a *Dunkirk's* prize which was a 24-gun ship, and while she was at the West Indies she made several captures. On 18th October, 1708, when in chase of a French ship she ran ashore at San Domingo and became a total wreck. Captain Purvis, who was in command, took his French opponent despite this and carried his crew in her back to Jamaica.

The present *Dunkirk* is a destroyer of the *Battle* class, and was built by Alex Stephens in 1945. She carries five 4.5-inch guns.

H.M.S. EAGLE

Description of Badge

FIELD: Blue.

BADGE: An eagle rising silver.

MOTTO: *Arduus ad Solem* (Arduous to the sun).

Badge is in allusion to the name.

BATTLE HONOURS

Portland	1653	
Gabbard	1653	June 3rd.
Lowestoft	1665	
Orfordness	1666	July 25th.
Barfleur	1692	May 19th—24th.
Gibraltar	1704	July 24th.
Velez Malaga	1704	August 13th.
Ushant	1747	October 14th.
Sadras	1782	February 17th.
Providien	1782	April 12th.
Negapatam	1782	July 6th.
Trincomalee	1782	September 3rd.
Calabria	1940	July 9th.
Mediterranean	1940	
Malta Convoys	1942	

The first *Eagle* was a Hansa ship, purchased in 1592, and converted to a hulk for taking ordnance out of ships. She was of 894 tons. In 1653 she was made into a careening hulk, and in 1675 laid up ashore at Chatham, being sold in 1683.

H.M.S. EAGLE—*continued*

Then came a Dunkirk vessel of 100 tons and 12 guns called *Aigle*, captured in 1650 and hired for the service of the Commonwealth Navy. She took part in the battle of the Kentish Knock, 1652, Blake's defeat of the Dutch off Portland in 1653, and the first battle of the Texel in the same year. In 1655 she was returned to her owners.

The third *Eagle*, a fifth rate of 299 tons and 22 guns, built at Wapping as the *Selby* and renamed *Eagle* at the Restoration in 1660. In April, 1665, she was at the blockade of the Zuyder Zee, and in June at the battle of Lowestoft under the Duke of York. Converted into a fireship in 1674, condemned in 1694 and sunk as a breakwater at Sheerness.

In 1666 the *Spred Eagle* of 240 tons and 6 guns, a fireship, was captured from the Dutch and renamed *Eagle*, and was expended in the Four Days' Fight, 1st-4th June, 1666.

The fifth *Eagle* was also a fireship of 50 tons and 6 guns, being taken from the Algerines in 1670 and expended in a night attack on Algerine corsairs in Bugia Bay on 2nd May, 1671.

Eagle number 6 of 208 tons was purchased in 1672 and fitted as a fireship, and foundered on passage to St. Helena in April, 1673.

There was an *Eagle* built at Portsmouth in 1679, and she was a third rate of 1,047 tons and 70 guns. In 1692 she was at the battle of Barfleur, and was also Rooke's flagship for boat attack on the French Fleet at La Hogue. She was rebuilt at Chatham in 1699. On 15th August, 1702, she took part in Rooke's attack on Cadiz; in 1704 at the capture of Gibraltar and the battle of Velez Malaga; in 1705 at the bombardment and capture of Barcelona; and in 1707, on 22nd October, when returning with Sir Cloudesly Shovell from the Mediterranean, she was wrecked and lost with all hands off the Scilly Islands.

There was another *Eagle* which was an advice boat of 153 tons and 10 guns, built at Arundel in 1696, and wrecked off the Sussex coast in the Great Storm of 27th November, 1703.

An *Eagle*, of 1,130 tons and 60 guns, was built at Portsmouth and launched on 1st December, 1744. She was originally named the *Centurion*, but was renamed *Eagle* in 1745. In 1746 she captured the Spanish privateer *Esperanza* of 16 guns and a French privateer —ex British *Shoreham*—of 22 guns. June, 1747, found her taking part in the capture of a French West India convoy. In

H.M.S. EAGLE—continued

July, 1747, in company with H.M. Ships *Edinburgh* and *Nottingham*, she captured the French privateer *Bellone* of 36 guns. October of 1747 found her in Hawke's action against the French under L'Etenduere. On 7th March, 1748, she assisted at the capture of a Spanish convoy off Morocco. In company with the *Medway* on 30th May, 1757, she captured the French Indiaman *Duc D'Acquitane* of 50 guns. In August, 1757, she joined Admiral Holbourne's fleet at Louisburg, Cape Breton, and in June, 1767, was sold.

Another *Eagle* was a third rate of 1,372 tons and 74 guns, built on the River Thames, and launched on 12th May, 1774. In 1776-1778 she was Lord Howe's flagship on the North America station, and took part in General Howe's defence at Sandy Hook against the French fleet under D'Estaing in 1778. In 1779 she joined the East Indies Squadron under Admiral Sir E. Hughes, and in 1782 was in Hughes' actions against the French under Suffren off Sadras, Providien, Negapatam and Trincomalee, and in 1783 in Hughes' action with Suffren off Cuddalore. In 1794 she was fitted for service as a lazareto, and in 1797 she was converted to a prison ship and renamed *Buckingham*. In 1812 she was broken up.

A later *Eagle* was a gunboat of 71 tons and 4 guns, and was purchased in 1794 for service in the Anti-Invasion Flotilla, finally being sold in 1802.

The *Ventura* captured from the French in 1803, a gunboat of 158 tons and 12 guns, was added to the Royal Navy as the *Eagle*, but was renamed *Eclipse* in 1804.

A third rate of 1,723 tons and 74 guns named *Eagle* was built at Northfleet, and was launched on 27th February, 1804. In 1804 she became the flagship of the squadron off the Texel, and in 1805 she was with Cornwallis's fleet blockading Brest; on 1st April, 1805, with Cochrane's squadron in chase of the French Rochfort squadron to the West Indies; in 1806 with Sir Sidney Smith's squadron in the Mediterranean, where she took part in the capture of Capri and the defence of Gaeta; in 1807-8 with Collingwood's fleet blockading Toulon; in July, 1809, with the expedition to Walcheren; in 1810 assisted in the defence of Cadiz against Marshal Soult; in 1811 ,on 27th November, captured the French *Corcyre* of 40 guns armed *en flute*; in 1812, July, destroyed French

H.M.S. EAGLE—*continued*

coast batteries at Ceste in the Adriatic; on 17th September boats captured two French gunboats and fifteen armed merchantmen off the mouth of the Po; on 13th July at the capture of Fiume; on 2nd August, 1813, captured 21 storeships off Rovigno, Istria, and landing parties stormed the forts; on 31st October, 1813, at the attack on and the capture of the Trieste forts. In 1832 she was cut down to a 50-gun ship, and from 1858 to 1862 served as a coastguard drill ship. After this service she was transferred to the Mersey Division of the R.N.V.R. in 1910, and in 1918 she was renamed *Eaglet*.

The next *Eagle* was an aircraft carrier of 22,790 tons, and was laid down as a battleship at Armstrong's in 1913 for the Chileans and was called *Almirante Cochrane*. She was purchased for the Royal Navy in 1917 for conversion to an aircraft carrier and renamed *Eagle*. Launched on 8th June, 1918, she was commissioned for trials in April, 1920. In 1940 she was at Calabria and in 1942 with the Malta Convoys. On 11th August, 1942, she was torpedoed and sunk in the Western Mediterranean by submarine.

The present *Eagle*, an aircraft carrier, is the logical outcome of such design started with the *Ark Royal* of 1936. Many lessons learned during the 1939-45 war have resulted in special features in her design. She is also the first carrier in any navy built to operate modern naval jet aircraft.

Note.—According to some lists there appears to have been 21 *Eagles*.

H.M.S. EARL OF PETERBOROUGH

Description of Badge

This is a circular plaque on which is a male bust, presumed to be a blackamoor from the arms of the Mordaunts. It is a rather crude casting, but better than many of this type. No colours indicated.

BATTLE HONOUR
Dardanelles 1915-16

The *Earl of Peterborough* was a monitor, and served in the Mediterranean and the Dardanelles under Captain Somerville in the war of 1914-1918.

H.M.S. EDINBURGH

Description of Badge
FIELD: White.

BADGE: Upon a mount of rock in base proper a castle triple towered black masoned white, the flags, windows and portcullis red.

MOTTO:

From the arms of Edinburgh. There is another badge showing a crowned cypher.

BATTLE HONOURS

Ushant	1747	October 14th.
Cape Francois	1757	October 21st.
Syria	1840	September 10th—December 9th.
Baltic	1854-5	
Norway	1940-1	
"Bismarck"	1941	May 23rd—27th.
Atlantic	1941	
Malta Convoys	1941	
Arctic	1941-2	

The *Edinburgh* was a sister ship to the *Belfast* and was a war loss, being sunk by torpedoes from a destroyer after damage by a U-boat in the Barents Sea.

H.M.S. ENCHANTRESS

Unofficial Badge: The field of the shield is red with a gold border. The anchor and cabling is gold. Above the shield is the naval crown. A blue scroll underneath has the name ENCHANTRESS in white letters.

Official Badge
 The official badge shows the flag of Admiralty.

BATTLE HONOURS
North Africa	1942-3
Atlantic	1939-1940-1-2-3-4-5
Mediterranean	1942

This vessel was an Admiralty Yacht of 3,470 tons, built at Belfast by Harland & Wolff, and launched on 7th November, 1903. She was laid up during the war of 1914-1918, and on 24th June, 1935, was sold and was the third *Enchantress*.

H.M.S. ENCHANTRESS—*continued*

The last *Enchantress* was built as the *Bittern* and was designated Admiralty Yacht (Escort Vessel), 1,190 tons and armed with four 4.7-inch guns. She was completed in April, 1935, and later refitted for the Second World War, being sold out of the Navy in 1946.

She was later renamed *Lady Enchantress* and used as a pleasure steamer, owned by the Three Star Shipping Company. She was the fourth Admiralty Yacht named *Enchantress* since 1862 and the seventh of the name since 1804.

H.M.S. ENDEAVOUR

Description of Badge
FIELD: Blue.

BADGE: A pair of compasses gold between four stars red.

MOTTO: *Nil intentaum* (Nothing unattempted).

The badge is derived from the medal to commemorate the discovery of New Zealand by Captain Cook in 1769, and the stars are from the flag of New Zealand.

BATTLE HONOUR
Cadiz   1596   June 21st.

The *Endeavour* was a survey vessel, and she was of 1,280 tons, carrying one 3-pdr. gun and built at Govan in 1912. There have been several of the name, including Captain Cook's *Endeavour*.

H.M.S. ESSEX

Description of Badge

Circular belt in yellow on which is the name in red; above is a naval crown gold with white sails, gems red and green. In the centre is a red shield on a gold field. Three white sea-axes in chief fess and base.

In allusion to the county of Essex (arms of Essex).

BATTLE HONOURS

Gabbard	1653	June 3rd only.
Four Days' Battle	1666	June 1st—4th.
Barfleur	1692	May 19th—24th.
Vigo	1702	October 12th.
Gibraltar	1704	July 24th.
Velez Malaga	1704	August 13th.
Passero	1718	July 31st.
Quiberon Bay	1759	November 20th.

The *Essex* was a twin-screw cruiser of 9,800 tons, 14 guns and a speed of 23 knots, and was launched at Pembroke in 1901. She served in the 1914-18 war, and in 1921 she was sold.

H.M.S. EURYALUS

Description of Badge
FIELD: Blue.
BADGE: The head and shoulders of a Greek warrior gold.
MOTTO:

The badge is derived from Greek mythology. Euryalus was a great friend of Nisus and one of the followers of Æneas.

BATTLE HONOURS

Trafalgar	1805	
Baltic	1854-5	
Heligoland	1914	August 28th.
Dardanelles	1915	
Sirte	1942	March 22nd.
Sicily	1943	July 10th—August 17th.
Salerno	1943	September 9th—October 6th.
Okinawa	1945	March 26th—May 25th.
Mediterranean	1941-3	
Malta Convoys	1941-3	

The first *Euryalus* was a third rate of 944 tons and 36 guns, built at the famous Buckler's Hard by Mr. Adams, and launched on 6th June, 1803. In 1804 she was on the coast of Ireland under Captain the Hon. Henry Blackwood and then off Boulogne under Lord Keith. On 15th September, 1805, she sailed from Spithead in company with Nelson in the *Victory* and joined the blockading squadron off Cadiz. After the battle of Trafalgar, Collingwood shifted his flag to the *Euryalus*, which took the *Royal Sovereign* in tow. In 1806 and 1807 she was employed in convoy work,

H.M.S. EURYALUS—continued

watching Carthagena, cruising in the Gulf of Lyons and escorting transports with troops under Sir John Moore to England.

Under Captain Hon. H. G. L. Dundas in 1808 in June her boats, assisted by those of the *Cruiser* (sloop), captured a Danish vessel and burnt two transports; in 1809 she was in the expedition to Walcheren, in November captured the French *L'Etoile* (14) off Cherbourg, and in 1813 was at the blockade of Toulon. In May, 1813, her boats, assisted by those of the *Berwick*, captured *La Fortune* (10) with twenty merchant vessels in Cavalarie Roads. During the American War in 1814 she was with Sir Alexander Gordon's squadron in the Potomac, and in 1815 she returned to England. From 1826 to 1844 she was a convict ship at Chatham, from 1845 to 1859 she performed the same service at Gibraltar, and in 1859 her name was changed to *Africa*, being sold at Gibraltar n 1860.

A screw frigate of 2,371 tons and 51 guns, fourth rate, of this name was launched at Chatham on 5th October, 1853. In 1854 she took part in the bombardment of Bomarsund; in 1855 at the bombardment of Sveaborg; on 24th October, 1862, at the capture of Kahding; 15th August, 1863, at the bombardment of Kagosima; and in 1864, during September, at the forcing of the Strait of Simonoseki. She was sold to Messrs. Castle & Sons in 1867.

Following her was a second-class screw cruiser of 4,140 tons and 16 guns, launched on 31st January, 1877. This vessel served on the East Indies stations as flagship and later at the Egyptian war. She was sold in 1897.

The next to be given the name was a first-class armoured cruiser of 12,000 tons, armed with two 9.2-inch and twelve 6-inch guns. She was built by Vickers at Barrow, and was launched on 20th May, 1901. From 1904 to 1906 she was the flagship on the Australia station, and in 1914 was with the Grand Fleet. In 1915, wearing the flag of Rear-Admiral Rosslyn E. Wemyss, she served in the Dardanelles at the landing on "W" beach, where she landed the Lancashire Fusiliers. Her next station was the East Indies, where she was flagship from 1916 to 1919, and in 1920 she was sold to Mr. Sidney Castle.

The present *Euryalus* is a cruiser of the *Dido* class, having been completed at Chatham in 1940.

H.M.S. EXETER

Description of Badge:
FIELD: White.

BADGE: A demi-lion red, crowned gold, holding an orb gold over wavelets gold and blue.

MOTTO: *Semper Fidelis* (Ever Faithful).

The badge is derived from the crest and the motto from the town arms of Exeter.

BATTLE HONOURS

Sadras	1782	February 17th.
Providien	1782	April 12th.
Negapatam	1792	July 6th.
Trincomalee	1782	September 3rd.
River Plate	1939	December 13th.

The *Exeter* was a cruiser designed by Sir William Barry and laid down in 1928, and completed at the end of 1930; her displacement was 8,390 tons, and she carried six 8-inch and four 4-inch A.A. guns. Her part in the famous battle with the *Admiral Graf Spee* in company with the *Achilles* and *Ajax* is well known. She was lost in action against the Japanese in Eastern Waters.

H.M.S. FALMOUTH

Unofficial Badge: A double-headed eagle with spread wings gold, on each wing a castle silver. On eagle's breast a stirrup silver and red. Blue scroll with letters in white.

Official Badge
FIELD: Red.
BADGE: A two-headed eagle silver, on his breast a castle gold.
MOTTO: Fail not.

Badge from the seal of Falmouth.

BATTLE HONOURS
Portland	1653	February 18th—20th.
Gabbard	1653	June 2nd—3rd.
Algiers*	1816	August 27th.

* A *Falmouth* was present at this action, but this vessel was a lighter or a hoy. The *Falmouth*, a frigate, being one of the ships guarding St. Helena, therefore does not qualify for this honour.

H.M.S. FALMOUTH—continued

| Heligoland | 1914 | August 28th. |
| Jutland | 1916 | May 31st. |

This vessel was a light cruiser of 5,250 tons and armed with eight 6-inch and four 3-pdr. guns, built by Messrs. Beardmore, Dalmuir, and launched on 28th September, 1910. In 1914, on 28th August, she was at Heligoland Bight, 25th December at the Cuxhaven air raid, at the battle of Jutland on 31st May, 1916, and on 19th August, 1916, she was sunk by an enemy submarine in company with H.M.S. *Nottingham* in the North Sea.

The last *Falmouth* was an escort vessel built in 1932 at Devonport, which became an R.N.V.R. drill ship in 1947.

H.M.S. FINISTERRE

Description of Badge

FIELD: Blue.

BADGE: A sea-horse gold supporting a flag white charged with a hurt, thereon a fleur-de-lis gold.

MOTTO:

The badge is derived from the supporters to the arms of Admiral Lord Hawke.

No battle honours are recorded for this ship.

The *Finisterre* is one of the *Battle* class of destroyer, built by Fairfield in 1944.

H.M.S. FORMIDABLE

Description of Badge

FIELD: Blue.

BADGE: Five tridents in saltire gold.

MOTTO:

Badge in allusion to the name.

BATTLE HONOURS

The Saints	1782	April 12th.
Matapan	1941	March 28th—29th.
Crete	1941	May 20th—June 1st.
Mediterranean	1941	
North Africa	1942-3	
Sicily	1943	July 10th—August 17th.
Salerno	1943	September 9th—October 6th.
Okinawa	1945	March 26th—May 25th.
Japan	1945	July 16th—August 11th.

The first *Formidable* was a French vessel of the same name, captured at Quiberon Bay on 20th November, 1759, and added to the Royal Navy in 1760. She was a third rate of 2,000 tons and 80 guns. No active service is recorded against her name, and she was broken up at Plymouth in 1767-8.

No. 2 was a second rate of 1,945 tons and 90 guns, built at Chatham and launched on 20th August, 1777. In 1778 she was in Keppel's action with French fleet under D'Orvilliers off Ushant; in April, 1781, at Admiral Darby's relief of Gibraltar; 12th April as the flagship of Sir George Brydges Rodney at the battle of the

H.M.S. FORMIDABLE—*continued*

Saintes; 1808 at the blockade of Toulon; and in 1813 was broken up at Portsmouth.

The third *Formidable* was a second rate of 3,594 tons and 84 guns, built at Chatham and launched on 19th May, 1825. In 1841-1845 she was on the Mediterranean station; 1854-1859 acted as guard ship at Sheerness; in 1869 she was loaned to the Bristol Training Ship Association as a training ship at Portishead, and was sold in 1906. There is a panel depicting the old *Formidable* in the chapel of the National Nautical School, Portishead, designed by Mr. Reginald Bell.

The fourth vessel of the name was a battleship of 15,000 tons, carrying four 12-inch guns, built at Portsmouth, and launched on 17th November, 1898. In 1901-1908 she was in the Mediterranean, 1909-1914 Atlantic Fleet and 2nd Fleet at the Nore; August, 1914, with the 5th Battle Squadron, Grand Fleet; and on 1st January, 1915, she was sunk by a German submarine off Start Point.

Formidable No. 5, an aircraft carrier of 23,000 tons, launched on 17th August, 1939. In 1941, on 28th March, she was at the Battle of Matapan and later at the evacuation from Greece and the evacuation from Crete, where she was severely damaged. Her battle honours show that she served in the Mediterranean and the Far East during the 1939-1945 war.

The *Formidable* reached the end of her days in 1953, being towed away from Portsmouth to the breakers on 7th May, 1953.

H.M.S. FORESTER

Unofficial Badge: A forester with bow silver, green habit and red trousers, brown boots, green hat with white plume, silver bugle, belt and band. Scroll yellow, gold edged, name of ship in black.

In allusion to the name.

Official Badge
FIELD: Green.

BADGE: Crossed woodmen's axes proper.

MOTTO: *Audax Potentes Caedo* (Boldly I cut down the mighty).

BATTLE HONOURS
Lowestoft	1665	June 3rd.
Sole Bay	1672	May 28th.
Martinique	1809	February 24th.

H.M.S. FORESTER—*continued*

Guadeloupe	1810	February 5th.
China	1856-60	
Heligoland	1914	August 28th.
Dogger Bank	1915	January 24th.
Narvik	1940	April 10th and 13th.
Norway	1940	
Spartivento	1940	November 27th.
Atlantic	1939, 1941, 1943-4	
Malta Convoys	1941	
Arctic	1942-3	
Normandy	1944	June 6th—July 3rd.
English Channel	1944	

A T.B.D. of 760 tons, carrying two 4-inch B.L., two 12-pdr. Q.F. guns, built at Cowes, I.O.W., and launched on 18th October, 1911. On 28th August, 1914, she was at Heligoland Bight, and in November at the bombardment of Zeebrugge. Then in 1915, on 24th January, she was at Dogger Bank, and in September, 1918, she operated on the Palestine coast in conjunction with General Allenby's army. On 5th November, 1921, she was sold to Mr. Edgar Rees of Llanelly.

The *Forester* of the Second World War was a destroyer of the *Escapade* class of 1,350 tons, built at Cowes in 1934.

H.M.S. FORTUNE

Unofficial Badge: Silver horseshoe enclosing a gold letter F. Naval crown above. Scroll red and gold with H.M.S. FORTUNE in white letters.

Official Badge
FIELD: Blue.

BADGE: A wheel gold with silver wing.

MOTTO: *Faveat* (May/Fortune/Favour You).

In allusion to the wheel of fortune.

BATTLE HONOURS

Armada	1588	Voluntary Ship.
Portland	1653	February 18th—20th.
Gabbard	1653	June 2nd—3rd.
Orfordness	1666	July 25th.
Jutland	1916	May 31st.

H.M.S. FORTUNE—*continued*

Atlantic 1939
North Sea 1940
Malta Convoys 1941-2

H.M.S. *Fortune* was a T.B.D. of 952 tons. Built at Govan, and launched on 17th May, 1913. In January, 1916, she assisted in the rescue of the crew of H.M.S. *King Edward VII*, which vessel had been sunk by a mine off Cape Wrath. She herself was sunk at the battle of Jutland, 31st May, 1916.

The official badge belonged to a later *Fortune*, built at Clydebank by John Brown in 1934. She was of 1,375 tons and her main armament was four 4.7-inch guns. She was transferred to the Royal Canadian Navy in 1943 and renamed *Saskatchewan*. There have been about 26 *Fortunes* in the Navy since 1522, mainly small vessels.

H.M.S. FRANKLIN

Description of Badge
FIELD: Blue.

BADGE: A dolphin embowed white pierced through the sides with two fishing spears in saltire gold.

MOTTO:

This vessel was named after Sir John Franklin, the famous Arctic explorer; he lost his life whilst on an expedition to discover the North-West Passage.

BATTLE HONOUR
Normandy   1944   June 6th—July 3rd (Surveying).

The *Franklin* is a survey vessel of 830 tons, built by the Ailsa Shipbuilding Company in 1937. Speed 17 knots.

H.M.S. FURIOUS

Description of Badge
FIELD: Black.

BADGE: An eagle's head white, langued red, armed gold.

MOTTO: *Ministrat Arma Furor* (Fury supplies arms).

BATTLE HONOURS
Crimea	1854-5
China	1856-60
Narvik	1940 April 10th and 13th.
Norway	1940-1941-1944
North Africa	1942-3
Malta Convoys	1942

The *Furious* was an aircraft carrier originally completed as a cruiser in 1917. The *Furious* did some useful service in the Second World War, her aircraft sinking many ships, and she ferried Spitfires to aid Malta in its defence.

H.M.S. GABBARD

Description of Badge
FIELD: Blue.

BADGE: Within a wreath of laurel gold a demi-dragon erased also gold, charged on the shoulder with a torteau, thereon a cross couped also gold.

MOTTO: *Fortiter, Fideliter, Feliciter* (Boldly, faithfully, successfully).

The badge is derived from the arms of the joint Commanders-in-Chief. The demi-dragon from the arms of Monck and the torteau from those claimed by Deane.

No battle honours are recorded for this name.

The *Gabbard* is one of the *Battle* class of destroyers, and was built by Swan Hunter in 1945.

H.M.S. GAMBIA

Description of Badge

FIELD: Per fess blue and green.

BADGE: An elephant in front of a palm tree proper.

MOTTO:

The badge is derived from the badge used by Gambia Colony.

	BATTLE HONOURS	
Sabang	1944	July 25th.
Okinawa	1945	March 26th—May 25th.

The *Gambia* is a cruiser of 8,000 tons and carries twelve 6-inch and eight 4-inch A.A. guns, and was built by Swan Hunter, being completed in 1942. Her battle honours indicate that she served in the eastern theatre of war.

H.M.S. GANGES

Description of Badge
FIELD: Blue.
BADGE: An elephant gold upon three wavelets silver.
MOTTO: Wisdom is strength.

Badge derived from the name.

BATTLE HONOURS
St. Lucia	1796	May 24th.
Copenhagen	1801	April 2nd.
Syria	1840	September 10th—December 9th.

The first *Ganges* was one of three ships presented to the Admiralty by the East India Company. Her name was originally the *Bengal* and was a third rate of 1,655 tons, armed with 74 guns. She was built on the Thames by Messrs. Randall & Co. Ltd., Blackwall, and launched on 30th March, 1782. On 20th October, 1782, she was in action off Cape Spartel and the final relief of Gibraltar by Lord Howe. In 1794 in the West Indies, in company with the *Montague*, she captured the French 26-gun corvette *Jacobin*; she was at the capture of St. Lucia, St. Vincent and Granada with Rear-Admiral Christian in May and June, 1796, and in 1801 at Copenhagen. Following this she was with Sir T. Louis's squadron at the capture of the French *Presidente* (40) on 27th September, 1806; the bombardment of Copenhagen in August, 1807; at the blockade of the Tagus in 1808; and in 1809 at the Walcheren Expedition. In 1811 she was converted into a prison ship, and loaned to the Transport Board in December, 1814. She was broken up at Plymouth in 1816.

H.M.S. GANGES—*continued*

The next *Ganges* was a second rate of 2,284 tons and 84 guns. Built of teak at Bombay and by the order of the Admiralty, it was directed that she should be a facsimile of the *Canopus*, which was originally the *Franklin* captured by Nelson from the French at the battle of the Nile on 1st August, 1798. She was launched on 9th November, 1821, serving on various stations. In 1828 Royal Marines of the squadron were landed at Rio de Janeiro for the protection of the Emperor of Brazil, and they were under the command of the Captain of *Ganges*. Captain Inglefield was presented with the Order of the Southern Cross in recognition of his services. She was at the Syrian campaign, where her captain, Barrington Reynolds, superintended the landing of troops at D'Journi, aided at the bombardment of Beyrout, and was present at the blockade of Alexandria. Just before the ship paid off in 1861 the captain addressed the ship's company and presented medals to those seamen of the *Ganges* who were present at the Crimea. The *Ganges* was the last sailing ship to be used as a sea-going flagship. On 5th May, 1865, the *Ganges* arrived at Devonport to be fitted out as a training ship for boys at Falmouth. Orders were issued for the whole of the boys belonging to the training ship *Wellesley* at Chatham to be transferred to the *Ganges*. The *Ganges* arrived at Falmouth on 20th March, 1866, in tow of the *Gladiator*, and was moored in Carrick Roads. Commander Frederick Hildebrand Stevens was the first Commanding Officer of the Falmouth Training Establishment, and Commander Walter Vernon Anson was the last Commanding Officer of the Falmouth Establishment.

In November, 1899, this establishment was transferred to Harwich, and after calls at Devonport and Sheerness she was finally towed to Harwich by the tugs *Hearty* and *Gladiator*. Commander Anson remained in command at Harwich until succeeded by Commander Joseph R. Bridson. From 1899 the *Ganges* and *Caroline* (fitted as a temporary hospital tender to *Ganges*) formed the Harwich Training Establishment for Boys. Then came a new establishment commissioned as H.M.S. *Ganges* and consisting of *Ganges*, *Caroline*, *Boscawen II* and *Boscawen III*. These two latter ships had been tenders to *Boscawen* at Portland. Various changes of name took place in the succeeding years, and now the *Ganges* is a shore Training Establishment at Shotley Gate, near Ipswich.

H.M.S. GLASGOW

Description of Badge
FIELD: Blue.
BADGE: The figure of St. Kentigern gold.
MOTTO: *Memor es tuorum* (Be mindful of your ancestors).

The badge of this ship is derived from the arms of the city of Glasgow.

BATTLE HONOURS

Lagos	1759	August 17th.
Havana	1762	August 13th.
Algiers	1816	August 27th.
Navarino	1827	October 20th.
Falkland Islands	1914	December 8th.
Norway	1940	
Biscay	1943	
Arctic	1943	
Normandy	1944	June 6th—July 3rd.

The first *Glasgow* was a sixth rate of 284 tons and 24 guns. She was originally the *Royal Mary* of the Scots Navy established by the Scots Parliament in 1696, built in London and first commissioned in June, 1696. After the Union in 1707 she was absorbed into the Royal Navy and renamed *Glasgow*, and sold on 20th August, 1719.

There was another sixth rate of the name launched at Hull on 31st August, 1757, of 451 tons and 20 guns. She was at Boscawen's victory at Lagos on 18th August, 1759; in June and July, 1762, at the siege and reduction of Havana, and in the course of the opera-

H.M.S. GLASGOW—continued

tion the *Glasgow* assisted the *Defiance* (60) to capture the Spanish *Venganza* (26) and *Marte* (18) in the harbour of Mariel. On 17th June, 1775, she cannonaded the enemy position at the battle of Bunker's Hill; on 6th April, 1776, she engaged an American squadron of fireships under Commodore Hopkin's for two hours; and on 19th June, 1779, was accidentally set on fire and destroyed at Montego Bay, Jamaica.

Then came a fifth rate of 1,260 tons and 40 guns, built and launched at Blackwall on 21st February, 1814. This vessel served at the bombardment of Algiers under Admiral Lord Exmouth, for which a naval medal was awarded, and at the battle of Navarino, where again a medal resulted. During her service she conveyed the remains of Queen Charlotte to Cuxhaven and took out Sir Edward Paget to India and brought home the Marquess of Hastings. She was broken up at Chatham in 1829.

A screw frigate of 3,037 tons and 28 guns bore this name, being launched at Portsmouth on 28th March, 1861, and after service in the East Indies was sold in December, 1884.

Fairfield's launched the turbine cruiser *Glasgow* of 4,800 tons and 25 knots on 30th September, 1909, and from 1910 to 1919 she served on the south-east coast of South America. On 1st November, 1914, she was at the Coronel battle, on 8th December at the sinking of the *Leipzig*, and on 14th March, 1915, at the destruction of the *Dresden* at Juan Fernandez Island. She became a stokers' training ship at Portsmouth, and in 1927 was sold to Messrs. T. W. Ward & Co.

The *Glasgow* in the present Navy List is a cruiser of the *Southampton* class of 9,100 tons, built by Scotts and completed in 1937. She served in various theatres of the Second World War, as her battle honours show.

H.M.S. GLORIOUS

Description of Badge

FIELD: Red.

BADGE: A rose gold with centre silver, and radiating rays silver.

MOTTO: *Explicet Nomen* (The name explains itself).

BATTLE HONOUR
Norway 1940

The *Glorious* was completed as a cruiser in 1917 by Harland & Wolff, Belfast. She completed her conversion into an aircraft carrier at Devonport in 1930. Her displacement tonnage was, like the *Courageous*, 22,500. This vessel was sunk by gunfire from the *Scharnhorst* and *Gneisenau* somewhere off Narvik on 8th June, 1940.

H.M.S. GLORY

Description of Badge
FIELD: Blue.

BADGE: A demi-lion erased gold holding between the paws a sun in splendour also gold.

MOTTO: *Per concordiam Glory* (Glory through unity).

The badge is in allusion to the name.

BATTLE HONOURS
First of June 1794 June 1st (and May 28th—29th).
Dardanelles 1915

The French *Gloire* of 748 tons, 44 guns, and a fifth rate, which was captured in Anson's victory over de la Jonquiere in the Bay of Biscay on 3rd May, 1747, was added to the Royal Navy as H.M.S. *Glory*. She saw service on the west coast of Africa and in the West Indies, and was commanded by Captain Richard, afterwards Earl Howe. In 1757 she was reduced to a 30-gun ship, and was sold at Portsmouth on 15th March, 1763.

Then there was a fifth rate of 679 tons and 32 guns, launched at Hull on 24th October, 1793. From 1769 to 1773 her service was in home waters, and on 30th August, 1774, she was renamed *Apollo*.

The next one of the name was a lugger of 8 guns and originally a French privateer named *La Gloire*, taken by H.M.S. *Scout* and added to the Royal Navy in 1781. In 1782 she was fitted out for use of the Commander-in-Chief, Plymouth, and broken up in 1783. (This vessel retained the name of *Gloire*.)

H.M.S. GLORY—*continued*

Another of the name was launched at Plymouth on 5th July, 1788, and was a second rate of 1,931 tons and 98 guns. This vessel served at the "Glorious First of June" in 1794 under Captain John Elphinstone, and in 1805 she was at the blockade of Cadiz as the flagship of Vice-Admiral Sir John Orde. On 22nd July, 1805, she was at Calder's action off Finisterre and was the flagship of Rear-Admiral Chas. Stirling. During the years 1809 to 1813 she was a prison ship at Chatham, and was broken up there in 1825.

Another French ship, *La Gloire*, a fifth rate of 877 tons and 42 guns, was taken by H.M.S. *Astræa* on 10th April, 1795, and added to the Royal Navy under her own name. She was, however, not put into commission, and was sold at Deptford, 24th March, 1802.

Yet another French *Gloire* was taken, this time by H.M. Ships *Centaur* and *Mars*, and added to the Royal Navy under her own name. She was of 1,153 tons, 40 guns, and was a fifth rate. In 1809 she served at the capture of Martinique, in 1810 at the capture of Guadaloupe, and in 1812 she was broken up at Chatham.

The French *Iphigenie*, a fifth rate of 1,066 tons, 38 guns, was captured off Madeira by H.M. Ships *Venerable* and *Cyane* on 16th January, 1814, and was taken into the Royal Navy as the *Gloire*, being sold at Plymouth on 10th September, 1817.

The battleship *Glory* of 12,950 tons, four 12-inch guns and twelve 6-inch guns, was built at Birkenhead by Laird Bros. and launched on 11th March, 1899. From 1901 onwards she served on various stations, and was at the Dardanelles in 1915, Egypt in 1916 and North Russia in 1917-18. She was renamed *Crescent* in 1920 and sold in 1922.

The Russian cruiser *Askold*, launched in 1900, was commissioned at Murmansk as H.M.S. *Glory IV* on 3rd August, 1918, for service with the Royal Navy in the White Sea, and was laid up in the Gareloch in 1919.

The latest *Glory* is an aircraft carrier of the *Colossus* class and is of 13,190 tons. She has already distinguished herself in the Korean campaign. Completed 1945 at Belfast.

H.M.S. GLOUCESTER

Description of Badge
FIELD: Blue.

BADGE: A trident white enfiled by a horseshoe gold.

MOTTO: *Prorsum* (Onwards).

From the arms of the city of Gloucester.

BATTLE HONOURS

Lowestoft	1665	June 3rd.
Orfordness	1666	July 25th.
Sole Bay	1672	May 28th.
Schooneveld	1673	May 28th and June 4th.
Texel	1673	August 11th.
Ushant	1747	October 14th.
Jutland	1916	May 31st.
Calabria	1940	July 9th.
Matapan	1941	March 28th—29th.
Crete	1941	May 20th—June 1st.
Mediterranean	1941	
Malta Convoys	1941	

The *Gloucester* was a cruiser of the *Newcastle* class and was a war loss in the Second World War. During operations in the Mediterranean near Crete she was severely damaged by attacking aircraft and sank afterwards.

H.M.S. GRAVELINES

Description of Badge
FIELD: Blue.

BADGE: Within a wreath of laurel gold a plate, whereon a saltire couped raguly red, in front of which a lion statant gardant, the tail extended, gold.

MOTTO: Zeal rests not.

The badge is derived from the red saltire of the former ensign of Spain, the lion from the crest of Howard, Lord High Admiral. The motto is the translation of the French motto of Lord Howard, *Desir N'a Repos*.

There are no battle honours recorded for this name.

The *Gravelines* is a destroyer of the *Battle* class, built by Cammell Laird. This vessel carries four 4.5-inch guns as her main armament and was built in 1944.

H.M.S. GREENWICH

Description of Badge
FIELD: Blue.

BADGE: An hourglass over a star, both silver.

MOTTO: *Tempore Utimur* (We use the opportunity).

The badge is derived from part of the arms of Greenwich, and of course this refers to the Observatory.

BATTLE HONOURS
Orfordness	1666	July 25th.
Sole Bay	1672	May 28th.
Schooneveld	1673	May 28th and June 4th.
Texel	1673	August 11th.
Barfleur	1692	May 19th—24th.
Marbella	1705	March 10th.

This vessel was a destroyer depot ship and was of 8,100 tons, completed by Swan Hunter and built in 1915. She carried as her armament four 4-inch and one 3-inch A.A. guns.

H.M.S. GRENVILLE

Description of Badge
FIELD: Black.

BADGE: A griffin gold upon a cap of maintenance proper.

MOTTO: *Deo Patriae Amicis* (For God, Country and Friends).

The motto at first used was Loyal Devoir, but the above motto *Deo Patriae Amicis* was transferred to her from *Revenge* in 1922 or a little later. The badge is derived from the crest of Sir Richard Grenville.

BATTLE HONOURS

Atlantic	1939	
English Channel	1943	
Mediterranean	1943-4	
Adriatic	1944	
Anzio	1944	January 22nd—31st.
Normandy	1944	June 6th—July 3rd.
Okinawa	1945	March 26th—May 25th.

The *Grenville* is one of the full conversion class of destroyers changed to anti-submarine frigate. Her tonnage is 1,710, and she was completed by Swan Hunter in 1943.

H.M.S. GUARDIAN

Description of Badge
FIELD: Black.

BADGE: A watchman's halberd and lanthorn gold and silver.

MOTTO: *Acer et Vigiland* (Keen and Watchful).

Badge in allusion to the name.

BATTLE HONOURS
Norway 1940
Sicily 1943 July 10th—August 17th.

The first *Guardian* was a fifth-rate vessel of 896 tons and she was fitted with 44 guns. She was launched on the River Thames on 23rd March, 1784, having been built by Robert Batson. On 24th December, 1789, whilst on the voyage out to New South Wales she struck an iceberg, and on 8th February, 1791, she was sold at the Cape of Good Hope.

The present vessel of the name was built as a netlayer and target-towing vessel, also for fleet photographic work, and was completed on 13th June, 1933. Her tonnage is 2,860 and her complement 181, and as armament she is supplied with two 4-inch and ten 20-mm. A.A. and six Lewis guns.

Her battle honours show that she served in the Second World War.

H.M.S. HAMPSHIRE

Description of Badge

A Tudor rose red. A naval crown above, gold with white sails and red and green gems. Underneath is a scroll blue on which is the name of the ship in white.

Badge from the arms of Hampshire.

BATTLE HONOURS

Gabbard	1653	June 3rd only.
Santa Cruz	1657	April 20th.
Lowestoft	1665	June 3rd.
Orfordness	1666	July 25th.
Schooneveld	1673	May 28th and June 4th.
Texel	1673	August 11th.
Havana	1762	August 13th.
Jutland	1916	May 31st.

A twin-screw four-funnelled cruiser of 10,850 tons, armed with four 7.5-inch, six 6-inch, two 12-pdrs., twenty-two 3-pdrs., two maxims and two torpedo tubes. Her speed was 23½ knots and she was launched at Elswick in 1903. This vessel was sunk in the Great War with the loss of her crew and Lord Kitchener.

H.M.S. HAWKINS

Description of Badge

FIELD: Blue.

BADGE: A demi-Moor proper, bound and decorated gold, arising out of wavelets black and silver.

MOTTO: *Nil Desperandum* (Never Despair).

The badge is derived from the crest and motto of Sir John Hawkins.

BATTLE HONOUR
Normandy   1944   June 6th—July 3rd.

The *Hawkins* was a cruiser of 9,800 tons and carried as her armament seven 7.5-inch and nine 4-inch guns. She was built at Chatham dockyard, completed in 1919 and was sold in 1946.

H.M.S. HERCULES

Unofficial Badge: This badge was carried by H.M.S. *Hercules*, battleship (super-Dreadnought) of 20,000 tons. Figure of Hercules proper. Scroll buff, gold edged, and with the words H.M.S. HERCULES in black.

Official Badge
FIELD: Blue.

BADGE: A lion and a man combatant both proper.

MOTTO:

The derivation of this badge is from Greek mythology and refers to the first labour of Herakles (Hercules), which was to slay a terrible lion which terrorized the country round about Nemea. Hercules went after the lion into its den and strangled

H.M.S. HERCULES—*continued*

it, for it could not be killed by sword, arrows or blows from a club. He later skinned the lion and wore its skin, thereby alarming Eurystheus, King of the Mycenæ and Hercules' taskmaster.

BATTLE HONOURS

Armada	1588	Merchant ship from the city of London.
Cadiz	1596	Hercules of Rye (merchant).
Quiberon Bay	1759	November 20th.
The Saints	1782	April 12th.
Jutland	1916	May 31st.

The first of the ships named *Hercules* in the Royal Navy appeared in 1588, and was one of the largest ships supplied by the city of London. Then there was a hired merchantman of 300 tons and 24 guns, which was at the 1621 Algiers expedition, where in conjunction with the *Bonaventure* she sunk one of the enemy's ships. There was another hired merchantman of this name at Blake's engagement with Tromp off the Kentish Knock in 1652, and she was captured by the Dutch.

Launched at Deptford in 1759 was a third rate of 1,608 tons which also bore this noble name. In the same year she became engaged in a running fight with the French *Souverain* (74), and was at Hawke's victory in Quiberon Bay. On 12th April, 1782, she was at the battle of The Saintes. On 17th August, 1784, she was sold.

Another third rate of 1,878 tons came along in 1798, which was originally the French *Hercule*, captured by the *Mars*. In 1803 she assisted at the capture of the French *Mignonne* (16) off San Domingo, in 1807 was at Copenhagen, and in 1810 was broken up at Portsmouth.

In 1815 another ship of this name was launched at Chatham. She was of 1,750 tons, 74 guns, and was a third rate. About 1855 she became a receiving ship in Hong Kong, and in 1865 was sold at this Crown Colony.

The *Hercules* of 1868 was an iron screw ship of 5,234 tons and carried 12 guns. In 1876 she was at the naval demonstration in the Dardanelles, where she was the flagship of Commander-in-Chief, Vice-Admiral Sir James Robert Drummond, K.C.B.;

H.M.S. HERCULES—*continued*

at Portsmouth in 1890 she was the flagship of the Admiral Superintendent of Naval Reserves, and in 1906 a floating barracks for dockyard employees at Gibraltar. Renamed *Calcutta* in 1909.

In May, 1910, the battleship *Hercules* of 20,000 tons was launched at Jarrow-on-Tyne by Palmer's Shipbuilding Company. On 31st May, 1916, she was at the battle of Jutland, and on 3rd December, 1918, she proceeded to Wilhelmshafen with the Inter-Allied Armistice Commission. In February, 1922, she was sold to the Slough Trading Co. for breaking up.

The *Hercules*, a 14,000-ton aircraft carrier, was laid down at Vickers-Armstrongs on the Tyne, and was commenced on 14th October, 1943.

H.M.S. HERMES

Description of Badge
FIELD: Blue.

BADGE: The head of Hermes with winged hat, all gold.

MOTTO: *Altiora Peto* (I seek higher things).

The name, of course, lends itself to having a badge from Greek mythology, Hermes being the same as Mercury, the messenger of the gods.

	BATTLE HONOURS
Burma	1852
Atlantic	1939

Vessels which have borne the name *Hermes* have included among them a variety of types, first of which was a sloop rigged as a brig, and was the Dutch vessel *Mercurious* of 201 tons and 14 guns captured by H.M.S. *Sylph* off the Texel on 12th May, 1796. She was added to the Royal Navy as the *Hermes*, and in 1797 foundered at sea with the loss of all her crew.

There was an armed vessel of 331 tons purchased in 1798 by the Royal Navy for service in the North Sea. This vessel was sold in 1802.

Then came a ship sloop of 339 tons and 16 guns. This vessel was built at Whitby in 1801 and was named the *Majestic*, a merchant ship. In 1803 she was purchased by the Royal Navy, serving on the Downs, North Sea, Channel and South America

H.M.S. HERMES—continued

stations until 1808, and in 1809 she was a store ship in the Mediterranean. In March, 1910, she was sold.

A sixth rate of 512 tons and 20 guns was launched at Portsmouth on 22nd July, 1811, which later saw service in the North Sea and Channel, and in 1813 she escorted a convoy to South America. On 15th September, 1814, she was disabled and went aground when taking part in an attack on Fort Bowyer, Mobile, U.S.A., and had to be destroyed to stop her from falling into enemy hands.

The Royal Navy purchased a vessel called *George IV* in 1830 which had been a merchant vessel, built at Blackwall in 1824, and called her *Hermes*. She was a steam vessel of 733 tons, and from 1830 to 1834 she was employed on packet service, after which she was converted to a coal hulk at Woolwich and renamed *Charger*, being broken up in 1854 at Deptford.

Following her was a paddle-wheel sloop of 830 tons, 6 guns, launched at Portsmouth on 26th June, 1835. After serving on the Mediterranean and North American stations she served at the second Burmese war, taking part in the bombardment and capture of Martaban on 5th April, 1852, and in the operations against Rangoon. After further service on other stations she was sold in 1864 for breaking up.

The *Minotaur*, a third rate of 1,726 tons, launched at Chatham in 1816, was renamed *Hermes* on 27th July, 1866, on taking up service at Gravesend as a cholera hospital, and was later broken up at Sheerness in 1869.

On 7th April, 1898, Fairfields launched the second-class protected cruiser *Hermes* of 5,600 tons and eleven 6-inch guns on the Clyde. After service on the West Indies and North American stations, and from 1900 to 1913 as a flagship on various stations, she became a depot ship for the Naval Wing of the Royal Flying Corps. On 31st August, 1914, she commissioned for service as a seaplane carrier, and on 31st October, 1914, she was torpedoed off Calais.

The first vessel specially designed as an aircraft carrier by the Admiralty was the *Hermes*, built at Armstrongs and launched on 11th September, 1919. She was completed at Devonport in 1923. In the Second World War of 1939 she saw service in the Atlantic, and her planes took part in an attack on the French

H.M.S. HERMES—*continued*

battleship *Richelieu* at Dakar. After operations in Iraq she was with the fleet under Sir James Somerville in the Indian Ocean, being sunk off Ceylon on 9th April, 1942, by Japanese aircraft.

The light fleet carrier *Hermes* was launched by Mrs. Winston Churchill on Monday, 16th February, 1953, at Vickers-Armstrongs Ltd., Barrow-in-Furness. The *Hermes* gives her name to the class of four carriers, the others being *Albion*, *Bulwark* and *Centaur*. All of these vessels incorporate many improvements, including the angle deck, etc.

H.M.S. HIBERNIA

Description of Badge

A circle of blue gold bordered on which is the harp of Ireland. Above it is a naval crown of gold with white sails and red and green gems. Issuing from the crown is the flag of a Rear-Admiral. Below is a green scroll with the name of the ship in black.

BATTLE HONOUR

Dardanelles 1915-16 February 10th—January 8th.

This vessel was of 16,350 tons, and was launched on 17th June, 1905, at Devonport; her main armament consisted of four 12-inch, four 9.2-inch and ten 6-inch guns. On this vessel, in 1912, a special superstructure was fitted on the forecastle, and from it was flown the first aeroplane to fly from a British warship. In 1914 she joined the Grand Fleet, and in October captured S.S. *Oscar* 2, which had on board the Austrian Ambassador and his staff, bound from Rome to Tokio. In 1915 she served in the Dardanelles operations, and in 1918 she became an accommodation ship for Chatham and Sheerness. She was sold in 1921 for breaking up in Germany.

H.M.S. HINDUSTAN

Description of Badge

An elephant proper. Scroll gold with white letters.

Description of Present Badge (1949) Royal Indian Navy.

FIELD: Red.

BADGE: An elephant silver on a base green, statant to sinister, within a border blue bearing EX ORIENTE LUX (Light from the East).

No battle honours are recorded for this vessel.

This vessel was an 18-gun twin-screw battleship of the *King Edward* class of 16,350 tons, and was launched in 1903 at Clydebank. H.R.H. Prince of Wales served in her in 1911 as a midshipman from August to October. In 1914 she was with the 3rd Battle Squadron, and in 1916 she was sent to Sheerness to cope with enemy coastal raids. In 1918 she was the parent ship for fitting out the raid on Zeebrugge, and in 1921 she was sold.

H.M.S. HOGUE

Description of Badge
FIELD: Blue.

BADGE: A chess rook white within a chaplet of laurel gold.

MOTTO:

Badge derived from the arms of Sir George Rooke.

	BATTLE HONOURS	
Baltic	1854-5	
Heligoland	1914	August 28th.

The first vessel to bear this name of *Hogue* was launched at Deptford in 1811, and she was of 1,750 tons. She took part in the war with America in 1813 and was commanded by Captain the Hon. Thomas Bladen Capel, who had been Nelson's signal lieutenant. The American privateer *Young Teazer* was driven ashore and destroyed by the *Hogue* at Lunenburgh Bay, Nova Scotia. In company with the boats from three other ships, boats from the *Hogue* went up the Connecticut river and destroyed 5,000 tons of American shipping, numbering 27 privateers. She then became a screw ship of 1,846 tons and 60 guns, having been fitted with a screw at Blackwall. This vessel was with Sir Charles Napier's fleet in the Baltic in 1854, and was at the attack on Bomarsund, when guns from the *Hogue* were landed with some officers and men to work them. She was broken up at Devonport in 1865.

H.M.S. HOGUE—*continued*

The next *Hogue* was a 14-gun twin-screw cruiser of 12,000 tons, launched at Barrow in 1900. On 22nd September, 1914, under the command of Captain Wilmot S. Nicholson and in company with the *Aboukir* and *Cressy* off the Dutch coast, all three ships being sunk by the German submarine U9.

The present *Hogue* is a destroyer of the *Battle* class and was built by Cammell Laird in 1944.

H.M.S. HOOD

Description of Badge
FIELD: Blue.

BADGE: A Cornish crow black holding an anchor gold.

MOTTO: *Ventis Secundis* (With the following winds).

The badge is derived from the crest and the motto from the coat of arms of Admiral Hood, 1724-1816.

BATTLE HONOUR
"Bismarck"   1941   May 23rd—27th.

The *Hood* was a battle-cruiser of 42,100 tons displacement, and carried eight 15-inch, twelve 5.5-inch, two 4.7-inch and four 4-inch A.A. guns. This vessel served in the force which went to immobilize the French fleet at Oran, and was later sunk by a hit from the *Bismarck*.

H.M.S. HOWE

(Ex *Beatty*, renamed 21st February, 1940)

Description of Badge

FIELD: Barry wavy of four white and blue.

BADGE: In front of a circle of chain gold a sword erect, point upwards, with a diamond-studded hilt proper, surmounted by a wolf's head couped black.

MOTTO: *Utcunque placuerit Deo* (God's Will be Done.)

In this badge the wolf's head is from the arms of the first Earl Howe; the gold chain from the supporters and the sword refers to the royal presentation on board the flagship after the 1st June, 1794.

BATTLE HONOURS

Arctic	1942-3	
Sicily	1943	July 10th—August 17th.
Okinawa	1945	March 26th—May 25th.

The second vessel to bear this name was a first rate of 2,619 tons and carrying 120 guns, being built at Chatham, and launched on 28th March, 1815. She was broken up at Sheerness on 23rd February, 1854.

Then came a screw ship of 6,557 tons and 12 guns. This ship was built at Pembroke, and was launched on 7th March, 1860. In 1885 she became a training ship and was renamed *Bulwark* on 3rd December, 1885, being renamed *Impregnable* on 27th September, 1886.

H.M.S. HOWE—continued

Following her was a twin-screw armour-plated barbette ship of 9,700 tons and carrying 10 guns, being launched at Pembroke on 28th April, 1885. During the years 1890-1902 she was in the Channel Fleet; on 8th December, 1892, she stranded at Ferrol; in 1893 and up to 1896 she was in the Mediterranean Fleet; from 1897 to 1901 she was the port guard ship at Queenstown, and was sold at Devonport on 11th October, 1910.

The present battleship *Howe* was completed in 1942 and is of 35,000 tons; her heaviest guns are 14-inch. She was originally named *Beatty*. The vessels of this class saw considerable service in the Second World War.

H.M.S. ILLUSTRIOUS

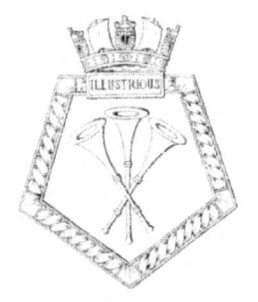

Description of Badge
FIELD: Blue.
BADGE: In front of a trumpet erect two trumpets in saltire gold.
MOTTO:

Badge in allusion to the name.

BATTLE HONOURS

Genoa	1795	March 14th.
Basque Roads	1809	April 11th.
Java	1811	September 18th.
Taranto	1940	November 11th.
Mediterranean	1940-1	
Malta Convoys	1941	
Diego Suarez	1942	May 5th—7th.
Salerno	1943	September 9th—October 6th.
Sabang	1944	July 25th.
Palembang	1945	January 24th.
Okinawa	1945	March 26th—May 25th.

The first *Illustrious* was a third-rate vessel of 1,616 tons and 74 guns, and was launched at Buckler's Hard on 7th July, 1789. In 1793 she sailed to join Lord Hood off Toulon, and on 14th March, 1795, she was in Hotham's action off Genoa. She suffered a very heavy concentration of fire and lost her masts and a large number of killed and wounded. After the action she was taken in tow, but broke loose in a gale, went ashore and was wrecked, the wreck being burnt.

H.M.S. ILLUSTRIOUS—continued

The next ship of the name to follow was a third rate of 1,746 tons and 74 guns, launched on the Thames on 3rd September, 1803. In 1804-5 she was at the blockade of Ferrol, then to the Leeward Islands on convoy duties; between 1807 and 1841 she was on various stations, Channel Fleet, Mediterranean and off Cadiz, North Sea, with Gambier at the destruction of the French vessels in the Basque Roads, East Indies, reduction of Mauritius, reduction of Java, North America and the West Indies. She became a training ship for seamen and boys in 1854, then in 1857-8 a training ship for cadets at Portsmouth. The *Britannia* was fitted out to take her place, and in 1858 she paid off. In 1861 she was attached to *Excellent* for instruction in Armstrong gun drill, and 1868 saw the end of her for she was broken up.

No. 3 was a battleship of 14,900 tons, and was launched at Chatham in 1896. This vessel was commissioned for the Mediterranean Fleet and was engaged in operations on the coast of Crete. In 1914 she was on the defence of Grand Fleet anchorages at Loch Ewe, in 1915 at Grimsby, ammunition store ship at the Tyne and Portsmouth, and in 1920 sold for breaking up.

The fourth *Illustrious* was launched at Barrow on 6th April, 1939. The work done by this aircraft carrier was varied, as can be seen by the battle honours. Her aircraft played havoc with the Italian Fleet at Taranto, and in the Mediterranean she had some extremely hot times—how hot can be imagined when in one month alone she was attacked fifty-eight times. Truly indeed could she be called *Illustrious*.

H.M.S. IMPLACABLE

Description of Badge
FIELD: Blue.

BADGE: A tiger's head erased proper.

MOTTO: *Saeva Parens Saeviorum* (Fierce parent of a fiercer offspring).

Badge is in allusion to the name and motto.

	BATTLE HONOURS	
Syria	1840	September 10th—December 9th.
Dardanelles	1915	
Norway	1944	
Japan	1945	
"Sevolod"	1808	26th August. Single ship action.

The first *Implacable* was the *Duguay Trouin* (74), and was one of the French van which escaped from Trafalgar and was captured by the squadron led by Sir Richard Strachan. She was bought for the Royal Navy on 28th April, 1806, and was given the name *Implacable*.

On 26th August, 1808, under the command of Captain T. Byam Martin she engaged the *Sevolod* (74), in the face of the Russian Baltic Fleet. However, the Russian Admiral Hanikoff came to the rescue: The *Sevolod* grounded and was compelled to strike her colours a second time to Sir Samuel Hood in the *Centaur*. On the arrival of further Russian ships she was set on fire and destroyed. In 1809 boats from the *Implacable* in company

H.M.S. IMPLACABLE—continued

with others went in to attack Russian gunboats at Hango Head in the Baltic. In 1840 she took part in operations on the coast of Syria. Later on, in 1855, she became a boys' training ship at Devonport, being incorporated with H.M.S. *Lion* at that port on 1st July, 1881. She was then, in 1908, placed on the sale list. On 12th March, 1912, she was lent to Mr. Wheatly Cobb as a training ship for sea scouts and similar organizations and was moored at Portsmouth, operating with the *Foudroyant* for use as a store depot. When she was no longer of any further service she was given an honourable burial in the English Channel. Her figurehead is to be seen outside the National Maritime Museum at Greenwich.

The next *Implacable* was a battleship of 15,000 tons, launched at Devonport in 1899, and was commissioned by Captain H.R.H. Prince Louis of Battenberg. This vessel served in the Mediterranean, Atlantic and Home Fleets. In the 1914-1918 war she saw service in the Channel, Mediterranean, Dardanelles and the Northern Patrol. In 1921 she was sold to the Slough Trading Co. Ltd.

In 1944 another *Implacable* came into being, an aircraft carrier. As her battle honours show, she saw service in Norwegian waters, and her aircraft destroyed or damaged 68,700 tons of enemy shipping in these waters. The German battleship *Tirpitz* was located by her aircraft, which led to the final destruction of this ship by the R.A.F. During the operations against the Japanese she was engaged in a variety of targets, and her aircraft sank or damaged 150,000 tons of enemy shipping and 113 enemy aircraft. Her first captain was Vice-Admiral The Mackintosh of Mackintosh, chief of the clan, and was sold in 1955.

H.M.S. INDEFATIGABLE

Unofficial Badge: This badge was carried by the battle-cruiser H.M.S. *Indefatigable* of 18,750 tons. The bee and ship in proper colours, the scroll in red with black letters.

MOTTO: Bee up and Doynge.

Official Badge
FIELD: Blue.

BADGE: Through a wreath of laurel proper a lion passant gardant gold.

MOTTO: *Deo adjuvante* (With God's Help).

Badge derived from the arms of Admiral Pellew, who was captain of the *Indefatigable* at the destruction of the *Droits de L'Homme*.

H.M.S. INDEFATIGABLE—continued

BATTLE HONOURS

Basque Roads	1809	
Jutland	1916	May 31st.
Palembang	1945	January 24th.
Japan	1945	July 16th—August 11th.
Okinawa	1945	March 26th—May 25th.
"Droits de L'Homme"	1797	January 13th. Single ship action.
"Virginie"	1796	Single ship action.

The first *Indefatigable* was a third rate of 1,384 tons and 64 guns, ordered to be built by Adams of Buckler's Hard in 1780. In 1794 on 8th September an order was made for her to be cut down a deck and she was made into a frigate, fifth rate, of 38 guns, and in 1795 Captain Sir Edward Pellew was appointed to command her and a frigate squadron cruising off Ushant. He remained in her on this service until February, 1799, and the squadron made several important captures, especially the *Virginie*, French 40-gun ship, and the famous engagements with the *Droits de L'Homme* in company with the *Amazon* (38), and in the capture of the French corvette *Vaillante* (20).

On 3rd October, 1804, the *Indefatigable*, commanded by Captain Graham Moore, with three consorts, took or destroyed a squadron of four Spanish treasure frigates off Cape Sta Maria; then on 16th July, 1806, her boats assisted at the cutting out of the French corvette *Cesar* (16) in the Gironde, in 1809 on 12th April she was at the Basque Roads, and in 1816 she was broken up.

The second ship of the name was a fourth rate of 2,047 tons and 50 guns, and was launched at Devonport on 27th July, 1848, and fitted as an "Advanced Ship." From 1849 to 1852 she was at North America and the West Indies, 1854 to 1857 on the southeast coast of America as the flagship of Rear-Admiral W. A. Hope Johnstone; in 1864 she was lent to Liverpool as a training ship for boys, and in 1914 she reverted to the Admiralty and was sold.

Indefatigable No. 3 was a second-class cruiser of 3,500 tons, launched in March, 1891. After serving in American and West Indian waters she eventually recommissioned at Bermuda, and in 1910 she became the *Melpomene*.

H.M.S. INDEFATIGABLE—continued

The fourth vessel was a battle-cruiser of 18,750 tons and eight 12-inch guns. She was launched at Devonport on 28th October, 1909, and commissioned for the 1st Cruiser Squadron. On 4th August, 1914, she was shadowing the *Goeben* in the Mediterranean; then she was the flagship of Admiral E. C. T. Troubridge, commanding the Dardanelles detached squadron, later hoisting the flag of Vice-Admiral Sackville Carden; in February, 1915, she joined the 2nd Battle-cruiser Squadron, Grand Fleet, Scapa Flow; and on 31st May, 1916, she was sunk in action at the battle of Jutland.

The fifth vessel of the name was launched at Clydebank as an aircraft carrier on 8th December, 1942, and completed on 3rd May, 1944. As the battle honours show, this vessel served in the attacks on the Japanese in the Far East theatre of the war of 1939-45 and was sold in 1955.

H.M.S. INDOMITABLE

Unofficial Badge: This badge was carried by H.M.S. *Indomitable*, a battle-cruiser of 17,250 tons. Gold field and cabling, red letters and dots. White feathers, green leaves, and gold scroll with black letters ICH DIEN. Buff scroll with red letters, H.M.S. INDOMITABLE.

Former badge of *Indomitable*, now superseded.

BATTLE HONOURS

Dogger Bank	1915	January 24th.
Jutland	1916	May 31st.
Malta Convoys	1942	
Diego Suarez	1942	May 5th—7th.
Sicily	1943	July 10th—August 17th.
Palembang	1945	January 24th.
Okinawa	1945	March 26th—May 25th.

H.M.S. INDOMITABLE—*continued*

Official Badge
FIELD: Blue.

BADGE: A dexter gauntlet of plate mail white.

MOTTO:

Badge in allusion to the name.

The first *Indomitable* was a battle-cruiser of 17,250 tons and carried eight 12-inch guns, and was launched by the Fairfield Company on 16th March, 1907. In 1908 she sailed with the Prince of Wales (late King George V) to Canada for the Quebec Tercentenary celebrations; in 1914 she was on operations in the Western Mediterranean, blockade of the Dardanelles, bombardment of forts; in 1915 at the Dogger Bank action, towed the *Lion* to Rosyth; on 21st November, 1918, she was at the surrender of the German Fleet, and in 1921 she was sold.

The second *Indomitable*, aircraft carrier, was launched in November, 1939. The battle honours show that this vessel fought in various theatres of the war of 1939-45. She was sold in 1955.

H.M.S. INFLEXIBLE

Description of Badge

Issuing from a naval crown gold, white sails, red and green gems, a demi-lion supporting a trident gold. Underneath in black the motto FIET. All above a scroll blue, gold edged, and having the name of the ship in gold.

Badge probably from the lion figurehead of eighteenth century.

BATTLE HONOURS
Lake Champlain	1776	October 11th and 13th.
Egypt	1801	March 8th—September 2nd.
New Zealand	1845-57	
Crimea	1854-5	
China	1856-60	
Alexandria	1882	July 11th.
Falkland Islands	1914	December 8th.
Dardanelles	1915	
Jutland	1916	May 31st.

The fifth vessel was a battle-cruiser of 17,250 tons, and was armed with eight 12-inch, sixteen 4-inch guns and five torpedo tubes. She was built by John Brown & Co., Clydebank, and launched on 26th June, 1907. In 1914 she was in the 2nd Battle-cruiser Squadron, Grand Fleet. Then she was detached from the Grand Fleet and sailed on 11th November with H.M.S. *Invincible* for South America. She was in the battle of the Falkland Islands, and in 1915 at the Dardanelles operations. In 1919 she was in the Reserve Fleet at the Nore, and was sold in December, 1921.

H.M.S. INVINCIBLE

Description of Badge

A lion on a mount proper, above a scroll red with the name of the ship in white. Scroll is black edged.

In allusion to the name and the symbol of the British lion.

BATTLE HONOURS

St. Vincent	1780	January 16th.
St. Kitts	1782	January 25th—26th.
First of June	1794	June 1st (and May 28th—29th).
Alexandria	1882	July 11th.
Heligoland	1914	August 28th.
Falkland Islands	1914	December 8th.
Jutland	1916	May 31st.

Battle-cruiser of 17,250 tons, eight 12-inch and sixteen 4-inch guns, 18-inch torpedo tubes. She was built by Armstrong Whitworth on the Tyne, and launched on 14th April, 1907. On 28th August, 1914, she was in action off Heligoland, and on 8th December in the battle of the Falkland Islands. In 1916 she was at the battle of Jutland, and on 31st May she blew up with the loss of Rear-Admiral Hood and all her complement except six. The ensign which she flew at the Falkland Islands engagement was placed in Portsmouth Cathedral.

H.M.S. IRON DUKE

Derived from an unofficial Badge: This badge was carried by H.M.S. *Iron Duke*, battleship (super-*Dreadnought*) of 25,000 tons. Red lion, gold crown, white flag with red cross. Scroll blue, gold loops, lettering IRON DUKE in white.

Official Badge
FIELD: Red.

BADGE: Profile head of the Duke of Wellington.

MOTTO: *Virtutis Fortuna Comes* (Fortune is the Companion of Valour).

Badge in allusion to the "Iron Duke".

BATTLE HONOUR
Jutland   1916   May 31st.

H.M.S. IRON DUKE—*continued*

The *Iron Duke* was a *Dreadnought* of 25,000 tons, built at Portsmouth in 1914, and carried ten 13.5-inch and twelve 6-inch guns. She was the famous flagship of Lord Jellicoe, serving at the battle of Jutland. Eventually she became a depot ship at Scapa Flow, and was badly damaged in an attack by German aircraft during the Second World War and was sold in 1946.

H.M.S. IRRESISTIBLE

Description of Badge

Interlaced initial letters R gold, I red. Above is a naval crown, white sails, red and green gems. Below is a scroll blue, gold edged, with the name of the ship in white.

In allusion to the name.

BATTLE HONOURS

Martinique	1794	March 22nd.
Groix Island	1795	June 23rd.
St. Vincent	1797	February 14th.
Belgian Coast	1914	
Dardanelles	1915	

The *Irresistible* was launched at Chatham on 15th December, 1898, and was a battleship of 15,000 tons and a speed of 18 knots. She was armed with four 12-inch and twelve 6-inch guns. This vessel served with the Mediterranean, Channel and Home Fleets, and in 1914, on 27th/28th August, she was engaged in the landing of Marines at Ostend. February-March, 1915, she was bombarding and attempting to force the entrance to the Dardanelles, and on 18th March was mined and sunk below Kephez Point.

H.M.S. JAMAICA

Description of Badge
FIELD: Red.

BADGE: A pineapple gold.

MOTTO: *Non sibi sed patriae* (Not for oneself but for one's country).

The badge is derived from the arms of Jamaica.

	BATTLE HONOURS	
Copenhagen	1801	April 2nd.
Barents Sea	1942	December 31st.
North Africa	1942	
North Cape	1943	December 26th.
Arctic	1942-4	

The first *Jamaica* was a sloop of 114 tons and 7 guns, four swivels, having been built at Deptford in 1710. She was wrecked in the West Indies on 2nd October, 1715.

The next vessel to have the name was also a sloop and she was of 273 tons and carried 10 guns. She also was built at Deptford, and was launched on 17th July, 1744. This ship was lost in the West Indies at Jamaica on 17th January, 1770.

Then came a sixth rate of 522 tons and 26 guns. She was originally the French *La Percante*, captured on 21st April, 1796, and added to the Royal Navy as H.M.S. *Jamaica*. In 1801 she was at Copenhagen, and on 15th-16th and 20th August her boats took part in operations against the Boulogne invasion flotillas. Her career was ended by being sold on 11th August, 1814.

H.M.S. JAMAICA—*continued*

The present *Jamaica* is a cruiser of the *Fiji* class, and her displacement is 8,000 tons. She was built by Vickers-Armstrongs at Barrow and completed in 1942. Her main armament is twelve 6-inch and eight 4-inch guns. Her war service in the Second World War ranged from the Arctic to North Africa. Recently 1955)) received the freedom of the city of Kingston, Jamaica.

H.M.S. JUTLAND

Description of Badge
FIELD: Blue.

BADGE: Within a wreath of laurel a sea griffin, all gold.

MOTTO:

No battle honours are recorded for this name.

Her badge is derived from the supporters of the arms of Admiral Sir John Jellicoe.

The *Jutland* ex *Malplaquet* is a destroyer of the *Battle* class, and was built at Alex Stephens' in 1946.

H.M.S. KELLY

Description of Badge

FIELD: Per fess wavy blue and white.

BADGE: A tower white supported by two lion's gambs gold, in base a bar wavy blue.

This badge is derived from the Kelly arms.

MOTTO:

BATTLE HONOURS

Atlantic	1939	
Norway	1940	
Crete	1941	May 20th—June 1st.
Mediterranean	1941	

The *Kelly* was a destroyer of the *Javelin* class, of 1,690 tons, and mounting six 4.7-inch and one 4-inch A.A. guns. She was sunk during the battle of Crete by aircraft bombing.

H.M.S. KEMPENFELT

Description of Badge
FIELD: Black.

BADGE: A sword proper between two wings green over two wavelets silver and blue.

MOTTO: *Fideliter* (Faithfully).

The badge is derived from part of the crest of Admiral Kempenfelt, and the wavelets to the incident of the loss of the *Royal George*.

	BATTLE HONOURS	
Jutland	1916	May 31st.
Atlantic	1939	
Anzio	1944	January 22nd—31st.
Normandy	1944	June 6th—July 3rd.
Okinawa	1945	March 26th—May 25th.

The *Kempenfelt* (ex *Valentine*) is a destroyer of the *Wager* class and is a leader. Her tonnage is 1,730 and, like the others, she carries as her main guns four 4.7-inch. She was built in 1943 at Clydebank. Converted to a frigate.

H.M.S. KENT

Description of Badge
FIELD: Red.
BADGE: The White Horse of Kent.
MOTTO: *Invicta* (Unconquered).

Badge from the arms and motto of Kent.

BATTLE HONOURS

Porto Farina	1655	April 4th.
Lowestoft	1665	June 3rd.
Orfordness	1666	July 25th.
Barfleur	1692	May 10th—24th.
Vigo	1702	October 12th.
Valez Malaga	1704	August 13th.
Passero	1718	July 31st.
Ushant	1747	October 14th.
Egypt	1801	March 8th—September 2nd.
Falkland Islands	1914	December 8th.
Atlantic	1940	
Mediterranean	1940	
Arctic	1942, 1943	
Norway	1944	

The *Kent* was a cruiser of 10,000 tons as refitted, and was completed at the Chatham yard in 1928. Her armament was eight 8-inch and eight 4-inch A.A. guns. At the Falkland Islands the previous *Kent* sank the *Nurnberg*; it was reported that during this battle a sailing ship passed across the scene.

H.M.S. KENYA

Description of Badge

FIELD: Barry wavy of six white and blue.

BADGE: A lion rampant gardant red.

MOTTO:

The lion is derived from the badge of the colony.

BATTLE HONOURS

Norway	1941	
"Bismarck"	1941	May 23rd—27th.
Sabang	1944	July 25th.
Burma	1944-5	
Atlantic	1941	
Malta Convoys	1941-2	
Arctic	1941-2	

The *Kenya* is a cruiser of the *Fiji* class and is of 8,000 tons, having as her main armament twelve 6-inch and eight 4-inch A.A. guns. She was built by Stephens and was completed in 1940.

Her service in the Second World War ranged from the Arctic to the east, and she was also in the *Bismarck* episode.

H.M.S. KING EDWARD VII

Description of Badge

The royal cypher ER entwined gold, figures VII in red. Above is a royal crown. A scroll blue with the name of the ship in gold is underneath.

This vessel has no battle honours recorded.

This ship gave her name to the class of eight ships. She was a battleship of 16,350 tons and 18 knots. Her armament consisted of four 12-inch, four 9.2-inch, ten 6-inch and some smaller guns and torpedo tubes. Built at Devonport, machinery by Harland and Wolff Ltd. She served during the first part of the Great War, and was mined and sunk off the north coast of Scotland on 6th January, 1916.

H.M.S. KING GEORGE V

Description of Badge
FIELD: White.
BADGE: Red cross of St. George charged with the head of H.M. King George V, gold.

Description of Badge
FIELD: Blue.
BADGE: The royal cypher of King George V ensigned by the royal crown proper.

Both these badges have been used as official badges.
MOTTO:

	BATTLE HONOURS	
Dunkirk	1940	(Personnel Ship)

H.M.S. KING GEORGE V—*continued*

Jutland	1916	May 31st.
Atlantic	1941	
"Bismarck"	1941	May 23rd—27th.
Arctic	1942-3	
Sicily	1943	
Okinawa	1945	March 26th—May 25th.

The first vessel to bear this name was launched on 9th October, 1911, by H.R.H. Princess Christian. She was a battleship of 23,000 tons, 21 knots, and carried as her main armament ten 13.5-inch and sixteen 4-inch guns. She was the flagship of the following in succession: Sir George Warrender, Bt., K.C.B., K.C.V.O.; Sir T. H. Martyn Jerram, K.C.B.; Sir John M. de Robeck, K.C.B. On 31st May, 1916, she was at the battle of Jutland, and on 19th August the same year in operations in the North Sea. In 1919 on 22nd November she became the flagship of Vice-Admiral Sir H. F. Oliver, K.C.B., K.C.M.G., M.V.O.; on 14th September, 1920, the flagship of Vice-Admiral Sir R. F. Phillimore, K.C.B.; in February, 1923, she became a seagoing gunnery training ship, stationed at Portland; and on 2nd December, 1926, she was sold to the Alloa Shipbreaking Company Limited.

The present vessel of the name was launched by H.M. King George VI in 1939 and is a battleship of 35,000 tons, mounting ten 14-inch and sixteen 5.25-inch guns. The first British battleship designed to carry aircraft and to have most of her big guns in quadruple turrets. Like the others of her class, she has done good service in the Second World War.

H.M.S. LAGOS

Description of Badge
FIELD: Blue.

BADGE: A falcon belled gold within a wreath of laurel gold.

MOTTO:

The badge is derived from the crest of Admiral Edward Boscawen, Commander-in-Chief in the battle of Lagos.

There are no battle honours recorded for this name.

The *Lagos* is one of the *Battle* class of destroyers, and was built by Cammell Laird. This vessel has for her main armament four 4.5-inch guns. She was launched in 1944.

H.M.S. LAUREL

Description of Badge

Circular wreath green, red berries, gold field with initial letter L in red. Above is a naval crown gold, white sails, red and blue gems. Underneath is a scroll red with the name of the ship in black.

Badge in allusion to the name and from an earlier badge which probably had an initial letter only.

BATTLE HONOURS

Portland	1653	February 18th—20th.
Gabbard	1653	June 2nd—3rd.
Scheveningen	1653	July 31st.
Heligoland	1914	August 28th.
Dogger Bank	1915	January 24th.
Jutland	1916	May 31st.
Belgian Coast	1914-16	
North Africa	1942	

This ship was a torpedo boat destroyer of 965 tons. The *Laurel* of the Second World War was a minesweeper of 590 tons (ex *Kingston Cyanite*).

There was a *Laurel*, a trawler bought in 1935 for service with the fleet.

H.M.S. LION

Unofficial Badge: This badge was carried by H.M.S. *Lion*, battlecruiser of 26,350 tons. Lion and mount, etc., in proper colours. Black letter ring. Red scroll with white letters LION.

Official Badge
FIELD: Black.
BADGE: A lion rampant gold.
MOTTO: *Concordant Nomine Facta* (The facts agree with the name)
Badge in allusion to the name.

BATTLE HONOURS
Armada	1588	(Golden) Lion.
Cadiz	1596	June 21st.
Portland	1653	February 18th—20th.
Gabbard	1653	June 2nd—3rd.
Lowestoft	1665	June 3rd.

H.M.S. LION—*continued*

Orfordness	1666	July 25th.
Schooneveld	1673	May 28th and June 4th.
Texel	1673	August 11th.
Barfleur	1692	May 19th—24th.
Ushant	1747	October 14th.
Java	1811	September 18th.
Heligoland	1914	August 28th.
Dogger Bank	1915	January 24th.
Jutland	1916	May 31st.
"Santa Dorotea"	1798	July 15th. Single ship action.
"Guillaume Tell"	1800	Single ship action.

The *Lion* was a 26,350-ton battle-cruiser, built by Vickers and completed in 1912. She was armed with eight 13.5-inch and sixteen 4-inch guns.

H.M.S. LIVERPOOL

Description of Badge

FIELD: Silver.

BADGE: A cormorant black, beaked and legged red, holding in its beak a branch of seaweed called lavergreen.

MOTTO: *Deus nobis haec otia fecit* (God gave us this ease).

The badge is derived from the arms of the city of Liverpool.

BATTLE HONOURS

Heligoland	1914	August 28th.
Calabria	1940	July 9th.
Mediterranean	1940	
Malta Convoys	1942	
Arctic	1942	

There have been a number of vessels bearing the name *Liverpool*, and the first one was a fifth rate of 681 tons and 40 guns. She was launched at Liverpool on 19th July, 1741, and from the time of commissioning to 1749 she was on service on the coast of Spain and in the Mediterranean. She was sold on 14th September, 1756.

A sixth-rate vessel of this name was launched on 1st February, 1758, of 590 tons and 28 guns. After serving on various stations she joined the fleet on the North America station in 1777 under Lord Howe, being wrecked off Long Island on 11th February, 1778.

Then came a fourth rate of 1,247 tons and 50 guns, built at Woolwich by Messrs. Wigram & Co. Ltd., which was launched on 21st February, 1814. From 1814 to 1816 she served on the

H.M.S. LIVERPOOL—continued

Cape of Good Hope station; from 1818 to 1822 she was on the East Indies station, and during this period in 1819 she took part in an expedition against the headquarters of Persian Gulf pirates at Ras-el-Khyma; and in 1822 on 16th April was sold at Bombay.

On 30th October, 1860, H.M. Dockyard, Devonport, launched a fourth-rate screw frigate of 1,195 tons and 51 guns of this name, which made a voyage round the world with the Flying Squadron in 1869-70, and in 1875 she was sold to Messrs. Castle & Sons for breaking up.

Vickers Sons and Maxim built a second-class protected cruiser called the *Liverpool* of 4,800 tons, which was launched on 30th October, 1909. On 28th August, 1914, she was at the Heligoland Bight action, and in February, 1915, she was searching off the African Coast for the German armed merchant cruiser *Kronprinz Wilhelm*. In part of 1915 to 1918 she served in the Adriatic, and on 8th November, 1921, she was sold for breaking up.

The present *Liverpool* was completed by Fairfield in 1938, and on 21st January, 1940, she intercepted the Japanese liner *Asama Maru* thirty-five miles from the coast of Japan and removed 21 German officers and men who were survivors from the German S.S. *Columbus*. She was then with the 7th Cruiser Squadron based at Alexandria escorting reinforcements from Alexandria to Malta. On 14th October whilst covering a Fleet Air Arm attack on Leros she was torpedoed by enemy aircraft south-east of Crete and was taken in tow by H.M.S. *Orion* to Alexandria. She then went to San Francisco for permanent repairs and later was covering Arctic convoys. Once again she was torpedoed, this time by Italian aircraft whilst escorting a convoy from the Clyde to Malta, and she was towed to Gibraltar by H.M.S. *Antelope*. In 1945 she returned to service, and was reduced to the reserve at Portsmouth in May, 1952.

H.M.S. LONDON

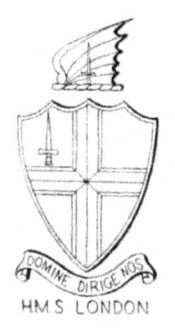

Unofficial Badge: Shield white field, red cross of St. George gold edged. Red and gold dagger. Crest gold with red dagger. Red scroll, black letters.

Description of Badge (official)
FIELD: White.

BADGE: A dagger red.

MOTTO: *Domine Dirige Nos.*

Badge and motto from the arms of London.

BATTLE HONOURS

Kentish Knock	1652	September 28th.
Scheveningen	1653	July 31st.
Gabbard	1653	June 2nd—3rd.
Lowestoft	1665	June 3rd.
Sole Bay	1672	May 28th.
Schooneveld	1673	May 28th and June 4th.
Texel	1673	August 11th.
Barfleur	1692	May 19th—24th.
Chesapeake	1781	March 16th.
Groix Island	1795	June 23rd.
Copenhagen	1801	April 2nd (not engaged).
Crimea	1854-5	
Dardanelles	1915	
Atlantic	1941	

H.M.S. LONDON—*continued*

Arctic 1941–2–3
"Marengo" 1806 March 13th. Single action.

This vessel was a cruiser of about 10,000 tons and originally resembled the *Devonshire* or *Sussex*, but underwent considerable alteration in her appearance when reconstructed. As her main armament she carried eight 8-inch and eight 4-inch A.A. guns. This vessel was completed at the Portsmouth yard in 1929, and sold in 1950 and broken up at Barrow. The unofficial badge shown is that of the *London*, a battleship of 15,000 tons.

H.M.S. LOWESTOFT

Unofficial Badge: Shield white, blue chevron charged with three white circles red centred, two Tudor roses red and an Eastern crown gold in chief, base rays of gold. Helm gold with gold and blue mantling, crest and figure of a saint in white. Scroll white with motto black underneath.

Official Badge
FIELD: Black.

BADGE: A Lowestoft plate proper, surmounted by an Oriental crown gold.

MOTTO: *Point du Jour* (Turn out early).

Badges from the arms of Lowestoft.

H.M.S. LOWESTOFT—*continued*

BATTLE HONOURS

Heligoland	1914	August 28th.
Dogger Bank	1915	January 24th.
Atlantic	1940-2-4-5	
North Sea	1940-1-2-5	

(There was a *Lowestoffe* whose Battle Honours are:—

Quebec	1759	September 13th.
Genoa	1795	March 14th.
"Minerve"	1795	Single ship action.)

The *Lowestoft* was a light cruiser of 5,440 tons and was armed with nine 6-inch guns, launched at H.M. Dockyard, Chatham, on 23rd April, 1913. On 28th August, 1914, she was in action off Heligoland, 1916 in the Mediterranean, 1917 in the Ægean, 1918 in the Adriatic, and during the years 1919, 1921 and 1923 was on the Africa station. In 1929 she was reduced to the reserve, and in January, 1931, she was sold to T. W. Ward for breaking up.

The last of the name was an escort vessel built at Devonport in 1934.

H.M.S. MAGPIE

Old Badge:
FIELD: White.
BADGE: A magpie proper.
MOTTO:

The badge in allusion to the name.

Official Badge
FIELD: White.
BADGE: Within an annulet black a magpie proper.
MOTTO:

This badge came from the magazine cover of the school magazine of Monkton Combe Junior School at Combe Down, Bath. Its adoption came in quite an unusual way. One of the boys of the school was home in Gibraltar for the holidays and was taken over

H.M.S. MAGPIE—*continued*

H.M.S. *Magpie* by the Commanding Officer of the ship, and in the course of the visit the boy produced the school magazine. The Commanding Officer thought it was better than the ship's badge and asked if he could use it. Following the necessary correspondence, the design was approved and accepted. This has resulted in a friendship being established between school and ship. The original design on the magazine cover was by the school's art mistress and was used because of the large number of such birds which are found in the vicinity of the school.

BATTLE HONOURS

Baltic	1855	
Benin	1897	February 8th—28th.
South Africa	1899-1900	(Medal but not battle honour).
Atlantic	1943-4	
Normandy	1944	June 6th—July 3rd.
Arctic	1944	

The first vessel to bear the name was a 4-gun cutter which was captured at Perros on 19th February, 1807. The second was a schooner and she was wrecked in Colorados Roads, Cuba, on 27th August, 1826. This vessel foundered in a squall and all but eight of the crew went down with the ship. Of these eight, six were drowned or eaten by sharks. The two men left, Meldrum and Maclean, were adrift in the boat. Meldrum tried to swim to a ship which they saw, but their shouts were heard and they were picked up.

A gunboat of this name was employed in the Russian war and was present at Sveaborg. A later *Magpie*, also a gunboat, was in service in the Gambia operations of 1894, the Benin expedition of 1897 and at South Africa during the Boer War.

The present *Magpie* is a sloop of the modified *Black Swan* class and built by Thornycroft. It was this ship which H.R.H. The Duke of Edinburgh commanded in the Mediterranean. She was launched in 1943.

H.M.S. MANXMAN

Description of Badge
FIELD: Blue.

BADGE: Three legs conjoined in armour proper, spurred and garnished in gold.

MOTTO: *Stabit Quocunque Jeceris* (It will stand, however it is thrown).

Badge derived from the arms of the Isle of Man.

BATTLE HONOUR
Malta Convoys 1941-2

The first *Manxman* was an aircraft carrier, the vessel being purchased from the Midland Railway Company in January, 1917. Up to October, 1917, she served with the Grand Fleet and then in the Mediterranean until the end of the 1914–18 war. In 1920 she was sold to the Isle of Man Steam Packet Company.

The present *Manxman* is a minelayer of 2,650 tons and was completed in 1941 at Cowes.

H.M.S. MARLBOROUGH

Description of Badge
FIELD: Black.

BADGE: A wyvern red with collar gold, therefrom a locket with St. Andrew's cross.

MOTTO: *S'en va t'en Guerre* (He goes to war).

Badge from the arms of Marlborough.

BATTLE HONOURS

Martinique	1762	February 16th.
Havana	1762	August 13th.
St. Vincent	1780	January 16th.
The Saints	1782	April 12th.
First of June	1794	June 1st (and May 28th-29th).
Jutland	1916	May 31st.

This vessel was a battleship (super-*Dreadnought*) of 25,000 tons. Her armament consisted of ten 13.5-inch and twelve 6-inch guns. She was launched at Devonport on 24th October, 1912. During 1914-1918 she was with the 1st Battle Squadron, Grand Fleet, 1919-1925 with the Mediterranean Fleet, 1926-1930 the Atlantic Fleet, and in May, 1932, she was sold for breaking up.

H.M.S. MARNE

Description of Badge

FIELD: Blue.

BADGE: Dolphin naiant white within a chaplet of laurel gold.

MOTTO:

The badge has been derived from the crest of Lord Ypres.

BATTLE HONOURS

Jutland	1916	May 31st.
North Africa	1942	
Malta Convoys	1942	
Arctic	1942-4	
Ægean	1944	

The *Marne* is a destroyer of the *Laforey* class, and was built by Vickers-Armstrongs. She was completed in 1941.

H.M.S. MARY ROSE

Description of Badge
FIELD: White.

BADGE: Within a wreath of laurel green a fleur-de-lis blue surmounted by a rose per pale white and red.

MOTTO:

The badge is derived from the following: first *Mary Rose* was named after Mary, the sister of Henry VIII. The rose and the fleur-de-lis were Tudor badges, and the laurel is in honour of the action of 17th November, 1917.

BATTLE HONOURS

Armada	1588	July 21st—29th Queen's ship.
Armada	1588	July 21st—29th Victuallers to the Westward.
Cadiz	1596	June 21st.
Lowestoft	1665	June 3rd.
Orfordness	1666	July 25th.
Sole Bay	1672	May 28th.
Schooneveld	1673	May 28th and June 4th.
Texel	1673	August 11th.
Jutland	1916	May 31st.
"The Seven Algerines"	1669	Single ship action.

The first *Mary Rose* was a great ship of 600 tons and carrying about 20 heavy guns and some 60 light. She was built in 1509 and named after Mary Tudor, the sister of Henry VIII. From

H.M.S. MARY ROSE—continued

1522 to 1525 she was in Henry VIII's first French war and was a favourite flagship owing to her good sailing qualities. She was said to have been rebuilt in 1536, and in 1544-5 she was in Henry VIII's third French war. On 19th July, 1545, she had an engagement with the French fleet off Portsmouth. When going into action she was swamped through her lower deck ports and sank with the loss of her captain, Sir George Carew, and nearly all hands.

Then came a vessel rated as 500 tons and carrying 36 guns, built in 1556 by Edward Bright, and in 1588 she was at the battle of the Armada. She was then rebuilt in 1589 and became 596 tons and was altered to the form of a galleon. In 1590 she was the flagship of Sir John Hawkins; at the expedition to and the capture of Cadiz on 21st June, 1596; in 1597 to the Islands (Azores) voyage; in 1599 in the general mobilization against the threat of Spanish invasion, at Leveson and Monson's expedition to the coast of Spain; and in 1618 was made into a wharf at Chatham.

Following her was a third rate of 394 tons and 26 guns, built in 1623 by Wm. Russell at Deptford. In 1625 she was in the Cadiz Expedition, and in 1650 was wrecked on the coast of Flanders.

A fourth rate of 566 tons and 40 guns named the *Maidstone* was built at Woodbridge in 1654 and renamed the *Mary Rose* in 1660. This vessel served in the Second Dutch War in 1665-7 and was at the Battle of Lowestoft, the Four Days' Fight, and the St. James's Day Fight. Captain John Kempthorne in the *Mary Rose* saved a convoy from an Algerine squadron of seven ships on 29th December, 1669, when they attacked him off Cadiz, beating them off after a severe action of four hours. The *Mary Rose* was very much damaged, and her captain was knighted for this very gallant action. Her battle honours show that she was at the third Dutch war, and in 1691 on 12th July she was taken by a French squadron when going with a convoy to the West Indies.

There was a destroyer called the *Mary Rose* of 1,010 tons and armed with three 4-inch guns. She was completed by Swan Hunter in 1916 and was at the battle of Jutland. In July, 1917, she began duty with Norwegian convoys. On 17th October, 1917, the Norwegian west-bound convoy was attacked by the German

H.M.S. MARY ROSE—*continued*

cruisers *Bremse* and *Brummer*, seventy miles east of Lerwick. The escorting destroyers *Mary Rose* and *Strongbow* were sunk, together with nine ships of the convoy.

The present *Mary Rose* is a fleet minesweeper of the *Algerine* class (ex *Toronto*), built by the Redfern Construction Company.

In the Cathedral Church of St. Thomas à Becket, Portsmouth, on Thursday, 7th November, 1929, a model of the fourth *Mary Rose* was dedicated as a lasting memorial of the heroes innumerable who through the seventeenth and eighteenth centuries and the early part of the nineteenth were certified as having made their Communion at that church before taking over their various commands in the King's ships, and more especially to commemorate those gallant men who lost their lives in the five successive men-of-war called by the name of *Mary Rose*.

H.M.S. MATAPAN

Description of Badge

FIELD: Barry wavy of ten white and blue.

BADGE: Within a laurel wreath proper a shakefork black.

MOTTO:

The badge is derived from the arms of Sir Andrew Cunningham, Commander-in-Chief at the battle.

No battle honours are recorded for this name.

This vessel is a destroyer of the *Battle* class, and was built at Clydebank. They are of 2,315 tons and the leaders of this class are of 2,325 tons. The main armament of the ship consists of five 4.5-inch guns. Her speed is 34 knots and she was launched in 1945.

H.M.S. MATCHLESS

Description of Badge

FIELD: Blue.

BADGE: In front of an estoile gold a plate charged with the astronomical mark of Saturn black.

MOTTO:

The badge is derived from the symbol of Saturn owing to the planet being known to astronomers as the Matchless Planet.

BATTLE HONOURS
Ostend	1918	April 23rd.
Belgian Coast	1916-1918	
Malta Convoys	1942	
Arctic	1942-44	
North Cape	1943	December 26th.

The *Matchless* is a destroyer of the *Laforey* class, and was built in 1939.

H.M.S. MAURITIUS

Description of Badge
FIELD: White. In chief and base a bar wavy blue.

BADGE: A key erect ward downwards red, surmounting the bar in chief and two branches of sugar-cane in saltire proper.

MOTTO:

The badge is derived from the arms of Mauritius.

BATTLE HONOURS

Atlantic	1941	
Sicily	1943	July 10th—August 17th.
Salerno	1943	September 9th—October 6th.
Mediterranean	1943-4	
Anzio	1944	January 22nd—31st.
Normandy	1944	June 6th—July 3rd.
Biscay	1944	
Norway	1945	

This vessel is a cruiser of the *Fiji* class and is of 8,000 tons, her armament being mainly twelve 6-inch and eight 4-inch guns. She was built by Swan Hunter and was completed in 1940. Her war service in the Second World War is shown in her lengthy battle honours.

H.M.S. MEDWAY

Description of Badge
FIELD: Silver.

BADGE: A lion black upon a bridge red.

MOTTO: *In Medio Tutissimus* (Midway (Medway) you will be safest).

The badge is derived from part of the arms and seal of the Rochester Bridge Commissioners, 1598.

BATTLE HONOURS
Quebec	1759	September 13th.
Ushant	1781	December 12th.

The *Medway* was a depot ship for submarines and was built by Vickers, being completed in 1929. Her displacement was 15,000 tons. She was torpedoed by a U-boat off Alexandria on 30th June, 1942.

H.M.S. MELBOURNE

Description of Badge

Shield light blue, red cross with crown and star gold in centre. First quarter, a lamb gold; fourth quarter, a sailing ship and sea proper; second quarter, a black swan; third quarter, a bull proper. Crest a wreath and kangaroo proper. Surrounded by wattle sprays, green tied with a bow. Scroll blue, gold edged, white lettering. Name of ship in red.

From the arms of Melbourne.

BATTLE HONOUR

Norway   1940

This vessel was an Australian cruiser of 5,600 tons and capable of a speed of 25½ knots. She carried eight 6-inch, one 3-inch and fifteen smaller guns, also two torpedo tubes. She was built in 1913. On completion of her service she was sold to the Alloa Shipbuilding Company Ltd., Greenock, for £2,500, and was broken up at Birkenhead. Her original cost was £405,000.

There was a *Melbourne* of 466 tons gross (a trawler), sunk by enemy aircraft off Narvik, Norway.

Present *Melbourne*, Royal Australian Navy aircraft carrier (ex *Majestic*), and was launched at Barrow in 1945.

H.M.S. MERMAID

Description of Badge
FIELD: Blue.

BADGE: On water barry wavy in base white and blue a mermaid proper.

MOTTO:

The badge is in allusion to the name.

		BATTLE HONOURS
Cadiz	1596	June 21st.
Dover	1652	May 19th.
Gabbard	1653	June 2nd—3rd.
Porto Farina	1655	April 4th.
Belgian Coast	1914-17	
Arctic	1944	

The *Mermaid* was a sloop of the modified *Black Swan* class, built by Denny Bros., the tonnage of the class varying from 1,430 to 1,490, and they carried six 4-inch dual-purpose guns. She was launched in 1943.

H.M.S. MILNE

Description of Badge
FIELD: Blue.

BADGE: A cross moline gold.

MOTTO:

The badge is derived from the arms of Admiral Milne.

BATTLE HONOURS

Dogger Bank	1915	January 24th.
Belgian Coast	1916	
North Africa	1942	
Atlantic	1942-3	
Arctic	1942-44	

The *Milne* is a destroyer of the *Laforey* class, and was built by Scott's. Her displacement tonnage is 1,935 and she was launched in 1941.

H.M.S. MONARCH

Description of Badge

A shield whose field is blue, gold edged, having sceptres in saltire on the centre of which is an orb, in chief a crown, three fleur-de-lis, all gold. Underneath a scroll red, with the name of the ship in white.

Badge in allusion to the Monarch.

BATTLE HONOURS

St. Vincent	1780	January 16th.
St. Kitts	1782	January 25th—26th.
The Saints	1782	April 12th.
Cape of Good Hope	1795	September 16th.
Camperdown	1797	October 11th.
Copenhagen	1801	April 2nd.
Baltic	1854	
Alexandria	1882	July 11th.
South Africa	1899-1900	
Jutland	1916	May 31st.

Monarch was a battleship (super-*Dreadnought*) of 22,500 tons, launched on the Tyne on 30th March, 1911. As she was passing down the river a very interesting incident occurred; all the boys on the *Wellesley* training ship swarmed the rigging of their ship and sang the National Anthem, accompanied by their band. She was sold in 1925.

H.M.S. MOON

Description of Badge
FIELD: Blue.

BADGE: Issuant from water in base barry wavy white and black a moon gold.

MOTTO:

The badge is in allusion to the name.

BATTLE HONOURS
Armada	1588	July 21st—29th. Queen's ship.
Cadiz	1596	June 21st. Queen's ship.
Jutland	1916	May 31st.

The *Moon* is an *Algerine* class of fleet minesweeper, built by the Redfern Construction Company, and she carries one 4-inch dual-purpose and some smaller guns and was built in Canada in 1943, (ex H.M.C.S. *Mimico*).

H.M.S. MUSKETEER

Description of Badge
FIELD: White.

BADGE: A demi-marine of 1805 affrontee proper.

MOTTO:

The badge is in allusion to the name.

	BATTLE HONOURS	
Arctic	1942-44	
North Cape	1943	December 26th.
Atlantic	1943	
Ægean	1944	

The *Musketeer* is a destroyer of the *Laforey* class of 1,920 tons, and was built by Fairfield in 1941. Her main armament consists of six 4.7-inch guns.

H.M.S. MYNGS

Description of Badge
FIELD: Red.

BADGE: Four naval cutlasses in saltire proper, pommels and hilts gold.

MOTTO:

	BATTLE HONOURS	
Zeebrugge	1918	April 23rd.
Norway	1944	
Arctic	1944-5	

This badge serves to symbolize the many actions in which Myngs fought. When killed in battle he was Vice-Admiral of the Red.

The *Myngs* is a destroyer of the *Zambesi* class, and is a leader of 1,730 tons, built by Vickers-Armstrongs in 1943.

H.M.S. NAPIER

Description of Badge

FIELD: White a fess wavy blue.

BADGE: A saltire engrailed red surmounted by a crescent white, within the horns a rose red.

MOTTO:

The badge is derived from the arms of the Napier family.

	BATTLE HONOURS	
Crete	1941	May 20th—June 1st.
Libya	1941	
Burma	1944-5	
Okinawa	1945	March 26th—May 25th.

The *Napier* is a destroyer which gave her name to the class. She was built in 1941 and transferred to the Royal Australian Navy. Her tonnage was 1,695 and she was a leader. Was used later for anti-submarine training. She was sold in 1955.

H.M.S. NATAL

Description of Badge

An elaborate badge in which the field is gold, the animals (Wildebeeste) proper. Above is a variation of the Royal Arms; below, a scroll blue with the name of the ship red. The badge is that of Natal in South Africa.

BATTLE HONOUR
North Sea   1945

This ship was an armoured cruiser of 13,550 tons. She was built in 1905 at Barrow, and sunk by an internal explosion at Cromarty Firth, 31st December, 1915.

H.M.S. NELSON

Description of Badge
FIELD: White.

BADGE: A lion rampant regardant holding in his paw a palm branch all proper.

MOTTO: *Palmam Qui Meruit Ferat* (Let him bear the palm who has deserved it).

The ship was named after Admiral Lord Nelson, and the badge adapted from one of the supporters of the arms of Nelson.

BATTLE HONOURS

Malta Convoys	1941-2	
North Africa	1942-3	
Sicily	1943	July 10th—August 17th.
Salerno	1943	September 9th—October 6th.
Mediterranean	1943	
Normandy	1944	June 5th—July 3rd.

The *Nelson* was a battleship of 33,950 tons displacement and carried nine 16-inch, twelve 6-inch and six 4.7-inch A.A. guns. The main armament was grouped forward, giving her a rather unusual appearance. In the Second World War *Nelson* was both mined and torpedoed. She and her sister the *Rodney* were the first British warships to mount 16-inch guns. She was sold in 1948 and broken up at Inverkeithing.

H.M.S. NEPAL

Description of Badge

FIELD: Barry wavy of six white and blue.

BADGE: A kukri and a trident in saltire white, in front of the centre prong of the trident a crescent gold, in chief a star of seven points also gold.

MOTTO:

The badge is derived from the arms of Nepal.

	BATTLE HONOURS	
Burma	1944-5	
Okinawa	1945	March 26th—May 25th.

The *Nepal* (ex *Norseman*) was built during the Second World War, and is a destroyer carrying six 4.7-inch guns as her main armament. She was built by Thornycroft and was completed in 1942. She was lent to Royal Australian Navy and sold in 1955.

H.M.S. NEWCASTLE

Unofficial Badge: This badge was carried by H.M.S. *Newcastle*, a light cruiser of 4,800 tons. Shield red, gold edged, castles in white, black lined. Blue scroll with gold letters H.M.S. NEWCASTLE.

Official Badge
FIELD: Red.

BADGE: A triple-towered castle silver.

MOTTO: *Fortitudine Vinco* (By strength I conquer).

The badge is from the Newcastle arms and motto.

	BATTLE	HONOURS
Porto Farina	1655	April 4th.
Santa Cruz	1657	April 20th.
Lowestoft	1665	June 3rd.
Orfordness	1666	July 25th.

H.M.S. NEWCASTLE—continued

Schooneveld	1673	May 28th—June 4th.
Texel	1673	August 11th.
Marbella	1705	March 10th.
Sadras	1758	April 29th.
Negapatam	1758	August 3rd.
Porto Novo	1759	September 10th.
Spartivento	1940	November 27th.
Burma	1944-5	

The first *Newcastle* was a fourth rate of 641 tons and 54 guns, and was built at Ratcliffe in 1653. She sailed from Plymouth under Blake for the Mediterranean on 29th October, 1654, and on 4th April, 1655, she led the frigates in the attack carried out by Blake on the Tunisian Fleet at Porto Farina. In 1657 she was at the attack on Santa Cruz, and in 1693 she was one of the Anglo-Dutch fleet of twenty-two sail under Sir George Rooke which, whilst acting as escort to the Smyrna convoy of 400 merchantmen, beat off an attack by a French fleet of eighty sail. In 1695 she was one of a small squadron which captured the French *Trident* (42) and *Content* (54) between Pantellaria and Sicily; and in 1703, on 27th November, when lying at Spithead, was one of 12 British men-of-war which foundered during one of the worst storms on record and lost, out of her complement of 233 men, 193 men.

Following her was another fourth rate of 676 tons and 50 guns. This vessel was in one of the combined fleets under Sir John Leake which defeated a French attempt to retake Gibraltar on 9th March, 1705. The whole of the enemy force, consisting of five sail of the line, was captured or driven ashore. On 3rd June, 1711, she engaged a French flotilla which consisted of a 36-gun ship and twelve smaller vessels with 2,000 men on board preparing for an attack on Antigua off St. Pierre, Martinique; the French force was smashed and driven back to St. Pierre. In 1732 she was rebuilt at Woolwich, and in 1746 broken up at Portsmouth.

H.M. Dockyard at Portsmouth launched a fourth rate of this name of 1,052 tons and 50 guns on 4th December, 1750. She took part in Pocock's action against the French off Cuddalore, and after the battle her captain, George Legge, was court-martialled for not giving sufficient support to the Admiral and was cashiered. On 3rd August, 1758, was at Pocock's action with Comte d'Ache

H.M.S. NEWCASTLE—continued

off Negapatam, her captain being the Hon. James Colville; at Pondicherry in 1759, in which her captain, Colin Michie, was killed. In 1761 she was captained by Richard Collins, and whilst engaged on the seizure of Pondicherry a violent hurricane swept down on the fleet and she became a total wreck.

There was another fourth rate of the name of 1,556 tons and 50 guns launched at Blackwall on 10th November, 1813. This vessel was specially built for coping with the large American frigates such as the *Constitution* and *President*. In 1814, in company with the *Leander* (50) and *Acasta* (50), she captured the privateer *Prince de Neufchatel* (American); and in 1816 the *Newcastle*, Captain Henry Meynell, arrived at St. Helena bearing the flag of Sir Pulteney Malcolm as Commander-in-Chief, and was especially appointed to enforce a rigid blockade of the island and to keep a close guard on Napoleon. She also brought out the commission appointed by Austria, Russia and France to reside at St. Helena during the captivity of Napoleon. In 1824 she was fitted as a lazaretto at Milford, in 1827 she was removed to Liverpool for a similar service, and in 1850 was sold for breaking up.

A screw frigate of 4,020 tons and 31 guns carried the name of *Newcastle* and was commissioned in 1874 at Sheerness for service in the detached squadron for particular service (Flying Service). Admiral Jellicoe commenced his sea career in this ship as a naval cadet. The squadron attended H.R.H. the Prince of Wales (King Edward VII) upon his visit to India in 1875, and afterwards the squadron visited Japan. In 1889 she was loaned to the War Department for service as a powder hulk at Devonport, and in 1929 was sold for breaking up.

In 1909, on 25th March, Armstrong Whitworths launched a second-class protected cruiser of 4,800 tons named the *Newcastle*. This vessel was sent to strengthen the force at Esquimault on 11th August, 1914, and in December cruised to Valparaiso, assisting in the search for the German armed merchant cruiser *Prinz Eitel Frederich*. She returned to England in 1919 after service from 1916 in the Adriatic and Mediterranean, and in 1929 was sold to Messrs. T. W. Ward for breaking up.

The present *Newcastle* (ex *Minotaur*) is a cruiser of the *Southampton* class of 9,100 tons and carrying as her main armament nine 6-inch and eight 4-inch guns.

H.M.S. NEWFOUNDLAND

Description of Badge
FIELD: White.

BADGE: Upon a mountain an elk statant proper.

MOTTO:

The badge is derived from the crest of Newfoundland.

BATTLE HONOURS
Sicily 1943 July 10th—August 17th.
Mediterranean 1943

This vessel is a cruiser of the *Uganda* class, and her displacement is 8,000 tons. Her armament consists mainly of nine 6-inch and ten 4-inch A.A. guns. She was built by Swan Hunter and was completed in 1942. She served at Sicily and in the Mediterranean.

H.M.S. NEW ZEALAND

Description of Badge

Oval field gold, royal crown in centre and the letters N Z blue on either side of crown. Above a scroll blue and gold with the name of the ship in white letters.

In allusion to the ship and the crown.

BATTLE HONOURS
Heligoland	1914	August 28th.
Dogger Bank	1915	January 24th.
Jutland	1916	May 31st.

This ship was a battle-cruiser of 18,000 tons. When this vessel was on a cruise to the Dominion a number of Maori chiefs were shown over her, and Sir Lionel Halsey (Admiral), who was in command, was given a Kiwi cloak and greenstone Tiki to wear if ever the ship went into action. He did this, much to the surprise of his officers and men, in action off Heligoland. He passed the robe on to Captain (late Admiral) Sir John Green, who wore it at Jutland. She was built in 1911 at Govan and sold in 1922.

H.M.S. NIGERIA

Description of Badge

FIELD: Barry wavy of six white and blue.

BADGE: Within two interlaced triangles green the imperial crown proper.

MOTTO:

The badge is derived from that of Nigeria.

	BATTLE HONOURS	
Norway	1941	
Sabang	1944	July 25th.
Burma	1944-5	
Atlantic	1941	
Malta Convoys	1942	
Arctic	1942	

This vessel is a cruiser of the *Fiji* class and is of 8,000 tons and carries as its main armament twelve 6-inch and eight 4-inch A.A. guns. She was completed in 1940 by Vickers-Armstrongs on the Tyne. Her service during the Second World War was widespread. She was sold to India in 1954.

H.M.S. NIZAM

Description of Badge
FIELD: White.

BADGE: In front of two bars wavy blue a quatrefoil white, charged with a demi-tiger erased proper.

MOTTO:

The badge is derived from the arms of the Nizam of Hyderabad.

BATTLE HONOURS
Malta Convoys	1941	
Crete	1941	May 20th—June 1st.
Libya	1941	
Okinawa	1945	March 26th—May 25th.

Nizam was built at Clydebank as a destroyer of the *Javelin* class and was completed in 1941. She was lent to the Royal Australian Navy during the Second World War, returning in 1945 to the Royal Navy, and was sold in 1955.

H.M.S. NOBLE

Description of Badge
FIELD: Blue.

BADGE: On water barry wavy white and blue in base the lymphad with armed figure reverse of the coin. Noble gold.

The badge is derived as given above, from a coin.

BATTLE HONOUR
Jutland   1916   May 31st.

The *Noble* (ex *Piorun—Nerissa*) was a destroyer of the *Javelin* class and her tonnage was 1,760, being built at Clydebank. She was completed in 1941 and spent some time under the Polish flag during the Second World War. The armament was six 4.7-inch guns. She was sold later on.

There was another *Noble* lent to the Royal Netherlands Navy and renamed *Van Galen*.

H.M.S. NORMAN

Description of Badge
FIELD: Blue.

BADGE: A Norman helmet proper, garnished gold.

MOTTO: *Cedere Nescio* (I know not how to yield).

The badge is in allusion to the name.

BATTLE HONOURS
Burma	1944-5	
Okinawa	1945	March 26th—May 25th.

The *Norman* is a destroyer of the *Napier* class of 1,690 tons, carrying six 4.7-inch and one 4-inch A.A. guns, built by Thornycroft. She was completed in 1941 and transferred to the R.A.N. She was returned in 1945 and sold in 1955.

H.M.S. NUBIAN

Unofficial Badge: The head of a Nubian in proper colours. A naval crown above. The scroll underneath is red with H.M.S. NUBIAN in black letters.

Official Badge

FIELD: Barry wavy of six white and blue.

BADGE: The head of a Nubian in profile proper.

MOTTO:

BATTLE HONOURS

Belgian Coast	1914-15	
Norway	1940	
Calabria	1940	
Mediterranean	1940-41-43.	
Libya	1940	
Matapan	1941	March 28th—29th.
Sfax	1941	April 15th—16th.
Greece	1941	April 24th—29th.
Crete	1941	May 26th—June 1st.
Malta Convoys	1941	
Sicily	1943	July 10th—August 17th.
Salerno	1943	September 9th—October 6th.
Arctic	1944	
Burma	1944-5	

This vessel was a torpedo boat destroyer, built by Thornycroft and launched in 1909. In 1916 on 27th October she was torpedoed in the Straits of Dover whilst in action with German destroyers.

H.M.S. NUBIAN—*continued*

Her bows were blown off, but the rest of the ship was salved and taken into port. Her sister ship, the *Zulu*, had her stern blown off and the two parts were joined together. This composite vessel was then renamed *Zubian*.

The last *Nubian* was built at Thornycroft's at Woolston, Southampton, and completed in 1938, 1,870 tons displacement, and her main armament was six 4.7-inch guns.

H.M.S. OBEDIENT

Description of Badge
FIELD: Blue.

BADGE: A sea-dog sejant proper collared gold.

MOTTO:

The badge is in allusion to the name.

BATTLE HONOURS
Jutland	1916	May 31st.
Barents Sea	1942	December 31st.
Arctic	1942-44	
Atlantic	1943	
Normandy	1944	June 6th—July 3rd.

The *Obedient* is a destroyer of the *Onslow* class and was built by Denny Bros. This class was the first to be built under the war construction programme. She did some very useful work during the Second World War, especially on one occasion when a convoy to Russia was being attacked by a German force which included the *Hipper*.

H.M.S. OBDURATE

Description of Badge
FIELD: Blue.

BADGE: A mule statant white.

MOTTO:

The badge is in allusion to the name.

BATTLE HONOURS
Jutland	1916	May 31st.
Barents Sea	1942	December 31st.
Atlantic	1943	
Arctic	1942-45	

This vessel is a destroyer of the *Onslow* class and was built by Denny Bros. She was, in company with other destroyers, protecting a convoy to Russia and helped to beat off an attack by heavier units of the German fleet, in the Arctic phase of her war service.

H.M.S. OCEAN

Description of Badge
FIELD: Blue.

BADGE: Issuant from water barry wavy in base white and blue a representation of Neptune white.

MOTTO:

The badge is in allusion to the name, showing as it does Neptune, King of the Ocean.

BATTLE HONOURS
Ushant	1781	December 12th.
Suez Canal	1915	February 2nd—4th.
Dardanelles	1915	

The first *Ocean* in the Royal Navy was a three-decker of 98 guns, built in 1761 in memory of how Boscawen, "Old Dreadnought," beat the French at Lagos and destroyed one of the two finest flagships in the French Navy, *L'Ocean* of 80 guns.

The second *Ocean* was a man-of-war of 98 guns, launched in 1805. From 1806 until 1809 she was in service as the flagship of Admiral Collingwood in the Mediterranean.

One of our earliest broadside ironclads also bore this name, and this vessel was built in 1863. Following her was a first-class battleship which was launched at Devonport on 5th July, 1898.

The present *Ocean* is an aircraft carrier of the *Colossus* class of 13,190 tons, and was completed in 1945. She has done very good service in the war in Korea.

H.M.S. OPPORTUNE

Description of Badge
FIELD: Blue.

BADGE: An hour-glass gold.

MOTTO: *Felix opportunitate pungæ.*

The badge is in allusion to the name.

BATTLE HONOURS

North Africa	1942	
North Cape	1943	December 26th.
Normandy	1944	June 6th—July 3rd.
Atlantic	1943	
Arctic	1942-45	

The *Opportune* is one of the *Onslow* class of destroyers of 1,540 tons, and was completed in 1942, having been built by Thornycroft. She carried two 4-inch and smaller guns.

H.M.S. ORION

Unofficial Badge: This badge was carried by H.M.S. *Orion*, a 22,500 ton battleship (super-*Dreadnought*). Field gold, figure of Orion in proper colours, lettering and dates black.

Official Badge
FIELD: Black.

BADGE: A half-length figure in semi-classical dress, holding a sword.

MOTTO: *Orb Circumcinto* (Over the World).

Badge derived from a figurehead carried by a previous ship of the name. (1789-1814).

H.M.S. ORION—continued

BATTLE HONOURS

First of June	1794	June 1st (and May 28th—29th).
Groix Island	1795	June 23rd.
St. Vncent	1797	February 14th.
Nile	1798	August 1st.
Trafalgar	1805	October 21st.
Baltic	1855	
Jutland	1916	May 31st.
Atlantic	1939	
Mediterranean	1940-43-4	
Calabria	1940	July 9th.
Malta Convoys	1941	
Matapan	1941	March 28th—29th.
Greece	1941	April 24th—29th.
Crete	1941	May 20th—June 1st.
Sicily	1943	July 10th—August 17th.
Salerno	1943	September 9th—October 6th.
Ægean	1944	
Anzio	1944	January 22nd—31st.
Normandy	1944	June 6th—July 3rd.
South France	1944	August 15th—27th.

This vessel is a cruiser of the *Leander* class, and her tonnage was 7,215, carrying as her main armament eight 6-inch and eight 4-inch A.A. guns. She was built at Devonport and completed in 1934. Her battle honours show the scope of her work in the Second World War. This vessel was sold in 1948. The name was given to the Reserve Fleet at Plymouth.

H.M.S. OROTAVA

Unofficial Badge: A triangle on which is a castle (single tower) on a wreath and the words H.M.S. OROTAVA. Colours not known. The triangle represents Mt. Teneriffe, on which half-way up is situated Orotava Castle. The ship was named after this place in 1899.

This vessel has no battle honours recorded.

The *Orotava* was a Royal Mail Steam Packet Company's liner, built in 1899, of 5,940 tons and capable of 14 knots. She was requisitioned as an armed merchant cruiser in December, 1914, and armed with five 6-inch and two 6-pounder guns. She was then converted into a seaplane carrier, and was released from service in 1919.

H.M.S. ORWELL

Description of Badge
FIELD: White.

BADGE: A sea-horse proper holding between the feet a roundell barry wavy blue and gold.

MOTTO:

The badge has been derived from the arms of Ipswich.

BATTLE HONOURS
Barents Sea	1942	December 31st.
Atlantic	1943	
Arctic	1942-45	
Normandy	1944	June 6th—July 3rd.
Norway	1945	

The *Orwell* is one of the limited conversion class of destroyers changed to an anti-submarine frigate. Her tonnage is 1,540, and she was completed at Thornycroft's in 1942.

H.M.S. OSEA

Unofficial Badge: This badge shows the devil afloat in an egg-shell with a sextant held up. Taken from Rudyard Kipling's poem. The devil is blue, the sea blue, and the sextant yellow and black.

No battle honours are recorded.

H.M.S. *Osea* was a shore establishment and base for motor launches and coastal motor boats on Osea Island in the River Blackwater, Essex. Paid off in 1919.

H.M.S. OWEN

Description of Badge

FIELD: Barry wavy of eight white and blue.

BADGE: A stag's head erased white, the antlers red, gorged with a naval crown gold.

MOTTO:

The badge is derived from the Owen crest.

There are no battle honours recorded for this name.

Survey vessel built at Aberdeen and completed at Chatham on conversion in 1949, of 1,640 tons (ex *Thurso Bay*, ex *Loch Muick*).

H.M.S. PACTOLUS

Description of Badge

Black shield, white and gold edged, thin red cross. In first quarter a submarine white; fourth quarter, three torpedoes white; second quarter, a mouse white; third quarter, a mouse white. A scroll red with letters black.

In allusion to the duties of the ship.

No battle honours are recorded for this vessel.

This ship was a depot ship for submarines, of 2,135 tons.

She was formerly a third-class cruiser built in 1896 and sold in 1921.

H.M.S. PALADIN

Description of Badge
FIELD: Blue.

BADGE: A sword erect white, pommel and hilt gold enfiled with two spurs in saltire also gold.

MOTTO:

Derived from the name paladin given to the peers of Charlemagne and also to medieval knights and heroes.

BATTLE HONOURS

Diego Suarez	1942	May 5th—7th.
Mediterranean	1943	
Sicily	1943	July 10th—August 17th.
Burma	1944-5	

The *Paladin* is one of the limited conversion class of destroyer changed into an anti-submarine frigate. Her tonnage is 1,540, and she was built by John Brown, completing in 1941.

H.M.S. PATUCA

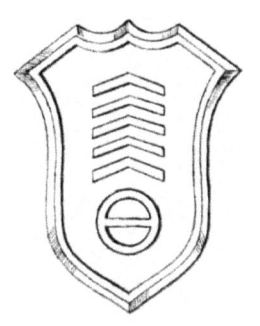

Unofficial Badge: A shield on which is placed five chevrons and a circle having a bar horizontally placed across the centre. Colours not known.

No battle honours are recorded for this vessel.

The *Patuca* was a liner belonging to Elders and Fyffes, a "banana boat." She was built in 1913, and commissioned as an armed merchant cruiser in December, 1914, being armed then with six 6-inch and two 3-pounders. This vessel was capable of a speed of 16 knots. Released from Admiralty service in December, 1918, and returned to her owners.

H.M.S. PEGASUS

Description of Badge

FIELD: Blue.

BADGE: A winged horse rampart gold.

MOTTO: Excelsior (Higher).

The badge is derived from Greek mythology, Pegasus being the winged steed which was created by Poseidon from the blood of the Medusa, for once upon a time, when the Gorgon Medusa was young and beautiful, Poseidon loved her.

BATTLE HONOURS

St. Vincent	1780	January 16th.
First of June	1794	June 1st (and May 28th—29th.)
Egypt	1801	March 8th—September 2nd.
Atlantic	1941	

The *Pegasus* (ex *Ark Royal*) was built by the Blyth Shipbuilding Co. Ltd. and purchased during 1914. Her displacement was 6,900 tons, and she was used as a seaplane carrier and for experimental air work.

H.M.S. PELICAN

Description of Badge

FIELD: Green.

BADGE: Upon water in base barry wavy white and blue a pelican proper.

MOTTO: What I have I hold.

Badge in allusion to the name.

BATTLE HONOURS

Armada	1588	July 21st—29th. Victualler to the Westward.
Kentish Knock	1652	September 28th.
Portland	1653	February 18th—20th.
Gabbard	1653	June 2nd—3rd.
Scheveningen	1653	July 31st.
Quebec	1759	September 13th.
St. Lucia	1778	December 15th.
St. Lucia	1796	May 24th.
Jutland	1916	May 31st.
Norway	1940	
North Africa	1942	
Normandy	1944	June 6th—to July 3rd.
Atlantic	1942-44	
English Channel	1944	
"Argus"	1813	Single ship action.

The first vessel to bear this name was of 150 tons and appeared about the time 1577-1580. She is famous for her voyage round

H.M.S. PELICAN—continued

the world made by Drake, and she was renamed the *Golden Hind*. On her return Queen Elizabeth ordered that she be preserved for ever and she was placed in a dock filled with earth at Deptford. Although she did not last "for ever" she was preserved for almost a hundred years.

There was a hired ship employed as a victualler bearing the name of *Pelican* in the Armada campaign, 1588.

Then there was a frigate of 60 tons and 12 guns, which probably came into the service by way of being a prize in the year 1647. In June, 1648, in the Civil War she was one of the ships carried off to join the Royalist Squadron in Holland.

A fourth rate of 500 tons carried the name, her armament being 34-42 guns. No date is given for the building of this ship, but it was launched before 1650. In November of that year she sailed with Penn for the Mediterranean in pursuit of Prince Rupert. Her battle honours show that she fought at various engagements from 1652 to 1653, and in February, 1656, was accidentally burnt at Portsmouth.

In January, 1653, a prize apparently having been taken by the *Tiger* had this name, and she was on convoy duties.

Then there was a fire-ship of 200 tons which was taken from the French by Sir Cloudesley Shovel in Dublin Bay on 17th April, 1690. She was then bought for the Royal Navy. On August 26th, 1692, she was made into a breakwater at Sheerness.

A bomb vessel of 234 tons and 8 guns had this name and was built at Shoreham or Topsham in 1754 as the *St. George* merchantman. She was bought at Shoreham in April, 1757, for the Royal Navy and renamed *Pelican*. She took part in the expedition to Quebec in 1759, and was sold in 1763.

In 1776 a schooner was bought at Antigua of 150 tons and with an armament of 8-10 guns and named *Pelican*. She was with Barrington's Squadron in 1778, and sold at Antigua in 1779.

The next was a sixth rate of 514-520 tons and 14-24 guns. This vessel was launched on the Thames on 24th April, 1777, and in August, 1781, was lost in a hurricane in Jamaica.

Then came the *Pelican*, a brig sloop of 202 tons and 18 guns, about which there seems to be a little indefinite information, for she may have been purchased in 1781 or launched at Plymouth in 1782. She was, however, sold at Deptford in 1783.

H.M.S. PELICAN—continued

A brig of 365 tons and 18 guns bore the name and was launched on the Thames on 17th June, 1795. She was at the capture of St. Lucia in 1796, and on 3rd September in the same year she was in an action with the French *Medee* (36) in the West Indies, and after a close action of two hours the Frenchman broke off the engagement. On 17th September, 1797, in company with the *Severn* (44), she sank the French privateer *Trompeur* (12) and captured the French *Republique Triomphante* (14) in the West Indies. In 1806 she was sold at Jamaica.

The *Voltiguer* taken from the French in 1806 was a brig sloop of 328 tons and 18 guns and named the *Pelican*, being eventually sold at Deptford in 1812.

Another brig sloop of 385 or 382 tons and 18 guns given the name of *Pelican* was launched at Topsham in August, 1812. This vessel captured the U.S. brig *Argus*, for which a medal was given, and in 1827 she was engaged in the suppression of piracy in the Levant. From 1839 to 1842 she was in the operations in China, and from 1847 to 1864 she was a Customs watch vessel at Rye, being sold there in 1865.

Now came a steam sloop called *Pelican* of 952 tons and 17 guns; she was launched on 19th July, 1860, at Pembroke, and in 1867 was sold to Arthur & Co.

The next *Pelican* was a composite screw sloop of 1,124 tons and her armament was two 6-inch and six 5-inch guns. She was launched at Devonport on 26th April, 1877, serving on various stations until sold in January, 1901, to the Hudson Bay Co.

The *Sir J. Jones* was built by Cox & Co., Falmouth, in 1880 as a special service vessel and given the name of *Pelican*; in 1906 taken over by the Navy from the War Department and employed as a tender to the Torpedo Depot at Malta. On 14th October, 1916, she was renamed *Petulant* and sold at Malta.

The torpedo boat destroyer *Pelican* of 1,005 tons and three 4-inch guns was launched at the Clyde yard of Beardmore's on 18th March, 1916. She served at the battle of Jutland and at operations in the North Sea, being sold in 1921.

The present *Pelican* is an escort vessel of 1,250 tons and armed with eight 4-inch dual-purpose guns, built by Thornycroft, employed surveying in the West Indies. In 1940 was very badly damaged by bombing in the Second World War.

H.M.S. PEMBROKE

Description of Badge

The badge of H.M.S. *Pembroke* (Royal Naval Barracks, Chatham) shows a naval crown of gold with red and green jewels. Issuing from it is a Commodore's broad pendant. The name ROYAL NAVAL BARRACKS CHATHAM in gold on blue and gold scroll.

BATTLE HONOURS

Lowestoft	1665	June 3rd.
Vigo	1702	October 12th.
Marbella	1705	March 10th.
Finisterre	1747	May 3rd.
Louisburg	1758	July 26th.
Quebec	1759	September 13th.
Havana	1762	August 13th.
Baltic	1855	April 17th—December.

The first ship to bear the name *Pembroke* was a fifth rate of 22 guns which was built at Woolwich in 1655, and this vessel was in service at the battle of Lowestoft in 1665. In 1667 she was in a collision and sank.

There was a *Pembroke* built at Deptford in 1689 which took part in an unsuccessful attempt on Martinique in 1693; later on, in 1694, she was captured by the French.

Another was built in 1694 and was a fourth rate of 60 guns. This vessel took part in the capture of ships in Vigo Bay laden with treasure. The action was under the command of Sir George

H.M.S. PEMBROKE—*continued*

Rooke, and it took place on 12th October, 1702. She was with Sir John Leake on 10th March, 1705, at the capture or destruction of a French squadron under Baron de Pointes; and when in company with the *Falcon* on 29th December, 1709, she was taken by a superior force of French vessels after a fierce action in which the captain of the *Pembroke* was amongst the heavy casualties.

The *Pembroke* which followed was a fourth rate of 50 guns built at Plymouth in 1710, and broken up at that port in 1726.

It was at Woolwich the next vessel to bear the name was built, and this took place in 1733. She was a fourth rate of 60 guns and took part in the victory by Anson over the French at Finisterre on 3rd May, 1747. The *Pembroke* took part in the blockade of Pondicherry in 1748, and was wrecked in the following year in a hurricane off Cuddalore.

Then another *Pembroke* came on the scene, being launched at Plymouth in 1757. She was a fourth rate of 60 guns. This vessel served at the reduction of Louisburg in 1758, the capture of Quebec in 1759, at the reduction of Havana in 1762, and in 1772 was converted into a hulk at Halifax, Nova Scotia, being broken up in 1793.

The next *Pembroke* was a third rate of 74 guns, launched at Blackwall in 1812 and converted into a screw steamship in 1855. She was in the Baltic campaign of 1855 and took part in the bombardment of Sveaborg, and after some years as a coastguard ship at Harwich she became flagship of the Commander-in-Chief the Nore in 1869. In 1873 she became reserve ship at Chatham, and in 1876 was the flagship of the Admiral Superintendent. In 1890, on being relieved by H.M.S. *Duncan*, she was renamed *Forte*, and then later changed her name to *Pembroke* again.

In 1891 the *Pembroke* was relieved by H.M.S. *Algiers* and was recommissioned for service as general depot at Chatham. Since then the name of *Pembroke* has been borne by Chatham Depot.

H.M.S. PENELOPE

Description of Badge
FIELD: Blue.
BADGE: A female head white.
MOTTO: *Constantia et Fide* (With constancy and faith).

The badge is derived from Greek mythology. Penelope was the wife of Odysseus and the mother of Telemachus. The story of the return voyage of Odysseus from the siege of Troy and of faith which Penelope had in his return is one of the most interesting in the tales from Greek mythology.

BATTLE HONOURS

Egypt	1801	March 8th—September 2nd.
Martinique	1809	February 24th.
Baltic	1854	
Alexandria	1882	July 11th.
South Africa	1899-1900	(entitled to medal but not battle honour).
Norway	1940	
Sirte	1942	March 22nd.
Sicily	1943	July 10th—August 17th.
Salerno	1943	September 9th—October 6th.
Ægean	1943	
Anzio	1944	January 22nd—31st.
Mediterranean	1941 and 1943	
Malta Convoys	1941-2	
"Guillaume Tell"	1800	Single ship action.

H.M.S. PENELOPE—*continued*

This vessel was a cruiser of 5,270 tons and carried six 6-inch and eight 4-inch A.A. guns. She was built in 1936, and during the Second World War had an exciting career. After one phase she was so full of holes from enemy attack that she was nicknamed the *Pepperpot*, finally being torpedoed inside the islands between Naples and Anzio on 18th February, 1944. The survivors from the sinking ship were picked up by L.S.Ts. which opened their doors and lowered the ramps down so that the men could get on—an example of quick appreciation of a tragic situation on the part of the L.S.T. commanding officers.

H.M.S. PERSEUS

Description of Badge

FIELD: Black.

BADGE: A dragon's head green and red pierced by a sword silver and gold.

MOTTO: *Fortiter* (Bravely).

Badge derived from Greek mythology. Perseus was the son of Zeus and Danæ. It was he who slayed the Medusa and also turned Atlas into a mountain. Andromeda, who was chained to a rock by her father as a sacrifice to a sea-monster, was rescued by Perseus, and she became the wife of Perseus. He also founded the Mycenæ.

No battle honours are recorded for this vessel.

The first *Perseus* was a sixth rate of 432 tons, built in 1776, and was present at the capture of Charleston in 1780. In 1789, whilst on the Lisbon station, she assisted in the capture of the Spanish ship *San Leon*, and in the same year was converted into a bomb vessel. In the year 1799 she served with Nelson in the Mediterranean and assisted at the blockade of Naples and Alexandria. During 1803 she made attacks on various vessels on the French coast, and in 1805 she was broken up at Sheerness.

There was another of the name of 522 tons and 22 guns, built at Sutton's Yard, Ringmore, in 1805. She served in the Mediterranean station and at Newfoundland. During the years 1818-1850 she was a receiving ship in London, stationed off the Tower. Later on broken up at Deptford.

H.M.S. PERSEUS—continued

The screw sloop *Perseus* of 955 tons and 15 guns was built at Pembroke and launched on 21st August, 1861. From 1863 to 1864 she was serving in the Japanese war, and was at the bombardment of Kagosima and at the forcing of the Straits of Simonoseki. In 1869 was in a punitive expedition against pirates' villages in Outingpoi Creek; 1886 found her fitted out as a tender to *Defiance* for instructional purposes with torpedoes, and in 1904 she was renamed *Defiance II*.

The Earle's Shipbuilding Co. launched a third-class protected cruiser of this name on 15th July, 1897, her tonnage being 2,135, and she carried eight 4-inch Q.F. guns. On her completion at Chatham in 1900 she was placed in reserve, and from 1901 to 1913 she saw service on the East Indies station, having engaged in the Somaliland operations 1902-1904. She was sold in 1914.

H.M.S. *Perseus*, a submarine of 1,475 tons, was launched at Barrow by Vickers-Armstrongs in 1929, and this vessel was lost in December, 1941.

The present *Perseus* was completed as an aircraft maintenance ship, having been built by Vickers-Armstrongs and launched on 26th February, 1944.

H.M.S. PETARD

Description of Badge

FIELD: Blue.

BADGE: A petard gold.

MOTTO:

The badge is in allusion to the name.

BATTLE HONOURS

Jutland	1916	May 31st.
Mediterranean	1942-3	
Sicily	1943	July 10th—August 17th.
Salerno	1943	September 9th—October 6th.
Ægean	1943	

The *Petard* (ex *Persistent*) is a destroyer of the *Onslow* class, and was built by Vickers-Armstrongs in 1941. This vessel has now been converted into an anti-submarine frigate.

H.M.S. PHOEBE

Description of Badge
FIELD: Blue.

BADGE: Over waves in base white and blue the moon proper.

MOTTO:

The badge is derived from Greek mythology. (1) The name of one of the Titanides, daughter of Uranus and Gaea. (2) Daughter of Zeus and Latona and the same as Artemis, Diana, Selene or Cynthia.

BATTLE HONOURS

Trafalgar	1805	October 21st.
Tamatave	1811	May 20th.
Java	1811	September 18th.
Benin	1897	February 8th—28th.
Zeebrugge	1918	April 23rd.
Belgian Coast	1917-18	
Greece	1941	April 24th—29th.
Crete	1941	May 20th—June 1st.
Malta Convoys	1942	
Ægean	1943	
Mediterranean	1944	
Sabang	1944	July 25th.
Burma	1944-5	
"Nereide"	1797	December 21st. Single ship action.
"Africaine"	1801	February 2nd. Single ship action.
"Essex"	1814	March 20th. Single ship action.

H.M.S. PHOEBE—continued

The first *Phoebe* was a fifth rate of 926 tons and 36 guns, built on the River Thames, and launched on 29th September, 1795. She took part in many operations and served with distinction. On 21st December, 1797, she captured the French 36-gun frigate *Nereide*, for which a naval medal was awarded; on 5th March, 1800, she captured the French privateer *Heureux* (22); on 19th February, 1801, she captured the French 40-gun frigate *Africaine*, for which a naval medal was awarded; on 21st October, 1805, she was at the Battle of Trafalgar; in July, 1806, she took part in operations north of Scotland for the protection of fisheries; at the capture of Mauritius on 29th November, 1810; in company with *Astrea*, *Galatea* and *Racehorse*, under Captain C. M. Schomberg, she was in an action off Madagascar with three French frigates, two of which were taken (naval medal awarded), August, 1811, at the capture of Java, and in action off Chili in company with *Cherub* (18) against the American frigate *Essex*, for which action a naval medal was awarded. In 1830 she became a "Slop" ship at Plymouth, and in 1841 was sold to Mr. J. Cristall.

The next *Phoebe* was a fourth rate of 2,044 tons and 50 guns, launched at Devonport on 12th April, 1854. In 1859 she was converted to a screw steamer of 2,896 tons and 30 guns, and in 1875 was sold to Messrs. Castle & Sons.

Following this vessel was a third-class cruiser of 2,575 tons and 8 guns, launched on 1st July, 1890, at Devonport. She served at the Benin River in 1894 under Rear-Admiral Bedford, and in 1897 under Rear-Admiral Rawson, being sold on 10th July, 1906, to Andrew J. Anderson, Copenhagen.

A torpedo boat destroyer of 1,044 tons and three 4-inch guns carried this name and was launched on 20th November, 1916, by Messrs. Fairfield & Co. In her Great War service she operated at Flanders Bight with the Harwich Forces and the blocking of Zeebrugge and Ostend. In November, 1921, she was sold to Messrs. J. Cashmore.

The present *Phoebe* is a cruiser of the *Dido* class and was built by Fairfield. Her service in the Second World War ranged from the Mediterranean to the Eastern theatres.

H.M.S. PIONEER

Description of Badge
FIELD: Blue.
BADGE: The badge of the Pioneer Corps, gold.
MOTTO:
In allusion to the name.

	BATTLE HONOURS
China	1856-60
Atlantic	1943

The first vessel to bear this name was built at Upnor in Kent, and was a schooner of 197 tons, the year being 1810. She served as a coastguard vessel, and was sold at Plymouth in 1849.

Then came a steamer (ex S.S. *Eider*) of 342 tons, purchased in 1850 for Arctic exploration. Foundered in the Arctic in 1854.

A screw gun vessel of 1,873 tons, built at Pembroke in 1856 and served in China in 1860, was another of the name.

The paddle river gunboat *Pioneer* of 142 tons was built at Rotherhithe for service on the River Zambesi and in 1860 served also in West African waters, and was sold in 1873 at Fernando Po.

There was a small steamer of this name hired in New Zealand for the Maori War in 1863.

The next *Pioneer* was a 6-gun composite steamer of 499 tons, built in 1874 at Sunderland, and served in West Africa at the blockade of Dahomey, 1876-7, and at the punitive expedition up the Niger river in 1879. She was sold and broken up in 1888.

Yarrow's built a *Pioneer* at Poplar in 1892 of 35 tons, and she was a screw river gunboat. This vessel was built in sections and

H.M.S. PIONEER—*continued*

shipped out to Lake Nyassa and re-erected at Fort Johnston, being commissioned in 1893. She was then in 1895 turned over to the British Central African Government.

There was a third-class protected cruiser of 2,000 tons launched at Chatham in 1899 given this name, and served first in the Mediterranean and then as a drill ship in Australian waters. She was then transferred to the Royal Australian Navy as a free gift and finally sold in 1926.

Two hired vessels had this name, one a small vessel hired in 1914 and another an armed motor yacht of 399 tons hired in 1915 and renamed *Pioneer II*.

During the 1939-45 war there was a *Pioneer* acting as a tender to the Manchester area, and her service earned the Atlantic 1943 honour.

The present *Pioneer* was laid down as a light aircraft carrier named H.M.S. *Mars*, of the *Colossus* class, but was altered during construction together with the *Perseus* and renamed. She was launched at Barrow-in-Furness by Vickers-Armstrongs in 1942, and sailed to the Far East in 1945 for attachment to the Fleet Train, as Commodore ship, Air Train, British Pacific Fleet. She was at Manus Island organizing when the Japanese surrendered and saw no active service, and was re-classified as a ferry carrier in May, 1953.

H.M.S. PORTIA

Description of Unofficial Badge: A circular plaque on which is representation of Portia from Shakespeare's "Merchant of Venice." Two circles of cabling surround the head, and in between are the words FIDELITY, WISDOM, JUSTICE and H.M.S. PORTIA. Colours not known.

The vessel has no battle honours recorded.

This badge is most likely from the torpedo boat destroyer *Portia*, built and commissioned during the Great War in 1916. She was sold in 1921.

H.M.S. PRIMROSE

Unofficial Badge: This is a circular badge surrounded by the familiar cabling. In the centre is a lion holding in its dexter paw a primrose. Underneath is the name of the ship. Colours not known.

This badge came from the crest of Lord Rosebery.

BATTLE HONOURS

Armada	1588	July 21st-29th (merchant ship of the City of London).
Armada	1588	July 21st—29th (*Primrose* of Harwich).
Cadiz	1596	June 21st.
North Sea	1942	
Normandy	1944	June 6th—July 3rd.
English Channel	1944	
Atlantic	1940-1-2-3-5	

This badge is most likely from the sloop *Primrose* which served in the Great War from 1915 to 1918. In April, 1922, this vessel was sold. There were also two auxiliary vessels during the war called *Primrose II* and *Primrose III*. During the Second World War there was also a corvette named *Primrose*. She was built at Renfrew and later on became a Norwegian whaler.

H.M.S. PRINCE OF WALES

Description of Badge
FIELD: White.

BADGE: On a red cross the badge of the Prince of Wales proper.

MOTTO:

It has been suggested that if the name of this ship is revived that a new badge should be designed, this one not being a very effective example.

BATTLE HONOURS

St. Lucia	1778	December 15th.
Groix Island	1795	June 23rd.
Dardanelles	1915	
"Bismarck"	1941	May 23rd—27th.
Malta Convoys	1941	

This vessel was one of the *King George V* class of battleships of 35,000 tons displacement, built by Cammell Laird & Co., and was lost when attacked by Japanese aircraft in 1941. She took part in the famous chase after the *Bismarck*.

H.M.S. PRINCESS ROYAL

Description of Badge

Royal cypher in red and crown of Sovereign's daughter. In allusion to name.

	BATTLE HONOURS	
Genoa	1795	March 14th.
Baltic	1854	
Crimea	1855	
Heligoland	1914	August 28th.
Dogger Bank	1915	January 24th.
Jutland	1916	May 31st.

This ship was a battle-cruiser of 26,350 tons. She was launched in 1911 at Barrow and was sold in 1923.

H.M.S. PROTECTOR

Description of Badge
FIELD: Red.

BADGE: A demi-gryphon gold.

MOTTO: Faith for duty.

Badge is derived from one of the crests of the Lord Protector of England, 1549, Edward, Duke of Somerset. His colours were red and gold.

BATTLE HONOURS

Sadras	1758	April 29th.
Negapatam	1758	August 3rd.
Cape of Good Hope	1806	January 18th.
China	1900	Entitled to medal, but did not land naval brigade nor take part in the capture of Taku Forts. Ineligible for battle honour.
Norway	1940	
Libya	1940-1	

This name was first given to a gun brig of 178 tons and 14 guns. She was launched at Brightlingsea on 1st February, 1805, and in 1806 took part in the capture of the Cape of Good Hope; in 1814 was fitted out as a survey vessel; from 1818 to 1830 was employed in surveying the east coast of England, being sold at Sheerness on 30th August, 1833, for breaking up.

H.M.S. PROTECTOR—*continued*

Then came a screw gunboat of 60 horsepower, ordered to be laid down at Portsmouth in 1862, but building was not proceeded with.

There was a ship of the East India Company which took part in the operations against Angria in 1756 and in Pocock's action with D'Ache off Pondicherry on 29th April, 1758.

A gunboat of 900 tons, built at Elswick in 1884, also bore this name; she was destined for South Australia and was in the service of the Commonwealth Government until 1921. She took part in the operations in China in 1900 and served in the Australian Navy during the Great War.

An auxiliary craft of this name was also commissioned for service with the Royal Navy during the Great War.

In 1780 there was a 28-gun ship captured from the Americans called the *Protector*, and which was subsequently added to the Royal Navy as the *Hussar*.

The present *Protector* is a net-laying and target-towing vessel similar to the *Guardian*, but handier and faster, having embodied in her design the experience gained with the *Guardian*. She was completed at the end of 1936 and is of 2,900 tons. She also served in the Second World War.

H.M.S. QUEEN

Unofficial Badge: Entwined letters **A A** in gold; above them is a royal crown with flying ribbons in proper colours. Underneath is a blue scroll with the ship's name in white.

Derived from an early unofficial badge.

Official Badge

FIELD: Gold.

BADGE: A lozenge purple charged with a gold orb.

MOTTO:

BATTLE HONOURS
Ushant	1781	December 12th.
First of June	1794	June 1st (and May 28th—29th).
Groix Island	1795	June 23rd.
Crimea	1854-5	
Dardanelles	1915	
Atlantic	1944	
Norway	1945	
Arctic	1945	

This ship was a battleship (pre-*Dreadnought*) of 15,000 tons.

During the Second World War there was an escort carrier named *Queen*, built in the U.S.A. in 1943, and which took part in strikes against the enemy on the Norwegian coast.

H.M.S. QUEEN ELIZABETH

Queen Elizabeth.—This badge was carried by H.M.S. *Queen Elizabeth*, a battleship (super-*Dreadnought*) of 27,500 tons. Proper colours. Scroll white, blue edged gold ends, H.M.S. QUEEN ELIZABETH in red letters.

Description of Badge

FIELD: Party per pale white and green.

BADGE: A Tudor rose red and silver between the letters E R under a Tudor crown gold.

MOTTO: *Semper Eadem* (Always the same).

The ship was named after Elizabeth Tudor, and the badge is adapted from the colours, badge and motto of the Queen.

350

H.M.S. QUEEN ELIZABETH—*continued*

BATTLE HONOURS

Dardanelles	1915	
Crete	1941	May 20th—June 1st.
Sabang	1944	July 25th.
Burma	1944-5	October 1944—April 1945.

The *Queen Elizabeth* was a battleship of 32,700 tons displacement and gave her name to the class; eight 15-inch and twenty 4.5-inch A.A. guns. She was built at Portsmouth and completed in 1915.

H.M.S. QUEEN MARY

Description of Badge

Royal cypher in black on a blue ground, royal crown above, scroll red and gold below with name of ship in black letters.

In allusion to the name.

BATTLE HONOURS
Heligoland	1914	August 28th.
Jutland	1916	May 31st.

This ship was a battle-cruiser of 27,000 tons, built in 1912 at Barrow, sister to the *Lion* and *Princess Royal*. She was sunk in action at the battle of Jutland.

H.M.S. QUILLIAM

Description of Badge

FIELD: Blue.

BADGE: Two quills in saltire and a trident erect and interlaced all gold.

MOTTO:

Badge in allusion to the name.

BATTLE HONOURS

Mediterranean	1943	
Sicily	1943	July 10th—August 17th.
Salerno	1943	September 9th—October 6th.
Sabang	1944	
Okinawa	1945	

The *Quilliam* was a destroyer of the *Queenborough* class and was transferred to the Royal Netherlands Navy. Her tonnage was 1,705 and her main armament was four 4.7-inch guns. This ship was built by Hawthorn Leslie, in 1941.

H.M.S. RAMESES

Unofficial Badge: The head of a Pharaoh or King of Egypt. Colour not known.

Badge in allusion to the name.

No battle honours recorded for this vessel.

The *Rameses* was a steel screw steamer of 2,490 tons, built in 1893 by R. Napier for the Moss Steamship Company Ltd., Liverpool. She was taken over by the Admiralty as a trooper and depot ship, and was stationed at Grangemouth during the war of 1914-1918.

H.M.S. RAPID

Description of Badge

FIELD: Red.

BADGE: A wheel, the axle tree winged gold.

MOTTO:

The badge is symbolic of the name.

BATTLE HONOURS

Atlantic	1943	
Sabang	1944	July 25th.
Burma	1944-5	

The following vessels have borne the name *Rapid*, starting from a gun brig of 177 tons and 12 guns which was launched at Topsham in October, 1804. This vessel whilst off Faro in Portugal, in company with H.M. Sloop *Grasshopper*, on 23rd April, 1808, captured two Spanish gunboats, drove two others ashore, and made prizes of two Spanish merchantmen from South America. She was sunk on 18th May, 1808, by gun batteries in the River Tagus.

In November of 1808 another vessel of this name was launched at Topsham, a sloop of 261 tons and 16 guns, and she was sold in December, 1814.

The next was launched at Portsmouth in August, 1829, and was a brig sloop of 231 tons and 10 guns, and she was wrecked off Crete on 12th April, 1838.

Then came a brig of 319 tons, 10 guns, launched at Portsmouth in June, 1840. During the years 1847-8 she was employed in the

H.M.S. RAPID—*continued*

suppression of the slave trade on the West Coast of Africa, and in 1856 she was sold at Singapore.

A screw sloop, second class, of 672 tons and 3 guns was the next one, and she was launched at Deptford in 1860. In 1873 she was concerned in operations against the Spanish Intransigentes, and in 1881 she was taken to pieces at Malta.

There was a *Rapid* built at Devonport in 1883 and which was a single screw composite sloop of 1,420 tons and 12 guns.

Then came a torpedo boat destroyer of 1,033 tons and capable of a speed of 35 knots. She was launched at Thornycroft's in July, 1916, and commissioned for the Grand Fleet at Scapa, where she was employed on convoy and patrol work. Sold at Portsmouth on 20th April, 1927.

In 1942 came a torpedo boat destroyer of the *Rotherham* class, and the present vessel is a fast anti-submarine frigate.

H.M.S. RELENTLESS

Unofficial Badge: This is a shield party per pale white and red, bordure black charged with the initial letter R in black.

This is a boat badge which was designed and adopted by the ship's officers (1916).

Official Badge

FIELD: Blue.

BADGE: A trident gold and a sword inflamed proper in saltire.

MOTTO:

This badge is in allusion to the name.

BATTLE HONOUR

Sabang   1944   July 25th.

357

H.M.S. RELENTLESS—*continued*

There was a torpedo boat destroyer of 880 tons and of 35-36 knots of this name ordered to be built at Yarrow's, and launched in April, 1916. She served at the Scapa base throughout the war, being with the 14th Flotilla on patrol, escort and screening duties. In November she was at the Heligoland Bight action screening the *Iron Duke*. In 1926, on 16th December, she was sold at Portsmouth.

Then came a torpedo boat destroyer in 1942 of the *Rotherham* class which is now a fast anti-submarine frigate.

H.M.S. RENOWN

Description of Badge
FIELD: Blue.

BADGE: A torch surrounded by a wreath all gold.

MOTTO: *Antiquæ Famæ Custos* (Guardian of Ancient Renown).

Badge and motto in allusion to the name.

BATTLE HONOURS

Gabbard	1653	June 2nd—3rd.
Scheveningen	1653	July 31st.
Ushant	1781	December 12th.
Egypt	1801	March 8th—September 2nd.
Atlantic	1940	
Norway	1940	
Spartivento	1940	November 27th.
"Bismarck"	1941	May 23rd—27th.
Mediterranean	1941	
Malta Convoys	1941-2	
Arctic	1942	
North Africa	1942	
Sabang	1944	July 25th.

The *Renown* was a battle-cruiser of 30,750 tons displacement, and carried six 15-inch and eight 4.5-inch (dual-purpose) guns, being completed by Fairfield in 1916. She had a wide and varied service during the Second World War.

H.M.S. REPULSE

Description of Badge
FIELD: Blue.
BADGE: A castle gold on which flies the flag of the Union proper on wavelets silver.
MOTTO: *Qui Tangit Frangatur* (Who touches me is broken).

Later Badge
FIELD: Blue.
BADGE: An eagle alighting on a rock, facing dexter, wings half raised.

First badge in allusion to the name.

BATTLE HONOURS

Cadiz	1596	June 21st.
Martinique	1762	February 16th.
The Saints	1782	April 12th.

H.M.S. REPULSE—*continued*

Atlantic	1940	
Norway	1940	
"Bismarck"	1941	May 23rd—27th.

The *Repulse* was a battle-cruiser of 32,000 tons displacement and mounted six 15-inch, fifteen 4-inch and four 4-inch A.A. guns, and was completed at Clydebank in 1916. She was lost when attacked by Japanese aircraft in company with the *Prince of Wales*, the *Repulse* being hit by five torpedoes and one bomb.

H.M.S. RESOURCE

Description of Badge
FIELD: Blue.

BADGE: A sea-unicorn silver, horn gold.

MOTTO: *Passim Ut Olim* (Everywhere as of yore).

The badge is derived from the fact that H.M.S. *Unicorn* was captured by the French in 1780 and renamed *Licorne*, being recaptured by the *Resource* on 20th April, 1781.

BATTLE HONOUR
Egypt   1801   March 8th—September 2nd.

The *Resource* was built by Vickers as a fleet repair ship, and her displacement tonnage is 12,300. She carried four 4-inch and four smaller guns.

H.M.S. REVENGE

Description of Badge
FIELD: Blue.

BADGE: A gryphon gold rising out of wavelets silver.

MOTTO: *Intaminatis fulget Honoribus* (Shines with untarnished honour).

The badge is derived from the crest of Sir Richard Grenville, 1541-1591, who was killed in the *Revenge*. This action was a very great one, for Sir Richard fought for fifteen hours against no less than fifty-three attackers. His ship was boarded fifteen times, but the invaders were thrown back. In the end he was forced to surrender after sinking four of the enemy.

BATTLE HONOURS

Armada	1588	July 21st—29th.
Armada	1588	July (*Revenge* of Lyme, Coaster).
Lowestoft	1665	June 3rd.
Four Days' Battle	1666	June 1st—4th.
Orfordness	1666	July 25th.
Bugia	1671	May 8th.
Schooneveld	1673	May 28th—June 4th.
Marbella	1705	March 10th.
Quiberon Bay	1759	November 20th.
Trafalgar	1805	October 21st.
Basque Roads	1809	April 11th.
Syria	1840	September 10th—December 9th.

H.M.S. REVENGE—*continued*

Jutland	1916	May 31st.
Belgian Coast	1914-15	
Atlantic	1939-1940	
English Channel	1940	
"Orphee"	1758	28th January. Single ship action.
Azores	1591	Single ship action.

This name will never be forgotten in British Naval history from the deeds of her illustrious forebear. The last was a battleship of 29,150 displacement; her armament consisted of eight 15-inch, twelve 6-inch and eight 4-inch A.A. guns, and she was completed by Vickers in 1916. Her battle honours show her service in the Atlantic and home waters, but she also served in the East and was part of Somerville's force in the Indian Ocean.

H.M.S. ROBERTS

Description of Badge
FIELD: Blue.

BADGE: A Field-Marshal's baton and a sword in saltire proper, pommel and hilt gold enfiled with an antique crown also gold, and in chief between the baton and sword an estoile also gold.

MOTTO:

Badge derived from the arms of Field-Marshal Lord Roberts

BATTLE HONOURS

Dardanelles	1915-16	
North Africa	1942	
Sicily	1943	July 10th—August 17th.
Salerno	1943	September 9th—October 6th.
Mediterranean	1943	
Normandy	1944	June 6th—July 3rd.
Walcheren	1944	November 1st.

The first *Roberts* was of 6,150 tons and was a monitor, carrying two 14-inch guns, ordered from Swan Hunters in 1914. She was originally named *Stonewall Jackson*, but was renamed *Lord Roberts*. On 22nd June, 1915, she was again renamed and this time she became the *Roberts*, serving in the Mediterranean and the Dardanelles. She then became a base ship at Yarmouth, and in September, 1936, she was transferred to T. W. Ward for breaking up.

H.M.S. ROBERTS—*continued*

The *Roberts* of the 1940 building programme was again a monitor, and this vessel was completed at Clydebank at the end of 1941. She was of 7,970 tons and carried two 15-inch, eight 4-inch, twelve 2-pounder and twenty 20-mm. A.A. guns. This ship and the *Abercrombie* were armed with guns which were formerly in the *Marshal Soult* and other discarded monitors.

H.M.S. ROCKET

Description of Badge
FIELD: Blue.
BADGE: The "Rocket" steam engine gold on a mount green.
MOTTO: Upward and Onward.

This badge represents the famous steam engine "Rocket."

BATTLE HONOURS
Baltic	1855	
English Channel	1943	
Sabang	1944	July 25th.
Burma	1944-5	

The first *Rocket* was a merchant ship of 62 tons which was bought for the Royal Navy in 1804 for service as a fire vessel. She did not, however, perform any service and she was sold in 1807.

Then came another of the name which was an iron steam vessel of 70 tons, built at Limehouse in 1842, and employed on towing duties at Portsmouth. She was then transferred to Sheerness in 1848, and was finally broken up at Woolwich in 1850.

A mortar vessel of 156 tons had this name, too, and she was built at Blackwall and launched on 5th May, 1855. In July she joined the Baltic Fleet and took part in the bombardment of Sveaborg. She was redesignated Mortar Vessel No. 20, and taken to pieces in 1865.

There was a third-class screw steam gunboat of 235 tons and two guns launched at Portsmouth on 21st August, 1856, which

H.M.S. ROCKET—continued

was specially built for the Russian war, but as she was not completed in time for the operations she went into reserve. This *Rocket* was broken up in 1864.

Following her was a twin-screw composite gun vessel of 464 tons, launched at Poplar on 8th April, 1868, and placed in reserve at Woolwich, and later commissioned for service on the Cape and West Africa stations. On 9th September, 1874, she was sent on to the Pacific station, and during this commission it fell to this ship to avenge an outrage on the crew of an American ship, the U.S. Steamer *George Wright*. This vessel was on a voyage in 1873 to Alaska and was lost at Queen Charlotte Sound in British Columbia. Fifteen of the ship's company who escaped to land were robbed and murdered by Indians. Early in 1877 some of the belongings of the victims were reported in the possession of a tribe at Deane's Inlet on the mainland. The *Rocket* was sent with an interpreter and a sergeant of police on 14th March, 1877, from Vancouver, and on arrival it was found that the men who had been implicated in the massacre were still on the spot. The commanding officer of the *Rocket* seized the chiefs as hostages and demanded that the murderers should be handed over. The request was refused and the village was shelled and burnt and two of the culprits taken. This vessel returned to England, and arrived at Sheerness on 11th June, 1883, and was sold in 1888.

The next *Rocket* was a torpedo boat destroyer of 280 tons and 27 knots launched on 14th August, 1894, on the Clyde. She was commissioned as a sea-going tender to the detached squadron in 1896 and again for the Naval Review in 1897. She then transferred to Reserve Fleet, Bermuda. In 1900 she was a tender to H.M.S. *Crescent*, in 1903 tender to the Vernon Torpedo School, where she remained until sold in 1912.

Another torpedo boat destroyer bore the name of *Rocket* and she was of 1,065 tons, built by Denny of Dumbarton, and was launched on 2nd July, 1916. She was employed on screening, convoy and patrol duties throughout the war, and after the Armistice assisted in bringing in surrendered German destroyers. After the war she was at Portsmouth, and sold for breaking up in 1927.

H.M.S. ROCKET—*continued*

The present *Rocket* was in action soon after her completion in 1943, for on 23rd October she took part in an engagement with German torpedo boats off Triagoz Island in which H.M. Ships *Charybdis* and *Limbourne* were lost. The *Limbourne* had to be sunk by *Rocket* and *Talybont*. In July, 1944, the *Rocket* was one of the surface ships of the Eastern Fleet that engaged Japanese shore defences during Admiral Somerville's air strike and bombardment of Sabang, Sumatra. In the following September the *Rocket* also took part in the air strike on Sigli, Sumatra, and in March, 1945, took part in the bombardment of Port Blair, Andamans. The *Rocket* is now a fast anti-submarine frigate.

H.M.S. RODNEY

Description of Badge
FIELD: White.
BADGE: Out of a ducal coronet gold, an eagle purple with beak and claws gold.
MOTTO: *Non Generant Aquilæ Columbas* (Eagles do not breed doves).

Badge from the crest of Rodney.

BATTLE HONOURS

Quebec	1759	September 13th.
Syria	1840	September 10th—December 9th.
Crimea	1854-5	
Norway	1940	
Atlantic	1940-1	
"Bismarck"	1941	May 23rd—27th.
Malta Convoys	1941-2	
North Africa	1942-3	
Sicily	1943	July 10th—August 17th.
Salerno	1943	September 9th—October 6th.
Mediterranean	1943	
Normandy	1944	June 6th—July 3rd.
English Channel	1944	
Arctic	1944	

This vessel was a sister ship to the *Nelson* and there was only about 50 tons difference in the displacements, the *Rodney's* being 33,900 tons. She was completed by Cammell Laird in 1927. In her war service she was with *King George V*, in the *Bismarck* episode.

H.M.S. ROEBUCK

Description of Badge
FIELD: White.
BADGE: A roebuck gardant proper.
MOTTO:

Badge in allusion to the name.

BATTLE HONOURS

Armada	1588	July 21st—29th. Merchant ship under Drake.
Cadiz	1596	June 21st. Merchant ship.
Portland	1653	February 18th—20th.
Gabbard	1653	June 2nd—3rd.
Barfleur	1692	May 19th—24th.
Velez Malaga	1704	August 13th.
Martinique	1794	March 22nd.
Egypt	1801	March 8th—September 2nd.
China	1860	
Sabang	1944	July 25th.
Burma	1944-5	

The first *Roebuck* fought in the Armada campaign of 1588 and was a hired ship of 300 tons. She was in Drake's squadron which joined with Howard at Plymouth.

Then there was another hired ship of 104 tons in 1596 and which was described as the *Roebuck* of London and was in Raleigh's squadron on the Cadiz voyage. Later was mentioned as being owned by him.

H.M.S. ROEBUCK—continued

Phineas Pett built a pinnace of this name of 90 tons and 10 guns at Woolwich, and he launched it on 28th March, 1637. On 26th May, 1648, this vessel was one of Rainborowe's Squadron which revolted to the Royalists and joined the Prince of Wales in Holland on 11th June. In October she came under the command of Prince Rupert, and in November, 1649, she fell into the hands of Parliament at the surrender of Kinsale. She then served in the Winter Guard, cruising against privateers, being cast from the service in 1651.

There was a prize of this name captured from the Dutch, so it is recorded, in 1652, and she carried 30 guns. During the year 1653 she served in the battles of Portland, Gabbard and the first battle of the Texel, and in 1657 she was sold.

In 1666 a sixth rate was built at Harwich called *Roebuck* of 129 tons and 16 guns which served in the second Dutch war of 1666-7 and the third Dutch war of 1672-4, and in 1683 she was sold.

There was another vessel of this name sunk to secure the graving place at Portsmouth on 26th August, 1692, having been originally a fire-ship of 70 tons and 6 guns, bought in 1688 and converted.

The next *Roebuck* had quite an interesting career and was a fireship of 276 tons and carried 8 guns. She was built at Wapping by Ed. Snelgrove and launched on 17th April, 1690. On 30th June, 1690, she was at the battle of Beachy Head, at the battle of Barfleur in 1692, and in operations on the coast of Brittany in 1694. In 1695 she was converted into a fifth rate of 26 guns at Kinsale. From 1699 to 1701 under Captain William Dampier she made a voyage to Australia and New Guinea, and when homeward bound sank at Ascension on 24th February, 1701.

In 1704 a fifth rate of 494 tons and 40 guns was built at Portsmouth carrying the name of *Roebuck*, and this vessel served at the battle of Velez Malaga on 13th August, 1704. She continued service on convoy work and cruising until 1713, and in 1742 she left the service.

There was a *Roebuck* built at Southampton in 1743 (though one record says rebuilt) of 708 tons and 44 guns, being a fifth rate. From 1743 to 1748 she was in the wars against France and Spain,

H.M.S. ROEBUCK—*continued*

and from 1756 to 1759 saw service in the Seven Years War. In 1759 she paid off and was out of commission in 1761.

Then came a fifth rate of 886 tons and 44 guns, built at Chatham in 1774. In 1778 she was with Howe on the North American station, and in 1780 she was at the capture of Charleston as the flagship of Arbuthnot. In 1781, on 14th April, in company with the *Orpheus* (32), she took the U.S. *Confederacy* (36), and in 1794 was in operations in the West Indies. In 1806 she became a guard ship after having been a store ship from 1798, and in 1811 she was taken to pieces.

In 1791 to 1796 there was a packet vessel named the *Roebuck*, and from 1793 to 1814 there was a revenue cutter of the same name.

A gun vessel of 865 tons and 6 guns followed on and was built at Millwall, and launched on 22nd March, 1856. In 1860 she was on service in the Red Sea, and in 1864 she was broken up.

Hawthorn Leslie built a torpedo boat destroyer of 360 tons and speed of 30 knots. She served in the Great War in Local Defence Flotilla at Devonport, and in 1919 was sold.

There was a balloon vessel in 1940 named *Roebuck II*, and in the building programme of 1942 another torpedo boat destroyer was ordered which later was converted to a fast anti-submarine frigate.

H.M.S. ROYAL SOVEREIGN

Description of Badge

FIELD: Red.

BADGE: The royal crest of England.

MOTTO: *Ducere Classem Regem Sequi* (to lead the fleet, to follow the king).

BATTLE HONOURS
Orfordness	1666	July 25th.
Vigo	1702	October 12th (not engaged).
First of June	1794	June 1st (and May 28th—29th).
Cornwallis Retreat	1795	June 17th.
Trafalgar	1805	October 31st.
Calabria	1940	July 9th.
Atlantic	1940-1	

This battleship, affectionately known as the "Tiddly Quid," was completed at Portsmouth in 1916 and was of 29,150 tons displacement. Her armament was eight 15-inch, twelve 6-inch and eight 4-inch A.A. guns. At one phase of the Second World War she was in the force under Admiral Somerville in the Indian Ocean. In 1944 she was transferred to the Soviet Navy, and was renamed on being returned later.

H.M.S. ROYALIST

Description of Badge
FIELD: White.
BADGE: A fleur-de-lis under a crown all gold.
MOTTO: *Surtout Loyal* (Loyal above all).

BATTLE HONOURS
Jutland	1916	May 31st.
Ægean	1944	
South France	1944	August 15th—27th.
Burma	1945	
"Weser"	1813	October 21st. Single ship action.

The first *Royalist* was probably named in sympathy with the French Royalists at the time of the Revolution, and the badge was derived from this source.

There was a *Royalist* launched at Sandwich on 10th January, 1807, and she was a brig sloop of 382 tons and 18 guns. On 1st May, 1809, she captured the French privateer *Princesse* (16), and on 17th November she captured another French privateer, the *Grand Napoleon* (18). From February to June, 1813, she assisted in coast operations off Northern Spain, and on 12th October assisted in the capture of a Franco-Dutch frigate, the *Weser* (40).

Another vessel to carry the name was a brig sloop of 231 tons and 10 guns, launched at Portsmouth on 12th May, 1823, and sold in November, 1838.

Then followed another brig sloop of 250 tons and 10 guns. She was launched at Bombay on 13th July, 1839, and was purchased

375

H.M.S. ROYALIST—*continued*

in 1842 as the *Mary Gordon* and renamed *Royalist*. From 1843 to 1847 and in May to June, 1849, she was engaged in operations against Borneo pirates; during the years 1852-1859 she was engaged in the surveying service, and in 1857 she was lent to the Thames Police as a floating headquarters at Waterloo Bridge, being sold in February, 1895.

There was a screw sloop, second class, of 669 tons and 11 guns, launched at Devonport on 14th December, 1861, and was on the North America and West Indies stations from 1862 to 1867, and in 1875 was broken up at Chatham.

A barque-rigged third-class cruiser of 1,420 tons and a speed of 13 knots bore the name. Her armament was two 6-inch and ten 5-inch guns. She was launched on 7th March, 1883, at Devonport. In 1886 she was sent on the Niger expedition, and from January to May, 1899, she served in operations at Samoa. In 1900 she became a receiving hulk at Haulbowline, and on 1st December, 1913, she was renamed *Colleen* and commissioned as a receiving ship at Queenstown.

Beardmore's launched a light cruiser of this name on 14th January, 1915; she was of 3,500 tons and had three 6-inch and four 4-inch guns. Her speed was 28.5 knots. Throughout the Great War she served with the 4th Light Cruiser Squadron and was at Jutland, Heligoland Bight and at the surrender of the German Fleet. She was sold in 1922.

The present *Royalist* is a cruiser of the *Dido* class of 5,700 tons, her armament being eight 5.25-inch guns. She was completed in 1943. Her Second World War service ranged from the Mediterranean to Burma.

H.M.S. RUBY

Unofficial Badge: The word RUBY displayed centrally outlined with what appears to be brilliants. Underneath a sailing ship with rayed lines extending upwards and outwards from ship. Above a naval crown and the letters H.M.S.

The badge appears to be in allusion to the exploits of a sailing ship *Ruby* accentuated by the design of the name.

BATTLE HONOURS

Cadiz	1596	June 21st (*Ruben* or *Ruby*).
Dove	1652	May 19th.
Kentish Knock	1652	September 28th.
Portland	1653	February 18th—20th.
Gabbard	1653	June 2nd—3rd.
Santa Cruz	1657	April 20th.
Orfordness	1666	July 25th.
Sole Bay	1672	May 28th.
Schooneveld	1673	May 28th and June 4th.
Texel	1673	August 11th.
Barfleur	1692	May 19th—24th.
Cape of Good Hope	1795	September 16th.
Baltic	1855	
English Channel	1942-3	
Normandy	1944	(Anti-submarine Trawler).

There was a 40-gun ship, a frigate, of this name, built at Deptford in 1652, and in the same year she served in the battle off

H.M.S. RUBY—*continued*

Dover. Later battles in which she played a part were North Foreland, Porto Farina, Bantry Bay and Barfleur. She captured the French *Entreprennant*, and was one of Benbow's squadron in 1702, and in the meeting with the French behaved in a most admirable manner. This *Ruby* is probably the one referred to in the badge which shows a sailing vessel. Another *Ruby*, a 64-gun vessel, captured the French 36-gun frigate *Prudente* off St. Domingo in 1779, and in 1782 she captured the French *Solitaire*, a 64-gun ship, after a brilliant engagement. Her commanding officer, Captain Collins, was knighted as a reward. There was a *Ruby* gunboat in service during the war against Russia. Later came a third-class cruiser, built at Hull in 1876, which took some part in the Egyptian war of 1882. The M.S. Trawler *Ruby* was purchased in 1935 and in 1936 served at Haifa. The battle honours show her service in the Second World War.

H.M.S. SAINTES

Description of Badge

FIELD: Blue.

BADGE: Within a laurel wreath gold a bezant, thereon an eagle displayed purple.

MOTTO:

The badge is derived from the eagle in the arms of Rodney, who was Commander-in-Chief in the battle.

No battle honours are recorded for this name.

The *Saintes* is one of the *Battle* class of destroyers, built by Hawthorn Leslie in 1944.

H.M.S. ST. JAMES

Description of Badge

FIELD: Paly bendy gold and blue.

BADGE: Within a wreath of laurel gold a white dragon statant.

MOTTO:

The field of this badge is from the colours of Prince Rupert, and the dragon is from the crest of the Duke of Albemarle, who were joint Commanders-in-Chief.

No battle honours are recorded for this ship.

The *St. James* is one of the *Battle* class of destroyers and was built by Fairfield in 1945.

H.M.S. ST. KITTS

Description of Badge

FIELD: Blue.

BADGE: A merman proper supporting with his hands a trident erect gold, all within a wreath of laurel also gold.

MOTTO:

The merman shown in this badge was one of the supporters of the arms of Sir S. Hood, who was the Commander-in-Chief in the battle.

No battle honours are recorded for this name.

The *St. Kitts* is one of the *Battle* class of destroyers and was built by Swan Hunter in 1944.

H.M.S. ST. VINCENT

Description of Badge
FIELD: Red.
BADGE: A winged horse silver, mane and hooves gold, wings blue charged with a fleur-de-lis gold.
MOTTO: Thus.

Badge is derived from arms of the Earl of St. Vincent.
Motto from the old steering order, "Keep her thus."

BATTLE HONOURS
Baltic	1854	March 24th—September.
Jutland	1916	May 31st.

The first vessel to bear the name *St. Vincent* was a fireship of 200 tons and carrying 8 guns. She was captured from the French in 1692, and served on various stations until sold in 1698.

A first rate of this name was launched at Plymouth on 11th March, 1815, and was named after Admiral the Earl of St. Vincent, then Commander-in-Chief of the Channel Fleet. She became the flagship of various Admirals and in 1859 became Reserve depot ship on the formation of the Royal Naval Reserve. On 1st January, 1862, she became a training ship for boys at Portsmouth, and in 1906 was sold.

The battleship *St. Vincent* of 19,250 tons, launched on 10th September, 1908, was armed with ten 12-inch and twenty 4-inch guns. She served at the battle of Jutland, and in 1921 was sold for breaking up.

Training Establishment. In 1927 became the Boys' Training Establishment, Forton, Gosport, and in 1942 was the Preliminary Air Training Establishment.

H.M.S. SATELLITE

Unofficial Badge: This badge has a representation of the world in clouds, and above there is a crescent moon. Above, the letters H.M.S., and below is a scroll having on it the word SATELLITE. No colours are known.

The derivation is obvious, being an allusion to the name.

BATTLE HONOUR
Abyssinia   1868   April 13th.

The *Satellite* of this badge was a screw cruiser, third class, of 1,420 tons, and which carried 8 guns. She was built at Sheerness, and launched on 13th August, 1881. For some time she served on the Pacific and China stations. During February-March, 1894, she served in the Gambia River operations, and from 1903 to 1906 she was the Royal Naval Reserve drill ship at North Shields, then being lent to the Tyne Division of the Royal Naval Volunteer Reserve.

H.M.S. SAVAGE

Description of Badge

FIELD: White.

BADGE: A savage affronte holding a club proper.

MOTTO:

The badge is in allusion to the name.

BATTLE HONOURS

Guadeloupe	1810	February 5th.
North Cape	1943	December 26th.
Normandy	1944	June 6th—July 3rd.
Arctic	1943-45	

The *Savage* is a destroyer of 1,796 tons and carries four 4.5-inch dual-purpose and six 40-mm. guns. Built by Hawthorn Leslie. The *Savage*, accompanied by other vessels of her class, attacked the *Scharnhorst* with heroic disregard of that vessel's powerful armament, allowing heavier forces to come up and finish the job. She was built in 1943, and sold to the Royal Netherland Navy in 1945.

H.M.S. SCORPION

Description of Badge

FIELD: Barry wavy of six white and blue.

BADGE: A scorpion gold.

MOTTO:

The badge is in allusion to the name.

BATTLE HONOURS

Quebec	1759	September 13th.
Guadeloupe	1810	February 5th.
Dardanelles	1915-16	February 19th—January 8th.
North Cape	1943	December 26th.
Normandy	1944	June 6th—July 3rd.
Arctic	1943-45	
"Athalante"	1804	31st March. Single ship action.
"Oreste"	1810	12th January. Single ship action.

This vessel is of the *Weapon* class and was originally named *Tomahawk*, then *Centaur* and finally *Scorpion*. The tonnage of this class is 1,980 tons, and they carry six 4-inch dual-purpose guns in twin mounts, and she was launched in 1946.

H.M.S. SCOTT

Description of Badge

FIELD: Barry wavy white and blue.

BADGE: A penguin proper.

MOTTO:

Badge in allusion to the Antarctic and Scott's expeditions.

	BATTLE HONOURS	
Zeebrugge	1918	April 23rd.
Norway	1941	
Normandy	1944	June 6th—July 3rd.

The *Scott* is a survey vessel of 830 tons, and capable of a speed of 17 knots. It was built by the Caledon Shipbuilding Company in 1938, and served as a minesweeper during the Second World War.

H.M.S. SEAGULL

Unofficial Badge: This shows a seagull proper with a background of sea and sky proper. Above is a naval crown gold with white sails, red and green gems. Light blue scroll white edged, the name in black.

Official Badge

FIELD: Barry wavy of six white and blue.

BADGE: A seagull flying proper.

MOTTO:

Badge in allusion to the name.

	BATTLE HONOURS	
Ashantee	1873	
Normandy	1944	June 6th—July 3rd.
Arctic	1941-44	

This ship was a first-class gunboat of 735 tons, built at Chatham, and launched on 31st May, 1889. In 1915 during the month of August she was engaged in the bombardment of the Belgian coast, and on 30th September, 1918, she was sunk in collision in the Firth of Clyde.

The *Seagull* of the Second World War was a fleet minesweeper of the *Halcyon* class, and was the Royal Navy's first all-welded ship. Now of *Franklin* class and is a survey vessel.

H.M.S. SEA ROVER

Description of Badge

FIELD: Blue.

BADGE: A mermaid swimming proper, her tail encircling a helmet gold.

MOTTO: *Subter Sed Super*.

Badge in allusion to the name.

BATTLE HONOUR
Atlantic 1945

The *Sea Rover* was an "S" class submarine, built by Scotts. She was completed in 1943. The tonnage of this class was 715/1,000 tons.

H.M.S. SHAH

Description of Badge
FIELD: Blue.

BADGE: A Shah's crown gold.

MOTTO:

Badge in allusion to the name.

BATTLE HONOUR
Burma 1945

The *Shah* was an aircraft carrier of the *Ruler* class, built by the Kaiser Company Incorporated at Vancouver, Washington.

H.M.S. SHANNON

Description of Badge: A shamrock leaf green, above which is a naval crown, gold with white sails, gems green and red. Underneath a red scroll showing the motto BE READY in white, the ship's name in black below.

Badge in allusion to Ireland.

BATTLE HONOURS
Louisburg	1758	July 26th.
Lucknow	1857-8	(Indian Mutiny).
Jutland	1916	May 31st.
"Chesapeake"	1813	Single ship action.

This ship was a first-class armoured cruiser of 14,600 tons. She carried as her main armament four 9.2-inch guns. Her complement was 712 men. She was built at Chatham, and launched on 20th September, 1906. On 31st May, 1916, she was at the battle of Jutland, and during 1917-18 she was employed in the protection of convoy routes between Lerwick and Norway. On 12th December, 1922, she was sold for breaking up.

H.M.S. SHARK

Unofficial Badge: A Viking ship gold with white sail and red flag. Sea and sky proper. Above a naval crown gold, white sails, red and blue gems. Underneath is a scroll blue, gold edged, with name in gold. This badge is similar to the one originally designed by Lady Scott for H.M.S. *Bulwark*.

Official Badge
FIELD: Blue.

BADGE: A shark silver.

MOTTO: *Celer et Tenax* (Swift and tenacious.

BATTLE HONOURS
Crimea	1854	
Jutland	1916	May 31st.
North Sea	1940	

H.M.S. SHARK—*continued*

The *Shark* was a torpedo boat destroyer of 935 tons, and carried three 4-inch guns. She was built at Wallsend-on-Tyne, and launched on 30th July, 1912. In December, 1914, she was in the German raid on the Yorkshire coast; on 31st May, 1916, at the battle of Jutland, and here she was sunk in the action. Her Commanding Officer, Commander Loftus Jones, was awarded a posthumous V.C. The six survivors of the crew were rescued by a Dutch steamer.

The *Shark* of the Second World War was a submarine of 670 tons, sunk by German aircraft off the Norwegian coast in 1940. There was also a destroyer lent to the Royal Norwegian Navy.

H.M.S. SHEFFIELD

Description of Badge
FIELD: Blue.
BADGE: Eight arrows interlaced, silver feathered and pointed gold.
MOTTO: *Deo Adjuvante Proficio* (With God's help I advance).

The badge is adapted from the arms and the motto of Sheffield.

BATTLE HONOURS

Norway	1940	
Spartivento	1940	November 27th.
"Bismarck"	1941	May 23rd—27th.
Atlantic	1941-43	
Arctic	1941-43	
Mediterranean	1941	
Malta Convoys	1941	
Barents Sea	1942	December 31st.
North Africa	1942	
Salerno	1943	September 9th.—October 6th.
North Cape	1943	December 26th.
Biscay	1943	

The *Sheffield* is a cruiser of the *Southampton* class, and was built by Vickers-Armstrongs at Barrow, being completed in 1937. Her displacement tonnage is 9,100, and her armament consists mainly of nine 6-inch and eight 4-inch A.A. guns. Her speed is 32 knots. During the Second World War she rendered yeoman service, and her activities ranged from the Arctic to the Mediterranean, and she was present at the famous hunt for the *Bismarck*.

H.M.S. SIRIUS

Description of Badge
FIELD: Blue.

BADGE: In front of a five-pointed estoile white a mullet gold.

MOTTO: Heaven's Light Our Guide.

The badge is derived from the star called Sirius—the Dog Star, the brightest star in the heavens.

BATTLE HONOURS

Trafalgar	1805	October 21st.
Ostend	1918	April 23rd.
Belgian Coast	1914	
Mediterranean	1942	
Malta Convoys	1942	
Arctic	1942	
North Africa	1942-3	
Sicily	1943	July 10th—August 17th.
Salerno	1943	September 9th—October 6th.
Ægean	1943-4	
Normandy	1944	June 6th—July 3rd.
South France	1944	August 15th—27th.

The first to have the name was originally the *Berwick*, an armed store ship bought in 1781. She was a sixth rate of 512 tons and 10 guns, and was renamed *Sirius* on 12th October, 1786, being used for employment in Botany Bay, sailing from Spithead in March, 1787, under Captain John Hunter. This vessel carried out the Governor for the foundation of New South Wales in 1788,

H.M.S. SIRIUS—*continued*

Arthur Phillips, who flew his broad pennant in the *Sirius* as Commodore of the expedition and escorting a convoy of transports, etc. On 19th March, 1790, she was wrecked at Norfolk Island after colonizing the island.

Then there was a fifth rate of 1,047 tons and 36 guns, built by Messrs. Dudman on the River Thames and launched on 12th April, 1797. On 24th October, 1798, under Captain Richard King she captured the Dutch vessels *Furie* (36) and the *Waakzaamheid* (24) off the Texel; she participated in the capture of the French *De Daigneuse* (36) off the coast of Portugal on 28th January, 1801. Captain William Prowse commanded her during Calder's action off Ferrol on 22nd July, 1805; the same captain commanded her at the battle of Trafalgar, and on 17th April, 1806, she had an action off Gaeta with French gunboats and captured the *Bergere* (18). From 1809 to 1810 she was at the capture of the island of Reunion and the later operations against Mauritius under Captain Samuel Pym. On 25th August, 1810, she was destroyed to prevent her falling into the hands of the French.

Another fifth rate of 1,090 tons bore the name and she carried 38 guns, being built by Messrs. Tyson and Blake at Bursledon, and launched on 11th September, 1813. In 1860 she had her sides fitted with plates for gunnery experiments, and was broken up in September, 1862, at Portsmouth.

Following her was a screw sloop, first class, of 1,268 tons and 6 guns, built at Portsmouth, and launched on 24th April, 1868. From 1869 to 1871 she served on the West Coast of Africa and the Cape of Good Hope stations, from 1871 to 1873 on the North America and West Indies stations, and from 1876 to 1877 on the Niger in the blockade of Dahomey. She was sold in 1885.

Then there was a screw cruiser, second class, of 3,600 tons and 8 guns, built by Messrs. Armstrongs at Newcastle-on-Tyne, and launched on 27th October, 1890. This vessel was at Rear-Admiral Hood's bombardment of the Belgian coast in October, 1914, at the Cameroons in 1915, and finally sunk as a blockship at Ostend on 23rd April, 1918.

The present *Sirius* was built at Portsmouth, and was completed in 1942. Her tonnage is 5,450 and she carries as her main armament ten 5.25-inch guns. Her service during the Second World War is well shown in her collection of battle honours.

H.M.S. SLUYS

Description of Badge

FIELD: Barry wavy of six white and blue.

BADGE: Within a wreath of laurel gold a torteau charged with a leopard's face, crowned with a crown of fleur-de-lis, also gold.

MOTTO: *Per Medium Illorum Ibat* (Through the midst of them he went his way).

The badge is derived from the arms of Edward II, who was Commander-in-Chief in the battle of Sluys in 1340.

No battle honours are recorded for this name.

The *Sluys* is one of the *Battle* class of destroyers, and was built by Cammell Laird in 1945.

H.M.S. SOLEBAY

Description of Badge

FIELD: Barry wavy of six white and blue.

BADGE: A rose white within a chaplet of laurel gold.

MOTTO:

Badge derived from the fact that the Duke of York was Commander-in-Chief at Sole Bay.

BATTLE HONOUR
St. Kitts   1782   January 25th—26th.

There have been several ships carrying the name of *Solebay* in the Royal Navy, and the first was a 32-gun frigate. This vessel was lost on Christmas Day, 1709, near Boston Neck, with the loss of all her crew.

Then came a vessel which was employed in the defence of Gibraltar in 1727. She was a 6-gun bomb vessel.

The *Solebay* which followed her was a 20-gun ship, and she was captured by the French in 1744. However, on 28th April, 1746, she was recaptured by the *Alexander*, a 20-gun English privateer. This act of daring so pleased the King that Captain Phillips, who commanded the *Alexander*, was presented with a gold medal and five hundred guineas. On 26th May, 1758, in company with the 24-gun ship *Dolphin*, the *Solebay* fought a very gallant action with the *Marechal de Belle Ile* of 44 guns. After an action of some three and a half hours the French ship escaped.

There was another *Solebay* built in 1763, a 28-gun frigate which

H.M.S. SOLEBAY—*continued*

took part in the attack on Charleston in 1776 and was in the actions off the Chesapeake in 1781 and St. Kitts in 1782.

The next vessel to bear the name was a 32-gun frigate, built at Deptford in 1785. She attacked a French squadron off San Domingo on 24th November, 1799, consisting of four vessels armed altogether with 58 guns and carrying 481 men. She captured them all! Then on 6th December she cut out from Cape Tiburon four French corvettes after a very gallant action. The *Solebay* was wrecked on 11th July, 1809, during the attack on Senegal, but the crew were saved.

The present *Solebay* is a vessel of the *Battle* class, and was built by Hawthorn Leslie in 1944.

H.M.S. SORCERESS

Unofficial Badge: This is a round plaque of pleasing design showing a female figure conjuring up a sinuous S from a cauldron. No colours are shown.

It has been stated that the badge was designed most likely by the ship's first Commanding Officer, Lieutenant Commander H. R. James, D.S.C., in allusion to the name.

No battle honours are recorded for this vessel.

This vessel was launched by Swan Hunter on 29th August, 1916. She was about 1,065 tons and had a speed of 36 knots.

H.M.S. SOUTHAMPTON

Description of Badge
FIELD: White.

BADGE: A figure of Justice crowned, holding sword in right hand, scales in left, all proper, arising out of a castle gold.

MOTTO: *Pro Justitia Pro Rege* (For Justice and the King).

This ship also had another badge. From arms of Southampton.

BATTLE HONOURS

Belle Ile	1761	June 7th.
First of June	1794	June 1st (and May 28th-29th).
St. Vincent	1797	February 14th.
Heligoland	1914	August 28th.
Dogger Bank	1915	January 24th.
Jutland	1916	May 31st.
Norway	1940	
Spartivento	1940	November 27th.
Malta Convoys	1941	
"Emeraude"	1757	12th September. (Under consideration: single ship action).

The *Southampton* was a cruiser of 9,100 tons, carrying as her armament twelve 6-inch and eight 4-inch A.A. guns. During the Second World War, whilst protecting a convoy, she was heavily damaged by dive-bombers and she had to be sunk.

H.M.S. SUPERB

Description of Badge
FIELD: Blue.
BADGE: A heraldic tiger statant gold charged on the shoulder with an anchor black.
MOTTO: With sword and courage.

The badge is derived from the crest of Admiral Sir Richard Goodwin Keats.

BATTLE HONOURS

Passero	1718	July 31st.
Sadras	1782	February 17th.
Providien	1782	April 12th.
Negapatam	1782	July 6th.
Trincomalee	1782	September 3rd.
Gut of Gibraltar	1801	July 12th.
San Domingo	1806	February 6th.
Algiers	1816	August 27th.
Alexandria	1882	July 11th.
Jutland	1916	May 31st.

The first to bear this name was a fourth rate of 1,021 tons, and was originally the French *Superbe*, taken by the *Kent* in the Channel on 29th July, 1710. On 23rd September, 1710, she was commissioned in the Royal Navy and served during Queen Anne's War in the Mediterranean; in 1717 she was in Sir G. Byng's fleet in the Baltic; at the destruction of the Spanish fleet off Cape Passero; and during 1726-7 she was in Vice-

H.M.S. SUPERB—*continued*

Admiral Hosier's squadron in the West Indies. On the death of Hosier on 28th August, 1727, Captain Ed. St. Lo of the *Superb* became the S.O. During 1733 to 1736 she was rebuilt and was now of 1,068 tons. In 1743 she wore the broad pennant of Commodore Peter Warren; on 28th June, 1745, she was at the Leewards Islands, at the capture of Louisburg; during 1748-9 she was in the Mediterranean, and in 1757 she was broken up.

Number 2 was a third rate of 1,612 tons and 74 guns, built at Deptford by A. Hayes in 1760. From 17th February, 1782, to 20th June, 1783, she was at Sadras, Providien, Negapatam, Trincomalee and Cuddalore. On 3rd November, 1783, she was wrecked at Telicherry, her crew being saved.

There was a *Superb* which was not registered in the list of the Navy which was taken by the *Vanguard* from the French and used as a prison ship at Martinique, and appears to have been disposed of in 1797-8. She was a corvette of 22 guns.

The third *Superb* was a third rate of 1,916 tons and 74 guns, built in 1798 on the Thames by Dudman. In 1801 this vessel served at Saumarez's action in the Gut of Gibraltar on 12th July. Her Captain was R. G. Keats. A medal was given for this action. During 1803 to 1805 she was in the Mediterranean and at the blockade of Toulon and in the chase to the West Indies. On 6th February, 1806, she was the flagship of Vice-Admiral Sir J. T. Duckworth in his victory off San Domingo—this victory resulting in a gold medal; Captain R. G. Keats also having a medal. In August-September, 1807, she was in the expedition to Copenhagen, and from 1807 to 1810 she flew the flag of Rear-Admiral R. G. Keats in the Channel and Baltic. Again a medal resulted. On 27th August, 1816, she was at the bombardment of Algiers, in which her captain Chas. Ekins was wounded; for this action there was a medal. She ended her career by being broken up on 17th April, 1826.

The fourth *Superb* was a second rate of 2,589 tons and 80 guns, built at Pembroke, 1838-1845. She served on various stations and in 1858 was lent to the War Department as a hospital. In 1866 she was a temporary cholera hospital at Sheerness, and in 1868 she was ordered to be used as a quarantine ship at Motherbank, but on the results of her survey she was ordered to be broken up, this being done in February, 1869.

H.M.S. SUPERB—continued

The next *Superb* was an ironclad of 9,492 tons, having as her armament two 11-inch M.L. and ten 9-inch M.L. guns and six 20-pounders. Her speed was 14 knots. She began building in Chatham in 1873, but on 4th March, 1874, she was renamed *Alexandra* and launched under this name on 7th April, 1874.

Then came an ironclad of 9,170 tons carrying sixteen 10-inch M.L. guns, and a speed of 14.5 knots, launched in 1875 at Blackwall for the Turkish Government as the *Hamidieh*. On 20th February, 1878, she was purchased for the Royal Navy and cost £443,000 with armament. The name *Superb* was given to her on 22nd February, 1878. On 11th July, under Captain T. Le Hunte Ward, she was at the bombardment of Alexandria. She then became a second-class battleship, carrying eight 10-inch guns and four 4.7-inch guns, and in 1902 rated as a third-class battleship, and sold in 1906.

Superb number 7 was a battleship of 18,600 tons and carried ten 12-inch and eleven 4-inch guns, and she had a speed of 20.75 knots. She was laid down at Elswick, and launched on 7th November, 1907, then in 1909 was commissioned for the Home Fleet. On 31st May, 1916, she served at the battle of Jutland; in 1918 she became the flagship of Vice-Admiral Hon. Sir S. Gough Calthorpe, Commander-in-Chief, Mediterranean. After serving in operations at South Russia, she became in 1919 Gunnery Training Ship, and in 1922 she was sold for breaking up.

The present *Superb* is a cruiser built under the 1941 supplementary programme, and is of 8,000 tons and carrying as her main armament nine 6-inch and ten 4-inch guns. She was completed in 1945.

H.M.S. SURPRISE

Description of Badge
FIELD: White.

BADGE: An ancient galley black.

MOTTO: *Sola Nobilitas Virtus* (Valour is the only nobility).

The badge is derived from part of the arms and the motto of Admiral Sir E. Hamilton, captain of *Surprise*, who cut out *Hermione* at Puerto Cabello.

BATTLE HONOURS

Dogger Bank	1781	August 5th.
China	1855-60	
Belgian Coast	1917	
Atlantic	1941-2	
North Sea	1942	
"Hermione"	1799	October 25th. Single ship action.

The first *Surprise* was a sixth rate of 508 tons and 24 guns, built at Bewley, and launched on 27th January, 1745. She was at the blockade of Dunkirk, and was sold at Deptford on 17th July, 1770. Another sixth rate followed her, this time of 594 tons and 28 guns, launched at Woolwich on 13th April, 1774. In 1775 she was at the relief of Quebec, and was sold at Woolwich on 17th April, 1783. Then came a sloop of 18 guns which was the American *Bunker's Hill*, taken by Admiral Barrington on 24th December, 1778, at St. Lucia and added to the Royal Navy as H.M.S. *Surprise*. She was sold at Sheerness in 1783. There was a cutter called the *Surprise* of 135 tons and 10 guns purchased in 1780, and was in Hyde Parker's action with the Dutch fleet off

H.M.S. SURPRISE—*continued*

the Dogger Bank in 1781, being sold in 1786. Another cutter called the *Surprise* was purchased in 1783, of 164 tons and 10 guns, sold at Sheerness on 2nd October, 1792. The French corvette *Unite* (28) was captured by H.M.S. *Constant* in the Mediterranean on 20th April, 1796, and added to the Navy as H.M.S. *Surprise*. She was a fifth rate of 597 tons. On 25th October, 1799, she carried out the exploit of cutting out the *Hermione* at Puerto Cabello in Venezuela. Captain E. Hamilton was knighted and a captain's gold medal awarded. This vessel was sold at Deptford in 1802.

There was a schooner which bore this name of 96 tons and carrying 1 gun and was the U.S.S. *Tigress*, captured on Lake Erie on 3rd September, 1814, and supposed broken up in 1833.

A fifth rate of the name was launched at Milford in 1812 and sold at Plymouth in 1837.

Then came a first-class screw vessel of 680 tons and 4 guns, built at Blackwall in 1856. In 1857 she was at the bombardment of Canton, and in 1858 in an attack on pirate junks near Hong Kong in which nineteen junks were destroyed and seven taken into Hong Kong. She was broken up in 1860.

A screw despatch vessel bore the name, built at Jarrow-on-Tyne, and launched on 17th January, 1885. Her tonnage was 1,650. Renamed *Alacrity* in 1913.

Next vessel to bear the name *Surprise* was a torpedo boat destroyer of 885 tons, built on the Clyde by Yarrows and completed in January, 1917. She was sunk by a mine in the North Sea on 23rd December, 1917.

A yacht of 1,142 tons built in 1896 and taken up for naval service carried the name of *Surprise*. She was fitted out for anti-submarine service in 1940, and caught fire and capsized in Lagos on 28th February, 1942.

The present *Surprise* is a despatch vessel of 1,590 tons, launched by Smith's Dock Co. on 14th March, 1945, and completed in September, 1946. She was originally called *Loch Carron*, was then named *Gerrans Bay* and finally *Surprise*. This vessel had the honour of bearing Her Majesty Queen Elizabeth and H.R.H. the Duke of Edinburgh at the Review of the Fleet at Spithead.

H.M.S. SUSSEX

Description of Badge

FIELD: Blue.

BADGE: A martlet gold.

MOTTO: *Fortiter In Re* (Won't be Druv—free translation).

From the arms of Sussex.

BATTLE HONOURS
Portland	1653	February 18th—20th.
Gabbard	1653	June 2nd—3rd.

The *Sussex* was a cruiser of 9,830 tons and carried as her main armament six 8-inch and eight 4-inch A.A. guns. She was built by Hawthorn Leslie and completed in 1929.

H.M.S. SWIFTSURE

Description of Badge
FIELD: Blue.

BADGE: A heraldic tiger rampant, winged gold.

MOTTO:

The badge is derived from the figurehead of the first *Swiftsure*, which was built in 1573.

BATTLE HONOURS

Armada	1588	July 21st—29th. Queen's ship.
Cadiz	1596	June 21st. Queen's ship.
Santa Cruz	1657	April 20th.
Lowestoft	1665	June 3rd.
Four Days' Battle	1666	June 1st—4th.
Schooneveld	1673	June 4th. Second action only.
Texel	1673	August 11th.
Barfleur	1692	May 19th—24th.
Vigo	1702	October 12th.
Gibraltar	1704	July 24th.
Velez Malaga	1704	August 13th.
Lagos	1759	August 17th.
Quiberon Bay	1759	November 20th.
Belle Ile	1761	June 7th.
Nile	1798	August 1st.
Egypt	1801	March 8th—September 2nd.
Trafalgar	1805	October 21st.

H.M.S. SWIFTSURE—continued

Suez Canal	1915	February 2nd—4th.
Dardanelles	1915-16	
Okinawa	1945	March 26th—May 25th.

The first *Swiftsure* was of 400 tons and 41 guns, built at Deptford in 1573. In 1588 she was at the battle of the Spanish Armada, commanded by Captain Ed. Fenner; in 1589 in the expedition to Corunna and Lisbon under Drake and Norreys. This vessel was then rebuilt in 1592, taking part in 1596 in the expedition to Cadiz, commanded by Captain Sir Robert Crosse; in 1597 in the Earl of Essex's squadron to the Azores, commanded by Captain Sir G. Meyricke; in 1602 from January to April she was the flagship of Sir Amyas Preston on the Irish coast, and from 27th August to 2nd December of the same year she was the flagship of Sir Wm. Monson on the coast of Spain. In 1607 she was rebuilt again and then called the *Speedwell*.

The next *Swiftsure* was a second rate of 898 tons and 60 guns, built in 1621 at Deptford. In the 1625 expedition to Cadiz she was the flagship of the Earl of Essex. She missed all the battles of the first Dutch war, for she was then being rebuilt at Woolwich. From 10th to 17th May, 1655, she was at the capture of Jamaica; in 1657 at Blake's attack on Santa Cruz, Teneriffe, and the destruction of the galleons there. The *Swiftsure* was in the squadron which went into the Bay under Stayner. This ship was the flagship of Vice-Admiral Sir William Berkeley at the battle of Lowestoft, and in the Four Days' Fight on 1st June, 1666, she was captured by the Dutch and Sir William Berkeley was killed.

Following her was the *Swiftsure*, third rate, of 978 tons and 70 guns, launched at Harwich in 1673. After serving at the second battle of Schooneveld and at Barfleur she was rebuilt at Deptford in 1696. She then served at Vigo Bay, the capture of Gibraltar and Velez Malaga, and in 1715, on 2nd January, she was renamed *Revenge*.

A third rate of 1,426 tons and 70 guns was launched in 1750 at Deptford bearing the name *Swiftsure*. This vessel in 1758, on 28th February, came up in time to receive the surrender of the French *Foudroyant*, already defeated by the *Monmouth* (64). In 1759 she was at Boscawen's action off Lagos and at Quiberon Bay, in 1761 at the capture of Belle Ile, and in 1773 she was sold.

The name was carried on by another third rate of 1,521 tons

H.M.S. SWIFTSURE—*continued*

and 74 guns, launched on the River Thames on 4th April, 1787. In 1794, on 5th May, she captured the *Atalante* (36), which was added to the Royal Navy, near Cork; she was at San Domingo in 1796; at the battle of the Nile, 1798, under the command of Captain Ben Hallowell; on 11th August, 1798, she took the French *Fortune* (18) off the coast of Egypt; and on 24th June, 1801, she was captured by Ganteaume's squadron in the Mediterranean. At the battle of Trafalgar the *Swiftsure* was recaptured and re-added to the Royal Navy as the *Irresistible*.

The next to have the name was a third rate of 1,724 tons and 74 guns which was launched at Buckler's Hard on 23rd July, 1804. In 1805 she was in pursuit of the French fleet to the West Indies and back, and was in the battle of Trafalgar under the command of Captain W. G. Rutherford. On the coast of Corsica on 26th November, 1813, her boats cut out the privateer *Charlemagne* (8). During 1816 she was made into a receiving hulk at Portsmouth; in 1845 she was used as a target and was then sold in October of that year.

A screw-battleship, third class, of 6,910 tons was the next, and she was armed with 18 guns. This ship was launched at Palmer's Yard at Jarrow-on-Tyne on 15th June, 1870. On 13th February, 1878, she was with Vice-Admiral G. P. Hornby at the passage of the Dardanelles, and in 1904 was renamed *Orontes*.

The battleship *Swiftsure* was of 11,800 tons and had a speed of 19 knots; she carried four 10-inch and fourteen 7.5-inch guns, and was launched on the Tyne by Armstrong Whitworth & Co. The ship commissioned in 1904, serving eventually on various stations. In August, 1914, she was in the Indian Ocean and convoyed the Indian Expeditionary Force to Aden; in 1915, on 3rd to 5th February, assisted in the repulse of the Turkish attack on the Suez Canal; in April of 1915 she covered the landing at W Beach, and after patrol duties in the North Atlantic during 1916 and 1917 she paid off at Chatham, to be finally sold for breaking up in 1920 to the Stanlee Shipbreaking Co.

The present *Swiftsure* is a cruiser of 8,000 tons displacement and carrying nine 6-inch and ten 4-inch A.A. guns. She was completed at Vickers-Armstrongs on the Tyne in 1944. Her battle honours indicate that she was in at the closing stages of the Second World War.

H.M.S. TEAZER

Description of Badge

FIELD: White.

BADGE: A thistle proper.

MOTTO:

The badge is in allusion to the name.

BATTLE HONOURS

Zeebrugge	1918	April 23rd.
Mediterranean	1943	
Ægean	1944	
Adriatic	1944	
South France	1944	August 15th—27th.

The *Teazer* is one of the limited conversion class of destroyers changed to anti-submarine frigate. Her tonnage is 1,710, and she was completed by Cammell Laird in 1943.

H.M.S. TEMERAIRE

Description of Badge: A lion rampant reguardant gold, having in its paws a banner blue with gold edging, standing on the top of a castle. A scroll red, gold edged, with the name of the ship.

BATTLE HONOURS

Martinique	1762	February 16th.
Belle Ile	1761	June 7th.
Havana	1762	June 6th—August 13th.
Trafalgar	1805	October 21st.
Alexandria	1882	July 11th.
Jutland	1916	May 31st.

The first, a third rate, was captured from the French at Lagos by Boscawen in August, 1759, and in 1761 was at the action off Belle Isle and in 1762 was at Martinique and Havannah. The next *Temeraire* was a second rate and is the subject of Turner's picture "The Fighting Temeraire," which showed her being brought up to Rotherhithe to be broken up. She fought at the battle of Trafalgar. A battleship of 8,540 tons also carried the name. Built at Chatham in 1876, she served in 1878 at Hornby's passage of the Dardanelles and the bombardment of Alexandria in 1882. This ship also landed a naval brigade for action at Tel-el-Kebir and at Khartoum. She was renamed *Indus II* in April, 1904, and later *Akbar*, and sold in 1921.

The badge shown was the one carried by the 18,600-ton battleship *Temeraire*, launched at Devonport in 1907, and which served at the battle of Jutland.

H.M.S. TENACIOUS

Description of Badge
FIELD: White.

BADGE: A bulldog's face proper.

MOTTO: Hold fast.

The badge is in allusion to the name.

BATTLE HONOURS

Mediterranean	1944	
Adriatic	1944	
South France	1944	August 15th—27th.
Okinawa	1945	March 26th—May 25th.

The *Tenacious* is one of the limited conversion class of destroyers changed to anti-submarine frigate. Her tonnage is 1,710, and she was completed by Cammell Laird in 1943.

H.M.S. TERMAGANT

Description of Badge
FIELD: White.

BADGE: A shrew mouse proper.

MOTTO:

The badge is in allusion to the name.

BATTLE HONOURS

Egypt	1801	March 8th—September 2nd.
Baltic	1854	
Jutland	1916	May 31st.
Zeebrugge	1918	April 23rd.
Belgian Coast	1918	
Arctic	1943	
Mediterranean	1943-4	
Ægean	1944	
Adriatic	1944	
South France	1944	August 15th—27th.
Okinawa	1945	March 26th—May 25th.

The *Termagant* is one of the limited conversion destroyers changed to anti-submarine frigate. Her tonnage is 1,710, and she was completed by Denny Bros. in 1943.

H.M.S. TERPSICHORE

Description of Badge

FIELD: White.

BADGE: A Greek woman poised for dancing proper.

MOTTO: *Saltando Ducam* (I'll lead them a dance).

The badge is derived from Terpsichore, the muse of choral song and dancing.

BATTLE HONOURS

South Africa	1899-1900	Qualified for medal but not for honour as the ship did not land a brigade.
Ægean	1944	
Adriatic	1944	
South France	1944	August 15th—27th.
"Mahonesa"	1796	Single ship action.

The *Terpsichore* is one of the limited conversion destroyers changed to anti-submarine frigate, and is of 1,710 tons. She was completed by Denny Bros. in 1943.

H.M.S. THESEUS

Description of Badge
FIELD: Blue.
BADGE: A demi-minotaur transfixed with a sword proper.
MOTTO: Action always.

The badge was derived from Greek mythology and represents the Minotaur, which was a monster kept in the labyrinth by Minos and which was slain by Theseus, who was the son of Ægeus and Æthra, husband of Phædra and the father of Hippolytus.

BATTLE HONOURS
Nile	1798	August 1st.
Acre	1799	May 20th.
Basque Roads	1809	April 11th.
Benin	1897	February 8th—28th.
Dardanelles	1915-16	
Korea	1950-51	

The first *Theseus* was a third rate of 74 guns and 1,680 tons, launched in 1786. On 5th July, 1797, she was at the bombardment of Cadiz, and at the attempt on Sta Cruz de Teneriffe was the flagship of Rear-Admiral Sir Horatio Nelson. The captain of the ship was Captain R. W. Miller, who also served on the ship at the battle of the Nile on 1st August, 1798, and in 1799 at the defence of Acre. On 14th May, 1799, Captain Miller was killed by an accidental explosion of shells on board the ship. This vessel served at the Basque Roads and at the blockade of the Scheldt, 1810-1813. In 1814 broken up at Chatham.

H.M.S. THESEUS—*continued*

Thames Iron works launched another vessel of this name on 9th September, 1892, and she was a first-class cruiser of 7,350 tons and carrying twelve 6-inch guns. In 1896 she was commissioned for the Flying Squadron and was the British answer to Kaiser Wilhelm's telegram to Kruger on the occasion of the Jameson raid. A naval brigade was landed by this ship in 1897 for the Benin Expedition under Rear-Admiral H. H. Rawson. During the years 1899-1905 she was in the Mediterranean and Channel, and tender to *Cambridge* as sea-going gunnery training ship. From 1907 to 1912 the same service was performed as tender to *Vivid*. In 1914, August to November, service with the 10th Cruiser Squadron; 1915-1916 in the eastern Mediterranean co-operating with the army at Gallipoli bombarding enemy positions, and covering the evacuation. From December, 1918, to November, 1919, she was in the force sent to the Black Sea and was stationed at Batum. In 1921 she was sold.

The present *Theseus* is a light fleet carrier of 13,350 tons belonging to the *Colossus* class, and was completed by Fairfield in 1946. This vessel has been doing yeoman service in Korea, serving with the navies of the United Nations in support of the ground troops.

H.M.S. THISTLE

Unofficial Badge: A circular field gold, a thistle proper, underneath it a scroll red and green with the motto in white letters. The name of the ship in black letters, this tablet being white edged.

Official Badge
FIELD: White.
BADGE: A thistle leaved and slipped proper.
MOTTO: In allusion to the name of the ship.

BATTLE HONOURS
Baltic   1855
Norway 1940

This vessel commissioned at Devonport in 1902 and in 1925 she was put on the sale list and was a gunboat of 710 tons.

In the Second World War there was a *Thistle* submarine of 1,090 tons (lost), and a drifter of the same name, 79 tons, also lost.

H.M.S. THUNDERER

Unofficial Badge: A figure symbolic of thunder, wild hair and beard, hammer in hand, lightning flashes and clouds all proper. Encircled with a scroll blue with the name of the ship in white Jove, the god of thunder.

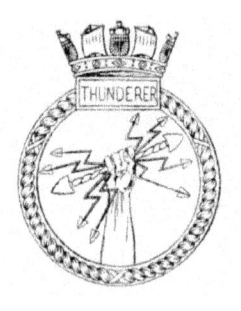

Previous Official Badge
FIELD: Black.

BADGE: A hand proper, grasping a thunderbolt, gold.

MOTTO: *Eripimus Jovi Fulmen* (We snatch the thunder from Jove)

Official Badge
FIELD: Blue.

BADGE: The figure of a man turned to the sinister grasping a

418

H.M.S. THUNDERER—*continued*

hammer over his shoulder. Vested proper and rising from clouds charged with forked lightning white.

MOTTO:

BATTLE HONOURS

Lake Champlain	1776	October 11th and 13th.
First of June	1794	June 1st (and May 28th—29th).
St. Lucia	1976	May 24th.
Trafalgar	1805	October 21st.
Syria	1840	September 10th—December 9th.
Jutland	1916	May 31st.
"Achille"	1761	Single ship action.

The first to carry this name was a third rate of 1,600 tons, launched at Woolwich. After varying services was supposed to have foundered in the great hurricane in the West Indies on 31st October, 1780. The next was a third rate serving in many operations, including the Glorious First of June, capture of the *Venus* and the battle of Trafalgar. Another third rate launched in 1831 served in the Mediterranean at the bombardment of Sidon and St. Jean D'Acre, and in 1863 was converted into a target ship for the trial of armour plate. The twin-screw armour-plated turret ship *Thunderer* launched in 1872 at Pembroke served in the Mediterranean and as guardship at Sheerness and Pembroke. King George V as Prince George of Wales served in this vessel for a while as a Lieutenant. 22,500-ton battleship carrying the name was the vessel which bore the badge shown, and was the flagship of Admiral Prince Louis of Battenberg, Commander-in-Chief, Blue Fleet, during the naval manœuvres in 1912, and in 1913 was the flagship of Vice-Admiral Sir John Jellicoe, Commander-in-Chief, Red Fleet. Whilst in the 2nd Battle Squadron, Grand Fleet, she served at the battle of Jutland. She ran ashore off Blythe on her way to be broken up on 24th December, 1926.

The present *Thunderer* is a shore establishment at Plymouth.

H.M.S. TIGER

Description of Badge

FIELD: Black.

BADGE: A tiger's head gold.

MOTTO: *Quis Erripet Dentes* (Who will draw my teeth?).

Badge in allusion to the name.

BATTLE HONOURS

Armada	1588	July 21st—29th.
Portland	1653	February 18th—20th.
Gabbard	1653	June 2nd—3rd.
Scheveningen	1653	July 31st.
Lowestoft	1665	June 3rd.
Orfordness	1666	July 25th.
Sole Bay	1672	May 28th.
Marbella	1705	March 10th.
Sadras	1758	April 29th.
Negapatam	1758	August 3rd.
Porto Novo	1759	September 10th.
Dogger Bank	1915	January 24th.
Jutland	1916	May 31st.

The *Tiger* was a 27,000-ton battle-cruiser built at Clydebank and completed in 1914; she carried eight 13.5-inch and twelve 6-inch guns.

A cruiser *Tiger* was laid down in October, 1941, but work was suspended. Originally designed to be 8,000 tons.

H.M.S. TORMENTOR

Unofficial Badge: An oval plaque surrounded by cabling and tied in a reef knot at the top. The badge is a flea. In allusion to the name.

BATTLE HONOUR
Martinique   1794   March 22nd.

This vessel was commissioned in 1917 at Scapa Flow for escorting and screening duties, and in 1929 was sold to Messrs. King of Liverpool.

H.M.S. TOTEM

Description of Badge

FIELD: Blue.

BADGE: The head of a totem pole gold decorated red.

MOTTO:

The badge is in allusion to the name.

No battle honours are recorded for this name.

The *Totem* is a submarine of the T class, and was built at Devonport dockyard. The displacement of this class is 1,090/1,575 tons. These are patrol types of vessels according to the official description.

The *Totem*, in addition to carrying a totem on her badge, also has a most impressive totem pole to carry in front of her conning tower.

H.M.S. TOURMALINE

Description of Badge
FIELD: Black.

BADGE: A pendant gold set with a geometrical design black.

MOTTO: *Ex Tenebris Lux* (Out of darkness light).

The badge is in allusion to the name. The tourmaline is a crystalline silicate, some forms of which are used as gems and others are used in optical instruments in connection with polarized light. The badge shown is that of the destroyer. The trawler badge was diamond shape.

BATTLE HONOUR
Atlantic   1943

The *Tourmaline* was a trawler of 641 tons and was sunk in action with enemy aircraft on 5th February, 1941.

The above badge belonged to the destroyer built in 1918, which was sold in 1931.

H.M.S. TRAFALGAR

Description of Badge
FIELD: Gold.

BADGE: A cross flory black within a chaplet of laurel green.

MOTTO:

The cross flory on this badge is derived from the arms of Nelson.

BATTLE HONOUR
Crimea 1854

The *Trafalgar* is one of the *Battle* class of destroyers and was built by Swan Hunter.

H.M.S. TRIBUNE

Description of Badge

FIELD: Blue.

BADGE: A unicorn white with a gold horn, holding a Roman standard marked S.P.Q. (It will be noted that the inscription is incomplete.)

MOTTO: *Par Droit d'armes* (By right of arms).

The unicorn is from the royal arms of Scotland. The tribune was, in ancient Rome, an officer elected by the plebs to preserve their liberties and protect them against tyranny.

BATTLE HONOURS

Baltic	1854	
Crimea	1854-5	
China	1856-60	
North Africa	1942	
Arctic	1942	
Sicily	1943	July 10th—August 17th.

The *Tribune* was a submarine of the *Trident* class and was of the patrol type used for general service. She was completed by Scotts in 1939, and was sold in 1946.

H.M.S. TRIDENT

Description of Badge

FIELD: Barry wavy of six white and blue.

BADGE: A trident gold.

MOTTO:

The badge is in allusion to the name. The trident was the three-pronged weapon which represents the god of the sea. Poseidon (Neptune).

BATTLE HONOURS

Quebec	1759	September 13th.
Cape of Good Hope	1795	September 16th.
Zeebrugge	1918	April 23rd.
Ostend	1918	May 10th.
Norway	1940-1	
Arctic	1941-2	
North Sea	1942	
Mediterranean	1943	
Sicily	1943	July 10th—August 17th.
Atlantic	1944	

The *Trident* gives her name to a patrol class of submarine, of which there were a number of war losses and a number scrapped. The *Trident* was completed by Cammell Laird in 1939. It was the *Trident* which scored a hit on the German vessel *Prinz Eugen*.

H.M.S. TRIUMPH

Unofficial Badge: This badge was carried by H.M.S. *Triumph*, a battleship (pre-*Dreadnought*), of 11,985 tons. Probably a gold mast with green leaves and red berries.

Official Badge
FIELD: White.
BADGE: A wreath of laurel green.
MOTTO: We shall triumph.

Badge is in allusion to the name.

BATTLE HONOURS

Armada	1588	July 21st—29th.
Dover	1652	May 19th.
Portland	1653	February 18th—20th.
Gabbard	1653	June 2nd—3rd.
Scheveningen	1653	July 31st.
Lowestoft	1665	June 3rd.

H.M.S. TRIUMPH—*continued*

Four Days' Battle	1666	June 1st—4th.
Orfordness	1666	July 25th.
Sole Bay	1672	May 28th.
Schooneveld	1673	May 28th—June 4th.
Texel	1673	August 11th.
Cornwallis Retreat	1795	June 17th.
Camperdown	1797	October 11th.
Dardanelles	1915	
Mediterranean	1941	
Malta Convoys	1941	
Korea	1950	

The first *Triumph* was a great ship of 1,100 tons and built in 1561. The armament of this vessel varied from time to time. She served at the battle of the Armada under Captain Martin Frobisher when, on the division of the fleet into four squadrons, Frobisher was made Admiral of the 4th squadron. On 26th July he was knighted by the Lord Admiral on board the *Ark Royal*, and on the 29th of that month the final battle was fought off Gravelines. In 1596 she was rebuilt, and in 1599 served during the mobilization of the fleet against a renewed threat of invasion by the Spaniards, under the command of Sir Fulke Greville, Captain and Rear-Admiral. In 1618 she was sold.

Durell of Deptford built a second rate of this name in 1623 of 921 tons and 42 guns. In 1627 she was in the expedition to Rhe as the flagship of the Duke of Buckingham, Lord High Admiral, and in 1636 she was the flagship of the Earl of Northumberland. When the first Dutch war commenced she was fitted out with 62 guns, and on 19th May, 1652, she was at the battle of Dover, where she was to have been joined by Vice-Marshal Wm. Penn and to be his flagship, but he did not join in time for the battle. On 28th September, 1652, she was at the battle of the Kentish Knock, and on 30th November she was at the battle off Dungeness, serving as flagship of Robert Blake, Admiral and General of the Fleet. On 18th February, 1653, she was at the battle off Portland as the flagship of Blake and Deane, Admirals and Generals of the Fleet. In this engagement her Captain, Andrew Ball, was killed. On 2nd-3rd June she was flagship of James Peacock,

H.M.S. TRIUMPH—*continued*

Vice-Admiral of the Red, at the battle of the Gabbard. At the first battle of the Texel on 29th-31st July, Vice-Admiral Peacock was killed. In 1665 she had 66 guns and was the flagship of Christopher Myngs, Vice-Admiral of the White, and on 3rd July was at the battle off Lowestoft. During 1666 she had 70 guns and was at the Four Days' Fight and the St. James's Day Fight. She was laid up when the Dutch came into the Medway in 1667 and was sunk in shallow water, but afterwards recovered. A succession of battles were served in before finally being sold to the office of Ordnance in 1688.

There was a second rate of this name of 1,482 tons and 90-96 guns, built in 1698 at Chatham by Robert Lee, and this ship served in the expedition to Cadiz in 1702, where she was the flagship of Rear-Admiral John Graydon, but the flag was shifted to the *Northumberland* for the attack on Vigo. In 1703 she was the flagship of Sir Cloudesley Shovell, Commander-in-Chief, Mediterranean; in June, 1705, she was with Vice-Admiral George Byng's squadron off Brest, then with the main fleet under Shovell and Peterborough to the Mediterranean. After other service she was renamed *Prince*, and in 1738 was broken up.

Another vessel of this famous name, though she did not appear on the list of the Navy, was a scow of 18 guns. This vessel surrendered to *Vernon* on 23rd November, 1739, at the capture of Portobello. She was commissioned, but in 1740 she was lost off the Samballa Islands, Darien.

A third rate called the *Triumph* of 1,825 tons and 74 guns was launched on 3rd March, 1764, at Woolwich. This vessel had quite an interesting career, serving in the Channel Fleet under Sir C. Hardy in 1779; 1780-1 in the West Indies with Rodney; on 8th June, 1795, in company with the *Phaeton*, captured part of a French convoy and engaged the batteries at Belle Ile; on 17th June at the Cornwallis retreat under Captain Sir Erasmus Gower; 11th October, 1797, at Camperdown, and in 1799 in the Channel fleet, but on the escape of Bruix from Brest in May she was detached as flagship of Rear-Admiral Cuthbert Collingwood which, with a squadron, joined Lord Keith in the Mediterranean.

She served with Lord Nelson's fleet at the blockade of Toulon in 1803-4; was at Calders' action off Ferrol on 22nd July, 1805, and in chase of Willaumez under Captain Sir T. M. Hardy in

H.M.S. TRIUMPH—*continued*

May, 1806. From 1815 to 1849 she was fitted for a lazarette (quarantine ship) at Milford and continued there until 1859, when she was broken up at Pembroke.

On 8th April, 1859, a vessel was ordered to be built at Pembroke to be named *Triumph*, but after starting as a second rate of 3,716 tons and 91 guns she was put into frame as an iron-cased ship of 50 guns and having her dimensions increased. On 14th February, 1862, she was renamed *Prince Consort*, and launched on 26th June.

On 27th February, 1868, a third rate armoured vessel of 5,026 tons was ordered to be built at Chatham and named *Triumph*, but on 11th March she was renamed *Sultan*.

Then an ironclad of 6,640 tons which was named *Sultan* on 27th February, 1868, was renamed *Triumph* on 11th March, and on 27th September, 1870, was launched. During the years 1873 and 1900 she served on various stations, and in 1901 on 24th June she commissioned as a depot ship for torpedo boats and torpedo boat destroyers at Devonport, being renamed *Tenedos* in April, 1904, and continuing in the same service until 28th February, 1905, when she paid off.

On 15th January, 1903, Vickers of Barrow launched a 11,985 ton battleship for the Chilean Government, but she was bought for the Royal Navy and renamed *Triumph*. From 1904 to 1914 she was engaged in various services, and later in the year of 1914 at the operations for the capture of Tsingtao and the bombarding of forts. In 1915 she was at the Dardanelles, later being switched to the Gulf of Smyrna for bombarding, and finally on 25th March she was sunk by submarine off Gabatepe.

There was a drifter built in Banff of 90 tons used as a netdrifter and for mine clearance. In 1920 she was returned to her owners. There was also another drifter used in the same type of service, built at Yarmouth; she was returned to her owners in 1919. Both these vessels bore the name of *Triumph*. During the 1939-45 war there were a number of small craft bearing this name.

The submarine *Triumph* of 1,090 tons, completed in 1939, was reported missing in January, 1942.

In 1944 on 2nd October a light fleet carrier of 13,350 tons was launched, and completed on 8th April, 1946.

H.M.S. TROUBRIDGE

Description of Badge

FIELD: Red.

BADGE: Upon water barry wavy in base white and blue a bridge of three spans turreted white, masoned black, flying therefrom, from a flagstaff proper, a flag blue.

MOTTO:

The badge is derived from the arms of Troubridge.

BATTLE HONOURS

Mediterranean	1943	
Sicily	1943	July 10th—August 17th.
Salerno	1943	September 9th—October 6th.
Ægean	1944	
Adriatic	1944	
South France	1944	August 15th—27th.
Okinawa	1945	March 26th—May 25th.

The *Troubridge* is a destroyer which gives her name to the class, and was built at Clydebank. Her tonnage is 1,730 and she carries as her main armament four 4.7-inch guns.

H.M.S. TRUCULENT

Description of Badge

FIELD: Gold.

BADGE: Three spiked maces black, two in saltire and one erect.

MOTTO:

The badge is in allusion to the name.

	BATTLE HONOURS	
Zeebrugge	1918	April 23rd.
Belgian Coast	1917	
Arctic	1943	
Atlantic	1944	

The *Truculent* was one of the T class submarines, known before as the *Trident* class, and was completed by Vickers-Armstrongs in 1942. The *Truculent* was sunk in the Thames by a Swedish vessel when she was undergoing trials after having been in dockyard hands.

H.M.S. TUMULT

Description of Badge
FIELD: Blue.

BADGE: Three bells gold, two and one, all conjoined by a ring.

MOTTO: *Tumultu Utamur* (Let us use this tumult (to our advantage)).

The badge is in allusion to the name.

BATTLE HONOURS

Sicily	1943	July 10th—August 17th.
Salerno	1943	September 9th—October 6th.
Atlantic	1943	
Mediterranean	1943-4	
Ægean	1943-4	
Adriatic	1944	
South France	1944	August 15th—27th.

The *Tumult* is one of the limited conversion destroyers changed to anti-submarine frigate. Her tonnage is 1,710, and she was completed by John Brown and Co. in 1943.

H.M.S. TUSCAN

Description of Badge

FIELD: Blue.

BADGE: A lion sejant gold, holding a shield bearing a fleur-de-lis red.

MOTTO: I hold what I take.

The badge is derived from the arms of Tuscany. The first *Tuscan* was captured from the Italian fleet of Napoleon in 1808.

BATTLE HONOURS
Ægean	1944	
Adriatic	1944	
South France	1944	August 15th—27th.

The *Tuscan* is one of the limited conversion destroyers changed to anti-submarine frigate. Her tonnage is 1,710, and she was completed by Swan Hunter in 1943.

H.M.S. TYNE

Description of Badge

FIELD: White.

BADGE: On a fess wavy red a triple-towered castle white, through the centre a trident counterchanged.

MOTTO:

Badge in allusion to the name.

	BATTLE HONOURS
Baltic	1854
Korea	1953

The *Tyne* is a destroyer depot ship of 11,000 tons and carries eight 4.5-inch and two multiple pom-pom guns, having been launched at Greenock in 1940.

H.M.S. TYRIAN

Description of Badge

FIELD: Red.

BADGE: An owl silver, with crook and flail gold.

MOTTO: Tireless ever.

The badge is derived from one of the coins of ancient Tyre.

BATTLE HONOURS

Sicily	1943	July 10th—August 17th.
Salerno	1943	September 9th—October 6th.
Atlantic	1943	
Mediterranean	1943	
Ægean	1944	
Adriatic	1944	
South France	1944	August 15th—27th.

The *Tyrian* is one of the limited conversion destroyers changed to anti-submarine frigate. Her tonnage is 1,710, and she was completed at Swan Hunter's in 1943.

H.M.S. ULSTER

Description of Badge

FIELD: Barry wavy of six white and blue.

BADGE: A dexter hand appaume red, dripping drops of blood also red.

MOTTO:

The badge is derived from the badge of Ulster.

BATTLE HONOURS

English Channel	1943	
Mediterranean	1944	
Adriatic	1944	
Normandy	1944	June 6th—July 3rd.
Okinawa	1945	March 26th—May 25th.

The *Ulster* is a destroyer which gives her name to the class, though perhaps this may now change in view of the fact that some of this class have now been converted to anti-submarine frigates. Her tonnage is 1,710, and she carries four 4.7-inch guns among her other smaller armament. This vessel was built in 1942.

H.M.S. ULYSSES

Description of Badge

FIELD: Barry wavy of ten white and blue.

BADGE: A ram's head affronte black in front of a stake erect inflamed.

MOTTO:

The badge is derived from Greek mythology and refers to the escape of Ulysses from the cave of Cyclops.

BATTLE HONOURS

Martinique	1794	March 22nd.
Egypt	1801	March 8th—September 2nd.
Martinique	1809	February 24th.
Normandy	1944	June 6th—July 3rd.
Arctic	1944	

The *Ulysses* is a destroyer of the *Ulster* class of 1,710 tons. She was built by Cammell Laird.

H.M.S. UNA

Description of Badge
FIELD: Blue.

BADGE: A woman proper habited white resting her sinister hand upon a lion statant gardant gold.

MOTTO:

This badge is in allusion to Una and the Lion from Spencers' "Færie Queen," Canto III. This refers to Una's encounter with the lion and how the animal went along with her as a strong guard when searching for her wandering knight.

BATTLE HONOUR
Burma   1945

There were two vessels given the name of *Una*, a submarine of the *Ursula* class built at Chatham Dockyard and completed on 27th September, 1941, and an unusual craft built in Burma. The badge depicted was for the submarine.

There was another, formerly a German yacht, captured by the Royal Australian Navy in 1914.

H.M.S. UNBEATEN

Description of Badge

FIELD: Per fess wavy blue and barry wavy of four white and blue.

BADGE: A figure of Britannia robed white with shield and trident, helm and trident gold.

MOTTO:

The badge is in allusion to the name and the shield is from the Union flag.

BATTLE HONOURS
Biscay 1942
Mediterranean 1941-2
Malta Convoys 1941-2

The *Unbeaten* was a submarine of 540 tons and was listed as missing in December, 1942. Official sources state that she may have been lost through the action of our own forces.

H.M.S. UNBROKEN

Description of Badge
FIELD: White.

BADGE: Issuant from water barry wavy in base proper a demi-horse salient black.

MOTTO: *Frango Infractus* (I break, but am not broken).

The badge is in allusion to the name.

BATTLE HONOUR
Sicily   1943   July 10th—August 17th.

The *Unbroken* was originally the P42, and was one of the *Ursula* class built by Vickers-Armstrongs. Her tonnage was 540/730.

This submarine was launched by Mrs. Linton, the wife of one of our ablest submarine commanders, at Barrow-in-Furness. She was commanded by Alastair Mars, D.S.O., D.S.C. and bar, serving with distinction in the Mediterranean. There she attacked merchant ships, cruisers, destroyers, shore targets, railway trains, etc. Also took agents in to the south of France where they landed in folboats. She sank some 30,000 tons of shipping and crippled two cruisers. This vessel was handed to the Russians in 1944 together with the *Ursula*, *Unison* and the battleship *Royal Sovereign*. She was returned to England in 1949 and was broken up at Newcastle in 1950.

H.M.S. UNDAUNTED

Description of Badge
FIELD: Blue.

BADGE: A falcon white hooded and belled gold.

MOTTO:

The badge is derived from the following: The French vessel *Bienvenue* was taken at Martinique, owing mainly to the distinguished conduct of Captain Robert Faulkner (1794), who was promoted to command the prize, "Renamed after you, sir, the *Undaunted*," as the Commander-in-Chief, Sir John Jervis, said in giving him his commission.

BATTLE HONOURS
China	1900	Entitled to medal but not battle honour.
Dogger Bank	1915	January 24th.
Belgian Coast	1916	
Normandy	1944	June 6th—July 3rd.
Okinawa	1945	March 26th—May 25th.

The *Undaunted* is one of the full conversion class of destroyers changed to anti-submarine frigate, and is of 1,710 tons. She was completed by Cammell Laird in 1944.

H.M.S. UNDINE

Description of Badge

FIELD: Blue.

BADGE: A mermaid gold diving into water in base barry wavy white and blue.

MOTTO:

The badge is derived from *Undine*, a female spirit of the water, without, but capable of, receiving a human soul.

BATTLE HONOURS

Adriatic	1944	
Normandy	1944	June 6th—July 3rd.
Mediterranean	1944	
Okinawa	1945	March 26th—May 25th.

The *Undine* is one of the full conversion class of destroyers changed to anti-submarine frigate. Her tonnage is 1,710, and she was completed by Thornycroft in 1943. The previous *Undine* was a submarine, sunk in Heligoland Bight in 1940.

H.M.S. UNICORN

Description of Badge
FIELD: Blue.

BADGE: A unicorn rampant white, armed and winged gold.

MOTTO:

The badge is in allusion to the name; the name is from one of the supporters of the royal arms.

BATTLE HONOURS

Armada	1588	Coaster of Bristol, under Lord High Admiral.
Armada	1588	Voluntary ship of Dartmouth.
Cadiz	1596	June 21st.
Porto Farina	1655	April 4th.
Santa Cruz	1657	April 20th.
Lowestoft	1665	June 3rd.
Orfordness	1666	July 25th.
Sole Bay	1672	May 28th.
Schooneveld	1673	May 28th—June 4th.
Texel	1673	August 11th.
Basque Roads	1809	April 11th.
Salerno	1943	September 9th—October 6th.
Okinawa	1945	
"Vestale"	1761	January 8th. Single ship action.
"Tribune"	1796	June 8th. Single ship action.
Korea	1950-3	

H.M.S. UNICORN—continued

The first *Unicorn* was captured from the Scots at Leith by the fleet under Lord Lisle in 1544, and she was a galleasse of 240 tons carrying 6 guns made of brass and 30 made of iron.

Another *Unicorn*, the *Unicorn* of Bristol, served at the battle of the Armada and was one of the coasters under the Lord High Admiral. This one was of 130 tons and her crew numbered 66. At the same battle was another of the name hailing from Dartmouth, and was one of the volunteer ships which joined the Royal Navy.

In 1633 a second rate of this name of 845 tons and 64 guns was built at Woolwich. She served in the Mediterranean and was at Blake's attack on Porto Farina in 1655, at Lowestoft, the Four Days' Fight, St. James's Day Fight, Sole Bay, Schooneveld, and in 1667 in action against the Dutch fleet in the Medway. She was sold on 27th January, 1687.

A fire-ship of 180 tons and 6 guns which was purchased in 1666 also bore this proud name. She was sunk as a bar at Chatham in 1667.

In 1665 there was a ship called the *Little Unicorn*, a Dutch prize commissioned in the Royal Navy as a frigate. She was later converted into a fire-ship and was expended in action in the Four Days' Fight.

The sixth rate of this name, built at Plymouth and launched on 7th December, 1748, was 481 tons and carried 28 guns. In 1757 she captured the French privateer *Invincible*, and the *Unicorn's* captain was mortally wounded in the action; she assisted the *Shrewsbury* (74) and *Lizard* (28) in an attack on a French convoy off Brest, and in this action one of the escorting frigates was driven ashore and many of the convoy taken or destroyed; on 8th January, 1761, she captured the French *Vestale* (32) off the Penmarc'h, and the captains of both ships were mortally wounded in the battle; she was then at the expedition to Belle Isle, and was finally broken up at Sheerness in 1771.

There was a *Unicorn* launched on the River Thames on the 23rd March, 1776, of 433 tons and 20 guns. This vessel, in company with the *Experiment* (50), captured the U.S. ship *Raleigh* (32) on 26th September, 1778. In 1779 she took part in

H.M.S. UNICORN—*continued*

Wallace's attack on the French in Canacale Bay; on 4th September, 1780, she was captured by two French frigates off Hispaniola, but on 20th April, 1781, she was recaptured by the *Renown*. She ended her days at Deptford and was broken up in 1787.

A fifth rate was launched as the *Unicorn* on 7th November, 1782, at Bursledon and was renamed the *Thalia* on 15th August that same year.

Another fifth rate of this name was launched at Chatham on 12th July, 1794, and was of 791 tons and carried 32 guns. On 8th June, 1796, she captured the French 40-gun frigate *La Tribune* (naval medal awarded for the action). In 1799 she took part in Rear-Admiral Morice Pole's attack on the Spanish fleet in Aix Roads; on 6th May, 1805, she captured the French privateer *Tape-a-Bord* off San Domingo. She was present at the capture of Monte Video in 1807, captured the French 22-gun vessel *Esperance* off the Isle of Rhe on 22nd April, 1808, and was with Lord Gambier's attack on 12th April, 1809, on a French fleet in the Basque Roads, for which a naval medal was awarded. This vessel was broken up at Deptford in 1815.

Yet another fifth rate, this time of 1,084 tons and 46 guns, was given the name of *Unicorn*, and she was launched at Chatham on 30th March, 1824. In 1856 she was loaned to the War Department for service as a powder hulk at Woolwich, in 1863 she was fitted as a drill ship for Naval Reserves to replace H.M.S. *Brilliant*, and on 5th November, 1873, she left Sheerness for Dundee in tow of H.M.S. *Salamander*. It was reported in 1939 that as the name *Unicorn* had been appropriated for the Fleet Air Arm supply and repair ship of the 1938 programme, the old ship of the name employed as the R.N.V.R. drill ship at Dundee would in future be known as *Unicorn II*. With the exception of the *Victory*, this is the oldest vessel still in service under the Royal Navy.

H.M.S. UPSTART

Description of Badge

FIELD: Blue.

BADGE: A man proper strapped to a wheel gold.

MOTTO:

The badge was suggested by the commanding officer of the *Upstart*. From Greek mythology and concerns the legend of Ixion.

BATTLE HONOURS

Atlantic 1944
Mediterranean 1944

This vessel is a submarine of 545 tons, and was completed in 1943. She was on loan to the Royal Hellenic Navy and was called the *Xifias*, and on return was re-named *Upstart*.

H.M.S. URANIA

Description of Badge
FIELD: Blue.

BADGE: A crescent white within a circle of estoiles.

MOTTO:

The badge is derived from Urania, the nurse of astronomy, who is usually represented with a globe in her hand to which she points with a rod.

BATTLE HONOURS
Normandy	1944	June 6th—July 3rd.
Okinawa	1945	March 26th—May 25th.

The *Urania* is one of the full conversion class of destroyers changed to anti-submarine frigate. Her tonnage is 1,710, and she was completed by Vickers-Armstrongs in 1944.

H.M.S. URCHIN

Description of Badge

FIELD: Barry wavy of eight white and blue.

BADGE: A hedgehog proper.

MOTTO:

The badge is in allusion to the name.

BATTLE HONOURS

Egypt	1801	March 8th—September 2nd.
Mediterranean	1944	
Adriatic	1944	
Anzio	1944	January 22nd—31st.
Normandy	1944	June 6th—July 3rd.
Okinawa	1945	March 26th—May 25th.

The *Urchin* is one of the full conversion class of destroyers changed to anti-submarine frigate and is of 1,710 tons. She was completed by Thornycroft in 1944.

H.M.S. URSA

Description of Badge

FIELD: Blue.

BADGE: A brown bear passant proper.

MOTTO:

The badge is in allusion to the name.

BATTLE HONOURS
Normandy	1944	June 6th—July 3rd.
Biscay	1944	
Okinawa	1945	March 26th—May 25th.

The *Ursa* is one of the full conversion class of destroyers changed to anti-submarine frigate. Her tonnage is 1,710, and she was completed by Vickers-Armstrongs in 1943.

H.M.S. VANGUARD

Unofficial Badge: This badge was carried by the battleship (super-*Dreadnought*) H.M.S. *Vanguard* of 19,250 tons. Field black, Nelson's head and shoulders proper, gold lettering and cabling, black scroll with white letters H.M.S. VANGUARD.

Official Badge

FIELD: Blue.

BADGE: Issuing from barry four white and green a demi-lion gold supporting a spear issuing white.

MOTTO: We lead.

The badge is derived from the custom of R.N. vessels to carry a lion figurehead, a custom which lasted for many years. The green and white bars are the Tudor colours referring to the first *Vanguard*, built in the reign of Queen Elizabeth I.

H.M.S. VANGUARD—continued

BATTLE HONOURS

Armada	1588	July 21st—29th.
Cadiz	1596	June 21st.
Portland	1653	February 18th—20th.
Gabbard	1653	June 2nd—3rd.
Scheveningen	1653	July 31st.
Lowestoft	1665	June 3rd.
Four Days' Battle	1666	June 1st—4th.
Orfordness	1666	July 25th.
Barfleur	1692	May 19th—24th.
Louisburg	1758	July 26th.
Quebec	1759	September 13th.
Martinique	1762	February 16th.
Nile	1798	August 1st.
Syria	1840	September 10th—December 9th.
Jutland	1916	May 31st.

The first of the vessels which bore the name *Vanguard* was a galleon rated as 500 tons and carrying 42 guns. She was built by Matthew Baker at Woolwich in 1586. In 1588 she served in the Spanish Armada campaign and was the flagship of Sir Wm. Wynter; at the taking of the Fort Crozon near Brest from the Spaniards in 1594, in which Sir Martin Frobisher, Captain and Admiral, was mortally wounded; in 1596 at the taking of Cadiz under Captain Sir Robert Mansell. She was rebuilt on two different occasions, one in 1599 and the other in 1615. During the Algiers Expedition in 1620 she was the flagship of Sir Richard Hawkins; in 1625 in the "affair of Pennington's ships"; in 1627 with Buckingham's expedition to Rhe, under Captain Sir John Burgh; and in about 1629 (the exact date is not known) she was cast from the service.

Then there was a second rate of 563-751 tons, 40-60 guns, launched at Woolwich in March, 1631. In the year 1652, on 16th July she was at Ayscue's action off Plymouth, on 28th September at the battle of the Kentish Knock, and on 30th November at the battle of Dungeness. The 18th February, 1653, found her at the battle off Portland as the flagship of Monck, on 3rd June at the battle off Gabbard, and on 29th—31st July at the first

H.M.S. VANGUARD—*continued*

battle of the Texel as the flagship of Vice-Admiral Joseph Jordan. Then came the battle off Lowestoft, 3rd June, 1665; the Four Days' Fight of 1666, 1st to 4th June, when her Captain, John Whitty, was killed; and on 25th July of the same year the St. James's Fight. In 1667 she was sunk at Chatham.

The next ship was a second rate of 1,357 tons and 90 guns, built at Portsmouth in 1678. This vessel was at the battle of Barfleur in 1692, and in 1703 she was overset in the Medway during the Great Storm of November, being rebuilt in 1710, and in 1728 she was renamed *Duke*.

There was a third rate of 1,419 tons and 70 guns, built in 1748 at Cowes, and this vessel took part in the capture of Louisburg in June, 1758; at the capture of Quebec with Saunder's Fleet in September, 1759; the relief of Quebec in May, 1760, as the flagship of Commodore Robert Swanton; at the capture of Martinique in February, 1762, and in May, 1774, she was sold.

The next one was not registered on the lists of the Navy but she was a gunboat bought at Gibraltar in 1781 by Sir Roger Curtis and was probably a Spanish prize; she served at Gibraltar during the siege and appears to have been sold in 1783.

Then came a third rate of 1,609 tons and 74 guns, built at Deptford in 1787. In June, 1794, she was at the attempt on Guadeloupe, and on 1st August, 1798, at the battle of the Nile as the flagship of Rear-Admiral Sir Horatio Nelson. On 25th July, 1803, captured the *Duquesne* (74) off San Domingo. During August and September of 1807 she was in the expedition against Copenhagen, and in 1821 she was broken up.

A "Symondite" was the next one, built at Pembroke in 1835, and was a second rate of 2,609 tons and 80 guns. She took part in the operations on the coast of Syria in September and November, 1840. She did not take part in the Russian war of 1854-5, and in 1867 she was renamed *Ajax*.

An ironclad of 3,774 tons and armed with 14 guns was the next to bear the name, and she was launched at Birkenhead in 1870. This ship was sunk in collision with the *Iron Duke* off the coast of Ireland on 1st September, 1875.

On 22nd February, 1909, the battleship *Vanguard* of 19,250 tons was launched at Barrow, being completed on 1st March,

H.M.S. VANGUARD—*continued*

1910. In 1914 she was in the 1st Battle Squadron, Grand Fleet, and took part in the battle of Jutland. She was blown up on 9th July, 1917, by an internal explosion at Scapa Flow.

During the 1914-18 war there were also hired motor drifters bearing the name.

The present *Vanguard* was launched in November, 1944, by Her Majesty The Queen, as Princess Elizabeth. She is of 42,500 tons and carries as her main armament 15-inch guns which were those first mounted in H.M.S. *Glorious* and H.M.S. *Courageous* in 1917. Designed by Sir Stanley Goodall.

H.M.S. VENGEANCE

Description of Badge
FIELD: Red.

BADGE: Three daggers in pile, points downwards, proper, pommels and hilts gold.

MOTTO: I strike, I cover.

Badge is in allusion to the name.

BATTLE HONOURS
Quiberon Bay	1759	November 20th.
Martinique	1794	March 22nd.
St. Lucia	1796	May 24th.
Crimea	1854	
Dardanelles	1915	

The first *Vengeance* was a sixth rate of 533 tons and 28 guns. This ship was the French *Vengeance* of 32 guns, captured off the Lizard by Captain John Elliott on H.M.S. *Hussar* (28). She was added to the Royal Navy under the same name, and eventually an order was given to make her into a breakwater at Plymouth.

The next *Vengeance* had quite an interesting history and was built on the Thames 1771-1774, being a third rate of 1,627 tons and 74 guns. On 27th July, 1778, under Captain Michael Clements, she was at the battle off Ushant; 17th April, 1780, at Rodney's action off Martinique, and in May of the same year at the action with de Guichen for the defence of St. Lucia. On 10th October, 1780, she was dismasted and damaged in the Great

H.M.S. VENGEANCE—continued

Hurricane, being sent to England in 1781 for repair, Commodore Hotham being in charge of the convoy carrying spoils of war from St. Eustatius. This convoy was intercepted by a greatly superior French squadron and many merchant ships were taken. In February, 1794, she was with Sir John Jervis at the capture of Martinique; February, 1797, at the capitulation of Trinidad; and in 1802 returned from the West Indies at the Peace of Amiens and was not commissioned again. She was then lent to the Transport Board for use as a prison ship for prisoners of war, and in 1816 she was broken up.

The name appeared again with an armed galleon of 4 guns which was bought at Ostend on 21st November, 1793, and was at first described as a Dutch hoy. There is no information available as to her services, but she may have been used experimentally, for in 1794 an anti-invasion gunboat flotilla was begun with other vessels of this type. The name remained on the Navy List until 1826, when it was suddenly removed without any explanation.

The French 40-gun frigate *Vengeance* of 1,370 tons, a fifth rate, was captured by the *Seine* (38) in Mona Passage and was used as a hulk for prisoners of war at Jamaica under the same name. Her name was removed from the Navy List in 1837, but it is believed that she was disposed of in Jamaica in 1814.

On 26th July, 1824, a second rate of this name and of 2,284 tons and 84 guns was launched at Pembroke. She served in the Mediterranean and was in the Black Sea in the Crimean War. From 1861 to 1897 she was a receiving hulk at Devonport, and then sold.

There was a battleship of 12,950 tons, carrying four 12-inch and twelve 6-inch guns and having a speed of $18\frac{1}{4}$ knots, of this name, launched on 25th July, 1899. In 1909 she was tender to Chatham Gunnery School; 1914, flagship of the 7th Battle Squadron at the Ostend Diversion of 28th August; from 11th November, 1914, to January, 1915, with the Cape Verde Squadron; 19th February to 22nd May, 1915, in operations at the Dardanelles; and in 1921 she was sold.

The *Vengeance* light fleet carrier was completed in 1945 and is one of the *Colossus* class.

H.M.S. VENUS

Description of Badge

FIELD: Blue.

BADGE: The symbol of the planet Venus gold.

MOTTO:

The badge is in allusion to the name.

BATTLE HONOURS

Quiberon	1759	November 20th.
St. Lucia	1778	December 15th.
First of June	1794	June 1st (and May 28th—29th).
Arctic	1942-44	
Normandy	1944	June 6th—July 3rd.
Malaya	1945	
Burma	1945	

The *Venus* is one of the full conversion class of destroyers changed to anti-submarine frigate. Her tonnage is 1,710, and she was completed by Fairfield in 1943.

H.M.S. VERULAM

Description of Badge

FIELD: Blue.

BADGE: In front of a saltire couped gold a sword erect proper, pommel and hilt also gold.

MOTTO:

The badge is derived from the arms of the city and the see of St. Albans.

BATTLE HONOURS

Norway	1944	
Normandy	1944	June 6th—July 3rd.
Arctic	1944	
Malaya	1945	
Burma	1945	

The *Verulam* is one of the full conversion class of destroyer changed to anti-submarine frigate. Her tonnage is 1,710, and she was completed by Fairfield in 1943.

H.M.S. VICTORIOUS

Description of Badge

FIELD: Red.

BADGE: A winged female figure habited and supporting with the hands uplifted a wreath of laurel white.

MOTTO:

Badge is in allusion to victory.

BATTLE HONOURS

Norway	1941-44	
"Bismarck"	1941	May 23rd—27th.
Arctic	1941-2	
Biscay	1942	
North Africa	1942	
Malta Convoys	1942	
Sabang	1944	July 25th.
Palembang	1945	January 24th.
Okinawa	1945	March 26th—May 25th.
Japan	1945	
"Rivoli"	1812	February 22nd. Single ship action.

The first *Victorious* was a third-rate vessel of 1,659 tons, launched at Blackwall on 27th April, 1785. In 1795 she was at the capture of the Cape of Good Hope, in 1796 she was in action off the north end of Sumatra in company with the *Arrogant* (74) with a French squadron of frigates, and in 1803 she was taken to pieces at Lisbon.

The next ship of this name was launched at Buckler's Hard in October, 1808, and was a 74-gun ship of 1,724 tons. She took part

H.M.S. VICTORIOUS—*continued*

in the Walcheren expedition of 1809; on 22nd February, 1812, she fought a single-ship action, capturing the French *Rivoli* (74) off the Gulf of Trieste; in 1835 she was fitted as a receiving ship and in 1868 was broken up.

The third *Victorious* was a first-class battleship of 14,900 tons, and was launched on 19th October, 1895, at Chatham. In 1898 she was ordered to China via the Suez Canal, going aground near Port Said, but she was lightened and proceeded on her way; by 1919 she had become a dockyard repair ship, and in 1923 was sold to a ship-breaking firm.

The aircraft carrier *Victorious* was built by Vickers-Armstrongs and completed in 1941. In 1941 aircraft from the *Victorious* made an attack on the *Bismarck* by night, making a long-distance attack and scoring one hit; her planes also found the *Tirpitz*, and an attack was made but the results were not known. On another sortie, in company with aircraft from the *Furious*, the combined force of planes sank a whole convoy off the Norwegian coast. More great work was accomplished in Pacific waters.

H.M.S. VICTORY

Description of Badge

This badge shows the stern view of the famous ship now preserved at Portsmouth Dockyard. Underneath is a scroll which carries the name.

BATTLE HONOURS

Armada	1588	July 21st—29th.
Dover	1652	May 19th.
Portland	1653	February 18th—20th.
Gabbard	1653	June 2nd—3rd.
Scheveningen	1653	July 31st.
Four Days' Battle	1666	June 1st—4th.
Orfordness	1666	July 25th.
Sole Bay	1672	May 28th.
Schooneveld	1673	May 28th—June 4th.
Texel	1673	August 11th.
Barfleur	1692	May 19th—20th.
Ushant	1781	December 12th.
St. Vincent	1797	February 14th.
Trafalgar	1805	October 21st.

The present H.M.S. *Victory*, Nelson's *Victory*, was launched a Chatham in May, 1765, of 2,162 tons, and carrying 104 guns and two carronades. She was a good, fast, manœuvrable vessel and was a great favourite as a flagship, many famous admirals having hoisted their flags in her. In 1798 the *Victory* was pronounced unseaworthy and was used at Chatham as a prison hulk. Nelson is supposed to have persuaded the Admiralty to prepare

H.M.S. VICTORY—*continued*

her for sea service again. In 1803 this work was completed and she became Nelson's flagship, where he remained in her until his death at Trafalgar. During her sea service she had been in many engagements, and it is a great tribute to British shipbuilding that she should have endured so well. From 1812 to 1922 the *Victory* was moored in Portsmouth Harbour and for a time was used as a training ship. Public interest and the work of the Society for Nautical Research resulted in the ship being preserved as a National Memorial. During the war, when war damage occurred at the Admiralty House in Portsmouth, the Commander-in-Chief used *Victory* as his Headquarters. During enemy air raids on Portsmouth the *Victory* had a 500-pound bomb dropped between her and the dock wall and which exploded underneath the fore part. Many thousands of people have visited this ship, and there is no doubt that she is a fine sight and calculated to stir the heart of any sea-minded boy.

The battle honours show the many engagements which the ships bearing the name *Victory* have taken a vigorous part in.

H.M.S. VIDAL

Description of Badge

FIELD: Green with barry wavy per fess two white and one blue.

BADGE: A grid-iron gold.

MOTTO:

Badge derived from survey work done by Admiral Vidal on the St. Lawrence river; the grid-iron being in allusion to St. Lawrence, who was roasted on a grid.

There are no battle honours recorded for this name.

This is a new type of survey vessel recently launched and fitted out at Chatham. She is of mostly welded construction and she has a platform for landing helicopters, being built in 1951.

H.M.S. VIGILANT

Description of Badge

FIELD: Blue.

BADGE: A dragon couchant gardant gold.

MOTTO:

BATTLE HONOURS

Abyssinia	1868	April 13th. Took part in campaign, but not eligible for honour as she did not land a naval brigade.
Arctic	1943-4	
Normandy	1944	June 6th—July 3rd.
Malaya	1945	
Burma	1945	

The *Vigilant* is one of the full conversion class of destroyers changed to anti-submarine frigate. Her tonnage is 1,710, and she was completed by Swan Hunter in 1943.

H.M.S. VIGO

Description of Badge

FIELD: Blue.

BADGE: Within a wreath of laurel gold a plate whereon a rook close proper.

MOTTO:

The badge is derived from the arms of Sir George Rooke, Commander-in-Chief.

No battle honours are recorded for this name.

The *Vigo* is one of the *Battle* class of destroyers, and was built by Fairfield's.

H.M.S. VINDICTIVE

Description of Badge

FIELD: Blue.

BADGE: Out of a cloud proper, an arm, the hand grasping a scimitar, all gold.

MOTTO: *Vindicavi* (I have made good).

The cloud refers to the attack on Zeebrugge having been made out of a smoke screen. The badge is the same as the earlier unofficial one.

BATTLE HONOURS
Zeebrugge	1918	April 23rd.
Ostend	1918	May 10th.
Norway	1940	

The *Vindictive* was built as a cruiser of the improved *Birmingham* class under the name of *Cavendish*, but she was renamed and completed as an aircraft carrier. She was later reconverted to a cruiser. She was then converted into a cadets' training ship and later into a repair ship.

The famous *Vindictive* was an armoured cruiser built in 1897 at Chatham.

H.M.S. VIRAGO

Description of Badge
FIELD: White.

BADGE: A demi-wild and dishevelled woman proper.

MOTTO:

The badge is in allusion to the name.

BATTLE HONOURS
North Cape	1943	December 26th.
Normandy	1944	June 6th—July 3rd.
Malaya	1945	
Burma	1945	
Arctic	1943-4	

The *Virago* is one of the full conversion class of destroyers changed to anti-submarine frigate. Her tonnage is 1,170, and she was completed by Swan Hunter in 1943.

H.M.S. VOLAGE

Description of Badge

FIELD: White.

BADGE: A red admiral butterfly proper.

The badge is derived from the name.

	BATTLE HONOURS	
Lissa	1811	March 13th.
Aden	1839	January 19th.
Baltic	1855	
Arctic	1944	

The *Volage* is one of the full conversion class of destroyers changed to anti-submarine frigate. Her tonnage is 1,710, and she was completed by Samuel White in 1944.

H.M.S. VULCAN (DEFIANCE)

Badges which ships connected by name with Defiance have borne also Battle Honours in other notes.

H.M.S. VULCAN

FIELD: Red.

BADGE: A hammer and spanner crossed, both gold, beneath wavelets blue and silver.

MOTTO: *Vis Fortibus Arma* (Strength is a weapon to the brave).

H.M.S. INCONSTANT

FIELD: Blue.

BADGE: A butterfly gold.

MOTTO: In Constancy Constant.

H.M.S. VULCAN (DEFIANCE)—*continued*

H.M.S. VULCAN (DEFIANCE)

BATTLE HONOURS

Barfleur	1692	May 19th—24th
Velez Malaga	1704	August 13th.
Finisterre	1747	May 3rd.
Crimea	1854-5	
China	1860	
Atlantic	1940	
Libya	1942	

The last vessel to bear this name was a trawler of 623 tons. (ex *Mascot*, ex *Aston Villa*) and acted as a depot ship for coastal craft.

H.M.S. INCONSTANT (DEFIANCE)

BATTLE HONOURS

Genoa	1795	March 14th.
Egypt	1801	March 8th—September 2nd
Jutland	1916	May 31st.
Diego Suarez	1942	May 5th—7th.
Arctic	1942-3-4	
Sicily	1943	July 10th—August 17th.
Atlantic	1943-4	
Normandy	1944	June 6th—July 3rd.
English Channel	1944	

The first *Inconstant* was a fifth rate of 890 tons and 36 guns. She was launched on the River Thames in 1783.

Then there was another fifth rate of 1,421 tons and 36 guns. This vessel was launched at Portsmouth in 1836.

Another one to have the name was the screw cruiser, second class, launched in 1868 at Pembroke. In 1897 she was an overflow ship for the Barracks at Devonport. In 1911 she was renamed *Impregnable II*.

The last *Inconstant* was a destroyer of 1,370 tons.

H.M.S. ANDROMEDA (DEFIANCE)

BATTLE HONOUR

St. Vincent	1780	January 16th.

Name from Greek mythology.

H.M.S. VULCAN (DEFIANCE)—*continued*

The *Andromeda* was a first-class protected cruiser of 11,000 tons and carrying sixteen 6-inch guns. She was launched at Pembroke in 1897 on 30th April, and from June, 1899, she was in reserve and on various stations until 1910. On 18th June, 1910, she was the parent ship of the Special Service Cruisers. In 1912, on 10th May, she became tender to *Euryalus* and renamed *Powerful II*, being added to H.M.S. *Powerful* on the commissioning of the *Powerful* as the Boys' Training Establishment at Devonport on 23rd September, 1913. She was subsequently renamed *Impregnable II*. H.M.S. *Impregnable* as a training ship was broken up in 1928. On 27th March, 1929, the *Impregnable II* was paid off into dockyard control at Devonport.

H.M.S. WAGER

Description of Badge

FIELD: White.

BADGE: A cross blue charged with five bezants within a horseshoe inverted red.

MOTTO: *Sponsione Provoco* (I challenge with a wager).

The badge is in allusion to the name and to the arms of Admiral Sir Charles Wager.

BATTLE HONOUR
Okinawa   1945   March 26th—May 25th.

The *Wager* is a destroyer which gives her name to the class. She was built at Clydebank.

H.M.S. WAKEFUL

Description of Badge
FIELD: Black.

BADGE: An eye proper with rays issuing therefrom gold.

MOTTO: *Si Dormiam Capiar* (Catch a weasel asleep).

The badge is in allusion to the name.

BATTLE HONOURS
Dunkirk	1940	May 26th—June 4th.
Atlantic	1939-40	
North Sea	1944	

The *Wakeful* is one of the full conversion class of destroyers changed to anti-submarine frigate. Her tonnage is 1,710, and she was completed by Fairfield in 1944.

H.M.S. WARRIOR

First Official Badge: A warrior in dress and helmet gold with sword and shield on a wreath blue and black. White scroll, gold edged, with motto ARMA FIRUMQUE in black.

Official Badge

FIELD: Green.

BADGE: A warrior's head proper, mustachioed crined and with armour gold, helmet white, winged also gold.

Based on a badge previously used by the ship.

BATTLE HONOURS

The Saints	1782	April 12th.
Copenhagen	1801	April 2nd. Support ship not engaged.
Jutland	1916	May 31st.

H.M.S. WARRIOR—*continued*

The first *Warrior* was a third rate of 1,621 tons and 74 guns, and was launched at Portsmouth on 18th October, 1781. She was at the battle of the Saintes in 1782 under Captain Sir James Wallace, at Copenhagen in 1801, and in 1805 at Calder's action off Ferrol. In 1809 she was at the occupation of the Greek Islands, and in 1857 was broken up.

Then followed an ironclad frigate of 6,121 tons and 40-68-pounder guns. She was launched at Blackwall in December, 1860, and served from 1861 to 1871 in the Channel Fleet, and in 1876 she was the coast-guard ship at Portland. From 1881 to 1883 she did the same duties at Greenock. This vessel was then re-rated as a third-class battleship in 1887, and in 1904 was renamed *Vernon III*.

The next vessel to carry the name was an armoured cruiser of 13,550 tons and having as her armament six 9.2-inch and four 7.5-inch guns. She was launched at Pembroke on 25th November, 1905, and in 1914 she joined the Grand Fleet at Scapa Flow. On 31st May she was at the battle of Jutland under Captain V. B. Molteno and was severely damaged in action. On 1st June the crew were taken off by the *Engadine* and she was abandoned and sunk.

There was a yacht *Warrior* of 1,266 tons and which carried two 12-pounders. She served from July, 1917, to November, 1918, on the North American and West Indies stations.

A trawler of 236 tons also carried this name, which was built at Grimsby in 1898. This vessel served from 1915 to 1918 on the Kingston Patrol.

The present *Warrior* is an aircraft carrier of the *Glory* class of 13,350 tons, and was completed in 1946. Modernized in 1952-3.

H.M.S. WARSPITE

Description of Badge
FIELD: Green.

BADGE: A ship's gun (*circa* 1600) gold.

MOTTO: *Belli dura despicio* (I despise the hard knocks of war).

There is another badge showing a woodpecker.

BATTLE HONOURS

Cadiz	1596	June 21st.
Orfordness	1666	July 25th.
Sole Bay	1672	May 28th.
Schooneveld	1673	May 28th and June 4th.
Texel	1673	August 11th.
Barfleur	1692	May 19th—24th.
Velez Malaga	1705	March 10th.
Lagos	1759	August 17th.
Quiberon Bay	1759	November 20th.
Jutland	1916	May 31st.
Atlantic	1939	English Channel, 1944.
Narvik	1940	April 10th and 13th.
Norway	1940	
Calabria	1940	July 9th.
Malta Convoys	1941	
Matapan	1941	March 28th—29th.
Crete	1941	May 20th—June 1st.
Sicily	1943	July 10th—August 17th.

H.M.S. WARSPITE—*continued*

Salerno	1943	September 9th—October 6th.
Normandy	1944	June 6th—July 3rd.
Walcheren	1944	November 1st.
Biscay	1944	Mediterranean 1940—41—43.

The *Warspite* was a battleship of 30,600 tons and carried eight 15-inch, eight 6-inch and eight 4-inch A.A. guns. Her speed was 15 knots and she was built in 1915. During the Second World War she made an attack on German craft in the fiord leading up to Narvik in company with a number of destroyers, bombarded the enemy's supply base at Valona in Albania, and was in the attack on the Italian fleet at Matapan, among other engagements. Her days were numbered, however, and she was sold for scrap, but when being towed round to the breakers went ashore on the Cornish coast.

H.M.S. WATERWITCH

Description of Badge

FIELD: Per fess wavy white and barry wavy of six blue and white.

BADGE: A witch on a broom proper.

MOTTO:

Badge in allusion to the name.

BATTLE HONOURS
China	1900	(Medal but not battle honour).
Anzio	1944	January 22nd—31st.

This vessel is one of the *Algerine* class of Fleet Minesweeper built by Lobnitz. Completed in 1943.

H.M.S. WELLINGTON

Description of Badge
FIELD: White.
BADGE: A dolphin blue and gold over a mural crown gold.
MOTTO: *Suprema Ut Olim* (Supreme as ever).

Badge derived from the arms of the City of Wellington in New Zealand.

BATTLE HONOUR
Atlantic   1939-40-1-2-3-4-5

The first *Wellington* was a sloop, rigged as a brig, and was of 312 tons and carried 16 guns. Her original name was the *L'Oreste*, captured from the French on 12th January, 1810, by the *Scorpion* off Guadeloupe. She was taken to pieces in September, 1812, at Portsmouth.

Then came a third rate of 1,757 tons and 74 guns which began building as the *Hero* at Deptford in 1813. This vessel was launched in September, 1816, and was named the *Wellington* on 4th December of the same year. In 1857 she was fitted as a coastguard ship, and on 10th May, 1862, replaced *Akbar* at Liverpool as a school ship and renamed *Akbar*. In January, 1908, came the termination of her loan to the Liverpool Juvenile Reformatory Association, and she was sold at Chatham in 1908 to Messrs. T. W. Ward & Co.

There was also a cutter named *Wellington* built at Cowes in 1815.

The *Wellington* which is now the Headquarters of the Honourable Master Mariners' Company was built at H.M. Dockyard, Devonport, and launched on 29th May, 1934. Most of her war service in the Second World War was in the Atlantic.

H.M.S. WEYMOUTH

Unofficial Badge: A shield, blue sky and green sea, with a lymphad charged with a shield party per fess chief gold and base red, three chevrons red in chief and three lions gold in base (presumed). Flags on lymphad dexter red with three gold lions, sinister white with red cross. Shield is gold edged. Scroll in blue and white, with name of ship in white.

Official Badge
FIELD: Blue.

BADGE: A bridge with two towers silver, surmounted by a fleur-de-lis gold.

MOTTO: Valour Buildeth the Bridge.

Badge from the arms of Weymouth.

H.M.S. WEYMOUTH—*continued*

BATTLE HONOURS

Sadras	1758	April 29th.
Negapatam	1758	August 3rd.
Porto Novo	1759	September 10th.

This ship was a light cruiser of 5,250 tons.

This vessel took part in chasing the *Goeben* and *Breslau*, and also convoyed the first Indian troops from Port Said to France in the 1914-18 war. She searched for and took part in the attack on the *Konigsberg*. One honour bestowed upon her was that of embarking the Prince of Wales at Port Said and taking him to Spezia.

H.M.S. WHELP

Description of Badge

FIELD: White.

BADGE: A lion's whelp sejant gardant proper.

MOTTO:

Badge in allusion to the name. The earliest whelps in the Royal Navy were *Lion's whelps*.

BATTLE HONOUR
Okinawa   1945   March 26th—May 25th.

The *Whelp* is a destroyer of the *Wager* class, built by Hawthorn Leslie in 1943.

H.M.S. WHIRLWIND

Description of Badge

FIELD: Blue.

BADGE: A head proper with wind issuant from the mouth.

MOTTO: *Tot Itinera Tot Venti* (Every voyage has its gales).

The badge is in allusion to the name.

BATTLE HONOURS
Zeebrugge	1918	April 23rd.
Ostend	1918	May 10th.
Atlantic	1939-40	
Norway	1940	
Okinawa	1945	March 26th—May 25th.

The *Whirlwind* is one of the full conversion class of destroyers changed to anti-submarine frigate. Her tonnage is 1,710, and she was completed by Hawthorn Leslie in 1944.

H.M.S. WIZARD

Description of Badge
FIELD: White.

BADGE: A pentacle red within an annulet also red.

MOTTO: Endless endeavour.

The badge is in allusion to the name.

No battle honours are recorded for this name.

The *Wizard* is a destroyer of the *Wager* class, and was built by Vickers-Armstrongs. Her tonnage is 1,710. Her main guns are four 4.7-inch.

H.M.S. WOOLWICH

Description of Badge

FIELD: Barry of three, yellow, blue, black.

BADGE: A cannon silver, with breach in form of lion's head gold.

MOTTO: *Sua Tela Tonanti* (Our bolts are those of the thunderer).

The badge is from the colours and motto of the Royal Military Academy badge from the town arms.

BATTLE HONOURS
Barfleur	1692	May 19th—24th.
Martinique	1762	February 16th.
Martinique	1794	March 22nd.
St. Lucia	1796	May 24th.
Egypt	1801	March 8th—September 2nd.

The *Woolwich* was a depot ship for destroyers and of 8,750 tons displacement. She was completed by Fairfield in 1935. She carries four 4-inch A.A. and 10 smaller guns. Her speed is 15 knots.

H.M.S. WRANGLER

Description of Badge

FIELD: Barry wavy of ten white and blue.

BADGE: A naval gun gold, the carriage red.

MOTTO: The first and last word.

The badge is in allusion to the name.

	BATTLE HONOURS
Baltic	1854
Crimea	1855

The *Wrangler* is one of the full conversion class of destroyers changed to anti-submarine frigate. Her tonnage is 1,710, and she was completed by Vickers-Armstrongs in 1944.

H.M.S. YARMOUTH

Unofficial Badge: Shield party per pale red and blue, demi-lions gold and fish tails silver. Scroll light blue with black lettering.

Official Badge
FIELD: Per pale red and blue.
BADGE: A demi-lion gold, ending in a fish-tail silver.
MOTTO: *Rex Et Jura Nostra* (Our king and laws).

Badges from the arms of Yarmouth.

BATTLE HONOURS

Lowestoft	1665	June 3rd.
Orfordness	1666	July 25th.
Sole Bay	1672	May 28th.
Schooneveld	1673	May 28th and June 4th.
Texel	1673	August 11th.

H.M.S. YARMOUTH—*continued*

Gibraltar	1704	July 24th.
Velez Malaga	1704	August 13th.
Finisterre	1747	May 3rd.
Ushant	1737	October 14th.
Sadras	1758	April 29th.
Negapatam	1758	August 3rd.
Porto Novo	1759	September 10th.
The Saints	1782	April 12th.
Jutland	1916	May 31st.

This ship was a light cruiser of 5,250 tons, built in 1911 at Glasgow and sold in 1929.

H.M.S. ZAMBESI

Description of Badge

FIELD: Gold, a chief blue.

BADGE: Over water barry wavy in base blue and white a crocodile proper.

MOTTO:

Badge in allusion to the Zambesi river.

	BATTLE HONOURS
Norway	1944
Arctic	1945

The *Zambesi* is a destroyer which gives her name to the class and was built by Cammell Laird. Her tonnage is 1,710, and she carries as her main armament four 4.5-inch dual-purpose guns, being launched in 1943.

H.M.S. ZEALANDIA

Description of Badge

Head of a Maori with a spear tipped red; above is a naval crown gold, white sails, red and blue gems. Scroll yellow and gold, black edged red letters.

In allusion to the name.

No battle honours are recorded for this vessel.

This ship was a battleship (pre-*Dreadnought*) of 16,350 tons.

H.M.S. ZEALOUS

Description of Badge

FIELD: Blue.

BADGE: A fret white charged with a bee volant proper.

MOTTO:

Badge in allusion to the name and to the arms of Captain S. Hood, who led the fleet into action at the battle of the Nile in the *Zealous*.

	BATTLE HONOURS	
Nile	1798	August 1st.
Norway	1945	
Arctic	1945	

The *Zealous* is a *Zambesi* class of destroyer, and was built at Cammell Laird's in 1944. In 1955 she was sold to Israel.

H.M.S. ZEBRA

Description of Badge

FIELD: White.

BADGE: A zebra statant proper.

MOTTO:

Badge in allusion to the name.

BATTLE HONOURS
The Saints	1782	April 12th.
Martinique	1794	March 22nd.
Copenhagen	1801	April 2nd.
Syria	1840	September 10th—December 9th.
Arctic	1945	

The *Zebra* (ex *Wakeful*) is one of the *Zambesi* class destroyers, and was built by Denny Bros. in 1944.

H.M.S. ZENITH

Description of Badge
FIELD: Blue.

BADGE: A sun in splendour gold.

MOTTO: This above all.

The badge is in allusion to the name.

There are no battle honours recorded for this name.

The *Zenith* (ex *Wessex*) is one of the *Zambesi* class destroyers, and was built by Denny Bros. in 1943, and was sold to Egypt in 1955.

H.M.S. ZEPHYR

Description of Badge
FIELD: Blue.

BADGE: A recumbent figure male to the sinister winged and draped white bearing flowers in the lap of his gown also white.

MOTTO:

The badge was derived from an antique carving.

BATTLE HONOURS

Quebec	1759	September 13th.
Martinique	1762	February 16th.
Copenhagen	1801	April 2nd.
Baltic	1864	
Arctic	1945	

The *Zephyr* is one of the *Zambesi* class of destroyers, and was built by Vickers-Armstrongs. This vessel is 1,730 tons and was built in 1943.

H.M.S. ZEST

Description of Badge

FIELD: White.

BADGE: A sprig of mustard plane leaved and flowered proper.

MOTTO:

Badge in allusion to the name. The motto suggested for the ship was "Keen".

BATTLE HONOURS

Norway	1945
Arctic	1945

The *Zest* is one of the *Zambesi* class of destroyers, and was built by Thornycroft.

H.M.S. ZODIAC

Description of Badge

FIELD: Blue.

BADGE: A bezant rayed gold, on each point a bezant charged with the zodiac signs black.

MOTTO: Faythe hath no fear.

Badge in allusion to the signs of the Zodiac.

BATTLE HONOUR
Arctic 1945

The *Zodiac* is one of the *Zambesi* class of destroyers and was, built by Thornycroft in 1943.

ILLUSTRATIONS

SHOWING SOME USES

OF

SHIPS' BADGES

[*Photo: Gale & Polden Ltd.*

THREE OF THE MEMORIAL WINDOWS IN THE CHURCH OF ST. GEORGE, ROYAL NAVAL BARRACKS, CHATHAM (showing ships' badges).

[Photos. *Gale & Polden Ltd.*

FIGUREHEADS LIKE THESE WERE SYMBOLIC OF THE SHIP OR HER ASSOCIATIONS JUST AS THE BADGES ARE TODAY.

[Photo: Gale & Polden Ltd.

FIGUREHEADS LIKE THIS WERE SYMBOLIC OF THE SHIP OR HER ASSOCIATIONS JUST AS THE BADGES ARE TODAY.

[*Crown Copyright Reserved*

A SELECTION OF EARLY UNOFFICIAL BADGES.
(H.M.S. *Tower* shown on this photograph was the first one to be designed by Major C. ffoulkes.)

A SELECTION OF EARLY UNOFFICIAL BADGES.

[Crown Copyright Reserved

A SELECTION OF EARLY UNOFFICIAL BADGES.

A SELECTION OF EARLY UNOFFICIAL BADGES.

[Crown Copyright Reserved

A SELECTION OF EARLY UNOFFICIAL BADGES.

[Crown Copyright Reserved

A SELECTION OF EARLY UNOFFICIAL BADGES.

[Crown Copyright Reserved

FIGUREHEAD AND BADGES USED ON ROWING BARGE IN ROYAL PAGEANT ON RIVER THAMES, 1919.

ENTRANCE, ADMIRAL SUPERINTENDENT'S OFFICE, R.N. DOCKYARD, CHATHAM.

MAIN GATE BADGE, R.N. DOCKYARD, CHATHAM.

BADGE OF QUEEN ELIZABETH ON ROYAL NAVAL ARMAMENT
DEPOT GATE PILLARS AT UPNOR.

ARETHUSA BATTLE HONOURS ON BOARD T.S. *ARETHUSA*
(EX *PEKING*).

BADGE ON A BUILDING NEAR ROYAL NAVAL COLLEGE,
GREENWICH.

EXAMPLES OF ARMS AND SCROLL WORK ON VESSELS OF THE
SAIL AND STEAM ERA OF THE ROYAL NAVY.

PULPIT, EX H.M.S. *NEW ZEALAND*, SHOWING THE ARMS OF NEW ZEALAND, NOW AT THE NAVAL BASE, AUCKLAND, NEW ZEALAND.